A University for the People
A History of the Institute for Christian Studies

Robert E. VanderVennen

Dordt College Press

Cover design by Willem Hart
Layout by Carla Goslinga

Copyright © 2008 by Robert E. VanderVennen
Those who are interested in sharing the author's insights and observations, so long as the material is not pirated for monetary gain and so long as proper credit is visibly given to the publisher and the author, may freely use fragmentary portions of this book. Others, and those who wish to use larger sections of text, must seek written permission from the publisher.

Printed in the United States of America.

Dordt College Press   www.dordt.edu/dordt_press
498 Fourth Avenue NE
Sioux Center, Iowa 51250
United States of America

ISBN: 978-0-932914-75-0

The Library of Congress Cataloging-in-Publication Data is on file with the Library of Congress, Washington, D.C.

Library of Congress Control Number: 2008926327

To the thousands of people who worked, prayed and
donated money to build a Christian university in
Canada that would bless all people and bring the
kingship of Christ to every area of
personal and communal life.

TABLE OF CONTENTS

Foreword i
Preface v
1 The Beginnings 1
2 Setting up the Institute 29
3 The Institute Opens 47
4 Growth and Turbulence in the Early Seventies 55
5 The Professors and their Courses 73
6 The Broader Context for Academic Courses 97
7 Books as a Vehicle for Leadership 123
8 Wedge and Book Publishing 141
9 Educational Services 151
10 Curriculum Development Centre and Patmos Art Gallery ... 161
11 Administrative Structure and Institutional Leadership 169
12 The Rough Road of Controversy 187
13 Development for the Institute 203
14 Finances 217
15 Accreditation and Relations with other Schools 225
16 Institute Appraisal and Influence 247
17 Today and Tomorrow 255

APPENDICES
1 The Institute Basic and Educational Creed 264
2 Speakers for Annual Summer Student
   Conferences 1959-1969 267
3 Summer Academic Conferences, Workshops and Seminars .. 269
4 Books Co-published for the Institute by University Press of
   America between 1983 and 1997 272

FOREWORD

The story that is told in these pages is an important one. The Institute for Christian Studies was birthed by the efforts of a post-World-War II immigrant community who had a vision for an academic institution that would bring something new to the North American environs that was now their home: a scholarly community guided by the kind of "reformational" understanding of reality that would provide guidance for those who desire to serve the Kingdom of Christ in all spheres of creaturely life.

Bob Vander Vennen's chronicle provides clear and abundant evidence that this vision has become a reality. Today's Institute can boast of an impressive roster of graduates, a superb record of published scholarship, and a profound impact on servants of the Kingdom around the world. And for all of that, its mission and influence continues to expand.

That the Institute for Christian Studies has not only survived, but has actually flourished, is not something that could have been taken for granted. For one thing, as anyone who understands the economics of higher education knows, it is difficult to support a graduate program—where individual mentoring is a necessity—without the income gained from large undergraduate classes. Nor was the Institute willing to compromise its original vision by moving in the direction of a more profitable "professional education" focus. And its life has also been complicated by many growing pains along the way, with the resultant controversies and shifting alliances that also are described—with refreshing candor!—in these pages. That the Institute has not only survived, but has also flourished in marvelous ways, is evidence of the Lord's blessing on its unique mission for embodying and pursuing scholarship "pro rege."

One of the special strengths of the Institute, as I view this history, is its possession of what is often referred to these days as convening power, the kind of magnetism that causes people to see your community as a strategic gathering place for important discussions. I am one of those persons who has benefited greatly from being "convened" by the Institute for Christian Studies. My own philosophical training was in the Anglo-American "analytic" variety, which did not permit me during my graduate studies to satisfy my desire to develop an approach to the intellectual life that was properly "reformational." I joined the Philosophy faculty at Calvin College shortly after the Institute was founded, and I soon found myself traveling frequently to Toronto for seminars, conferences and individual scholarly collaborations. Through the Institute's programs I was initiated into an international network of Christian scholars who had a significant impact on my philosophical development.

This fine chronicle of the Institute's four decades of service tells the exciting story of the flourishing of a unique academic community. For those of us who have been aligned with the Institute for some or all of this time, this chronicle also keeps the memories alive of a cloud of witnesses who have provided inspiration and nurture through their Kingdom service. And for some of us—and this is my testimony—it also makes it clear that our own journeys would have been much impoverished if we had not been frequently "convened" by this creative and engaging center of Christian scholarship.

Richard J. Mouw
President and Professor of Christian Philosophy
Fuller Theological Seminary

PREFACE

The history of the Institute for Christian Studies is a story with many dimensions. On a philosophical level, the ICS has brought into existence an enriched understanding of God's hand in all the world, including academic research and teaching, a viewpoint unprecedented as the leading motif in any other Christian college or university. On a more fundamental level, because freestanding independent colleges and universities were almost unknown in Canada, except for seminaries and Bible colleges, finding the legal room for the Institute to exist is an extraordinary story. The new ground opened by the Institute was often controversial. The Institute and its story show how Christian higher education can move beyond the dichotomistic view of Christians who demonstrate personal faith even as they teach material that assumes God's absence from the subject matter.

Dutch immigrants to Canada in the early 1950s had an urgent vision for preparing Christian leaders to serve their subculture and other Canadian Christians. They understood that a Christian university was essential to give leadership to their people in a new world. They wanted scholars to work out the meaning of Christ's rule over all of the world, especially in higher education and theoretical study, but also for the benefit of all people. They wanted the benefits of this higher education to reach down to all people of their culture, educated or not, and in that sense the Institute was designed to serve all the people within that culture. The culture these immigrants had left following the Nazi devastation in the Netherlands gave them the hope that the new world would be open to their unique vision.

This manuscript is the story of how that vision unfolded over the first fifty years of the Institute. People who embraced this vision set up an independent graduate school that reached throughout the world, even though it remained almost invisibly small. Along the way, the Institute shaped the culture of Dutch Reformed immigrants in Canada. Its vigorous publishing program has reached surprising places in every continent, including Asia, Africa, and Latin America, bringing to its Toronto classrooms many international students in addition to Americans. And in 2006, its alumni held academic positions in thirty North American colleges, universities, and seminaries and in fourteen universities overseas.

Structure of the Book

This book begins by describing the eleven-year gestation period from the first private conversations about the Institute to its opening (with only one professor) in 1967.

This book presents the ways in which the Institute's unique Christian insights are expressed by its professors and organized in their courses. Books are identified that give expression to Institute research by faculty members and graduate students, as well as special Christian insights brought to the Institute by visiting scholars at academic conferences. The heart of the Institute's educational conviction is that nothing in the world is secular, and that God's law underlies and gives unity and meaning to all the world and all education. In the tradition of Calvin, Kuyper, and Dooyeweerd, all academic and philosophical systems are understood to be ultimately and inevitably rooted in religious belief. The Institute is unique in centering its graduate program on philosophy rather than theology or ethics. This book shows how this special vision for Christian higher education became a reality, but it also opens room for disagreement about the validity of these insights.

Included is the Institute's special initiative to include worldview studies in its curriculum, which includes a special department offering a degree called Master of Worldview Studies. This program and its publications have drawn wide interest among Christian scholars and have developed through contact with people like James Sire and Arthur Holmes.

The People of the Institute

This book is written as a tribute to the people who wanted the Institute to exist—they prayed for it, worked for it, and were willing to pay for it. They had a vision of Christ's rule over the world, and, in their new nation, a graduate school like the Institute was at the heart of their vision. Many of the people who rallied to this vision and paid money to build it did not themselves have a higher education. This book about the development of that vision is written to be read by people without advanced education as well as by academicians.

I am not a Dutch immigrant, but I served as an executive administrator at the Institute from March 1974 until 2000. I started as Executive Director of the nonacademic work of the Institute and continued that service in a variety of positions until my retirement. I was close to much of the work of the Institute during those years and was strongly engaged in the vision behind it. Consequently, this history of the Institute is not objective (though it should be noted that the vision behind the Institute insists that no one's work is truly objective). Nor is this book a critical history. You will find criticisms on these pages, but they are muted because the people involved are my friends, people with whom I worked very closely. Rather, this is an anecdotal recollection, the account of one who has long been involved with the Institute and its vision.

Terminology

There are some issues of terminology in writing about this school, terminology that has undergone some changes over the years. The Institute is often called ICS, and throughout the text I have used Institute and ICS interchangeably.

The school was started by a nonacademic association, first called the Association for Reformed Scientific Studies, later the Association for the Advancement of Christian Scholarship. That association was disbanded in 1983 when the Institute received its charter to grant degrees from the government of Ontario. These names are cumbersome and the enabling body itself no longer in force, so I have simply referred to it throughout as the Association. The Association began with the aim of advancing Christian higher education to give leadership to a certain group of people and to educate some of its people for leadership service.

In the early years, the faculty decided to refer to each other as Senior Members and to the graduate students as Junior Members. The faculty had a vision of a graduate school as an academic community in which senior and junior partners work together and learn together in shared commitment to the development of quality Christian scholarship. Together they would embody and advance a Christian tradition of scholarship in critical dialogue with leading contemporary schools of thought. This aim is largely realized, though in practice the professors and graduate students at the Institute relate together in much the same close and congenial way as do professors and students at any other small graduate school. I generally use the ordinary terms *professor* and *student* because the meaning and implication of these terms are more widely understood.

This text has no footnotes, though there are numerous citations. Nearly all citations are taken from reports and minutes originating at the Institute and from its published newsletters. Though these are not generally secret or confidential documents, neither are they readily accessible to a scholarly reader, so citation in the style of academic footnotes is inappropriate. In certain places, I use expressions that were first written by someone else, but explicit credit in all of those cases has not seemed appropriate.

Acknowledgments

The help of many people was needed to produce this record of Institute history. I am thankful to the Board of Trustees of the Institute for Christian Studies and to its President, Harry Fernhout, for their readiness to give me access to Institute records and historical papers. I give special thanks to Hendrik Hart, Calvin Seerveld, John Meiboom, and my son Mark Vander Vennen for their careful review of the text and suggestions of many corrections and improvements. Bert Witvoet, Gerald Vandezande, and Calvin Seerveld gave special service by preparing the personal vignettes of early people who helped bring the Institute to reality. Harry Fernhout was very helpful, and I thank him especially for his insights and information on the status of the Institute in 2005 and his sense of how it might develop in the future, contained in Chapter 17.

Behind the scenes is the very great support I have received from my loving wife Mary, who has walked with me every part of the way and whose help is beyond measure.

1

The Beginnings

The Institute for Christian Studies could only have started with immigrants of the Reformed tradition arriving in Canada from the Netherlands in the early 1950s. Who else would have thought of starting a Christian university in Canada with so few resources?

The Dutch Immigration

As we begin the story of ICS, we need to know what life was like for these immigrants in the Netherlands before they left. They had just lived through five brutal years under the heel of the murdering Nazis. World War II was the second time in twenty-five years that Germany had rampaged western Europe. The situation was full of uncertainty. Would the communists from Russia be the next occupiers of the Netherlands? Money and the necessities of life were in very short supply. Everything was smashed during the Nazi occupation and needed to be rebuilt. Who had the heart for doing that? Besides, the postwar Dutch government had all kinds of restrictions on what its citizens could do. After being squeezed for five long war years, who needed their own government to tell them constantly what they could not do?

If everything in the country needed to be rebuilt from scratch, why undertake that under hard conditions where it could be destroyed again a generation later? It would be better to immigrate to a land of openness and freedom. Canadian soldiers had freed the country from the Nazis. Canada had lots of room and welcomed farmers to wide spaces with lots of opportunity. So Dutch immigrants streamed to Canada by the boatload, 185,000 of them between 1947 and 1970.

A high percentage of the Dutch immigrants to Canada were Christians who were members of Reformed churches. The next step in understanding the background of ICS is to know what the society of Dutch Reformed Christians was like in the years before 1939.

Dutch society in those prewar days was "pillared." Early in the twentieth century, the Dutch government accepted the petitions of its citizens that it should offer the opportunity for the cultural institutions of its people to develop in line with their faith and their committed worldview. So the government made room for separate social institutions for Protestant Christians, Catholic Christians, socialists, humanists, and other major affinity groups. Each group was free to set up its own schools from kindergarten through doctoral study; radio stations, newspapers, and magazines; labour unions; political parties; and so on, provided they could demonstrate that they had a large enough group of supporters. All this was legal, and money to support this structure was made available. That meant, for instance, that Dutch Calvinists could meet each other in all these institutions as well as in church. If they wanted, they could lead much of their lives rubbing shoulders only with people sharing their own religions beliefs.

This was the kind of culture the Dutch immigrants grew up with. Upon arriving in Canada, they set up their own churches, and they built Christian day schools as quickly as they built churches. They started a Christian labour union, Christian farmers' organizations, a Christian mental health service, a Christian political advocacy organization, and Christian newspapers and magazines to work toward the Christian reform of Canadian culture and to keep in contact with one another across Canada's vastness.

The central vitalizing engine for this Christian subculture was seen to be the Christian university. Such a school was essential to provide educated leaders for all these enterprises as well as pastors for the churches. It was also needed to develop Christian understanding for all areas of life. In the Netherlands, the Christian university was the Free University located in Amsterdam, officially opened by Abraham Kuyper in 1880. As Andrew Kouvenhoven, himself an immigrant, expressed it at the twenty-fifth anniversary of the first discussions about the start of the Institute, "The founding of the Institute was inevitable among the militant Calvinists who had adopted Canada as their homeland. Unaccustomed to being merely tolerated as a religious island in a secular sea, they desired the pulpit for the prophet, the lectern for the scholar and a seat at the table where decisions are made, all in the name of a gospel as big as God and wide as the world." When these immigrants didn't see such an institution in their new land, they decided to start one to provide leadership to their faith-borne cultural witness.

Canada seemed to many of the immigrants to be a rather new country, lacking the long-developed history of the Netherlands and other countries in western Europe. It appeared rather unformed, without its own established institutions and ways of doing things. In this, they were wrong—Canada had well-established mainline churches, schools, and a political system. But by the middle of the twentieth century, the country had become so secularized that most churches did not act as though the Christian faith had anything to do with education or public affairs.

Canada affirmed the cultural traditions of its immigrants, but also generally accepted that new immigrants needed to assimilate into Canadian culture. Mainline churches, public schools, and mass media were major means of Canadianizing newcomers. The Dutch immigrants, however, had a different idea of their place in Canada.

The Planning Starts

In October 1955, four men started meeting together to see whether a Christian university could be started in Canada. This might have seemed to be a foolhardy thing to do. The immigrants of the Dutch community were dirt poor. Many of them were young, and even if some of the older ones had a bit of money, the Dutch government had let them take only a small amount out of the country. The Dutch immigrants were trying to establish themselves, to build churches, Christian schools, and more. Many of them could hardly speak English.

The group of four consisted of two pastors, François Guillaume and Henry Venema, and two businessmen, Peter Speelman and Casper

---

Peter Speelman was a man who loved the Reformed faith and who strongly supported Christian action early on in the days of immigration. He was on the Board of the Christian Labour Association as well as on the  Board of the Association for Reformed Scientific Studies (precursor of the AACS). He ran a Christian book and record store in the 1950s and 1960s, in the basement of his home in Rexdale, a suburb of Toronto. You could often hear him sing or whistle Psalm tunes as he did his work. He was also deeply involved in the promotion of the local Christian schools. I remember how he used to visit Toronto District Christian High School and talk to us teachers. He had a soft heart for the underdog; he was worried sometimes that we would fail too many students. Peter could be quite emotional and leaned toward sentimentalism. He was good-hearted but not always wise. He was indefatigable, sometimes fiery. Some thought he lacked real knowledge of what a university was, but he deeply wanted to help students and enable them to be true to the Lord.

—Bert Witvoet

Vanderiet. What they were discussing was impractical, but they had a vision. They wanted to proclaim the Kingdom of God in all areas of life in Canada. To do that, they needed leadership that could only be provided by a Christian university that embodied their ideals.

A "university"? They may not have had a clear idea of the scope of the school they felt was needed. In the Netherlands, universities did not give bachelor's and master's degrees, and all academic education beyond high school was given in a university. Thus, they were thinking of academic higher education as education beyond high school in certain limited areas of leadership. They were not thinking of duplicating the University of Toronto. Yet in 1968, Casper Vanderiet wrote, "We had no idea how big a task it would be. It was an act of faith."

These four had several sessions together starting in the fall of 1955 and through that winter. Later, Rev. Guillaume said, "We prayed every time for guidance. We always closed our discussions with thanksgiving. The Lord was really in our midst. We did it by him. And we agreed, the four of us, 'We have to do it! This must be done!'"

To move the vision toward a school, it was necessary to spell out what kind of foundation the school would stand on and to organize the project. The four men drafted a preliminary constitution for an association for fostering a school of Calvinist academic studies, which was formally adopted in the following year in a public meeting. The constitution in Article 3 stated that "The basis of the society in all its activities is the infallible, all-sufficient and only authoritative Word of God, according to the interpretation of the Reformed Confessions, namely: the Belgic Confession, the Heidelberg Catechism, the Canons of Dort, the Westminster Confession of Faith, the First and Second Scottish Confession, the Second Helvitic Confession and the Thirty-nine Articles of the Anglican Church."

The purpose of the association was identified as "the advancement of Reformed higher education, which it seeks to accomplish (a) by establishing and maintaining a college(s) and graduate school(s); (b) by encouraging and supporting various activities which can be considered to stimulate Reformed science, provided that such activities remain within the limits circumscribed by Article 3 on the basis of the Society."

The four initiators soon invited four other leaders to discuss their vision and the proposed constitution. The four were pastors A. B. C. Hofland, Alvin Venema, and Maarten Vrieze and businessman Peter Nienhuis. The eight met on May 28, 1956, and they approved the ideas expressed in the preliminary constitution. They set themselves up as a committee and decided to invite a larger number of people to meet to consider their ideas.

The eight of them sent an invitation, written in Dutch, to fifty-six others to participate in a meeting on June 16, 1956. Peter Speelman chaired the meeting. His opening address, also in Dutch, was titled in English as "For the King and for the Neighbour" and included these words in an English translation:

> Our leading motif has been, that if in the future we are going to contribute to this land, and above all to the Kingdom of God, we who have been brought up in Calvinistic homes, who desire to hold fast the tradition of the Reformed confessions, regardless of which church denomination one belongs to, then we shall need leaders, men of science who will allow the light of God's Word to shine upon all the problems of our modern and increasingly complicated life. We wholeheartedly hope that our God and Christ in whose name we have begun this gathering may so direct, that what transpires today may tend to the greater glory of his ineffable name.

Speelman explained the need for a distinctively Reformed witness in Canada and the North American world. He said that this age was one of secularism with all its counterparts of humanism, socialism, communism, and materialism. To combat these influences, Christians need knowledge, which thus calls Christians to advanced academic study in every sphere of life for the honour of the King. He stated that his listeners must be willing to deny themselves and live by faith, for only then would they succeed in establishing a Reformed university.

The discussion led to the decision to establish an Association for Reformed Scientific Studies to be based upon the Word of God as interpreted by the historic Reformed confessions. A Board of Trustees was elected, and Peter Speelman was chosen as chairman. He continued as chairman until January 1957, when ill health forced him to resign this position and he became secretary instead.

While the meeting was in progress, three pastors from western Canada entered and asked how people and churches in western Canada could be included. A committee was appointed to consider this and report to the Board. There was general agreement both in the East and in the West that this activity should engage people from all parts of Canada, especially in Alberta and British Columbia where a number of Dutch immigrants had settled. The committee's first moves were to appoint some Board members from western Canada and include the West in the lecture tours that were being planned.

The first meeting of the Association open to the general public was held in Toronto on November 3, 1956. Professor Ned Stonehouse of Westminster Theological Seminary in Philadelphia spoke on the subject "Why a Christian University?" A telegram of good wishes was received from the American group called Reformed Fellowship. At that meeting, it became clear that three distinct groups were present: there were Dutch immigrants to Canada; Calvin College students of H. Evan Runner who were members of Runner's study group called the Groen Club; and American Christian Reformed pastors serving in Canada to help organize churches among the immigrants. By and large, those American pastors did not favour work toward a Christian university in Canada.

In 1958, Herman Dooyeweerd from the Free University visited Toronto and met with the Board. He said that Canada might have too few reformational people to be successful in developing a Christian university. He also thought that basing the Association on the church creeds was not a good idea and suggested instead writing a new statement that the work be based directly on the teachings of the Bible. This was well received, and H. Evan Runner was asked to draft an Educational Creed for the Association. He wrote most of the creed, but its preamble was largely written by Dutch professor Dirk Vollenhoven, a colleague and brother-in-law of Dooyeweerd who was visiting Runner at the time.

The Educational Creed, adopted in 1961, was a landmark statement requiring a submission, led by the Holy Spirit, to what the Scriptures in Jesus Christ require in the field of learning. It was used later with modifications in other Christian organizations. (See Appendix 1.) At the heart of the Educational Creed is the belief that there is no religious neutrality in life or scholarship; that life is integral, of one piece; and that synthesis of Christian and non-Christian thought is to be rejected. As Runner, the writer of the creed, said, "All of life is religion." (He agreed that the grammar of the phrase was wrong, but justified it by saying that the meaning of a statement is more important than its grammar.)

None of these immigrant people had ever been involved in starting such a school. Some had helped start Christian elementary and secondary schools, but a university was quite a different matter. It was pioneering work. Bert Witvoet, himself a Dutch immigrant, later wrote, "So what do you do when you have just landed in a new country and hardly speak English, and nobody has any money because every one of them is poor (which is why most of them immigrated)? Why, of course, you get together and envision a free Christian university to serve Canada and the United States, like the Free University of Amsterdam. There was some craziness in starting a university right then," Witvoet added, "but their religious vision was sound and clear-headed."

Members of the Association brought two strengths to this task. One was insight into Christian scholarship, into the unification of faith and learning, which had been worked at institutionally for the past hundred years by Dutch Calvinists in the Netherlands and in other parts of the world. This was put into practice using the methodology of what was then called the Philosophy of the Law-Idea developed by Herman Dooyeweerd and his coworkers. The other strength, which was not specifically academic, was the Kuyperian concern for the biblical integrity of all of life. This was in contrast to the practice of separating divine grace from "worldly" matters, a nature-grace duality. One approach to express this integrality is to operate Christian organizations, formed separately from churches but rooted in the biblical notion of God's all-embracing Kingdom, that are engaged in educational, political, and cultural activities.

The Dutch brought with them from the Free University in Amsterdam a pattern of institutional structure that could be followed. The Free University itself was unique among Dutch universities by not having its own incorporation. The name of its corporate entity, translated into English, was The Association for Higher Education on a Reformed Foundation, which founded and operated the university. The immigrants chose the same structure in Canada. They formed the Association for Reformed Scientific Studies, which launched the Institute for Christian Studies. But the Association's articles of incorporation gave it room for other educational activities as well as starting and operating a school. What they did not know was that under British Common Law, no one could operate a Canadian postsecondary school (except for Bible colleges and seminaries) without official approval granted in a bill passed by the provincial legislature.

From the perspective of the year 2000, John Hiemstra, Institute graduate and professor at The King's University College in Edmonton, wrote that the Dutch Reformed immigrants of the 1950s firmly believed that children must be taught to serve God and their nation as they grew up. He wrote that those immigrants tried to contribute to Canada the view that culture always reflects one of several possible religious visions, and that Christians are called by God to contribute to the larger society not only as individuals but also communally by way of Christian organizations.

Student Conferences

At this point, there was a group of people who want to start a new university, a Board, and a constitution. What was the next step in setting up a freestanding school?

At first, it was agreed that the Association should offer evening courses, but nothing came of that. Later, the Association's primary motivation to help students develop Christian insight into academic studies became its breakthrough activity. The organizers realized that most of the students who would become future leaders were attending secular universities where they would not be able to develop a Christian perspective on learning. John Hultink, while working to promote the Institute, wrote that at that time there were 600 Dutch Reformed children of immigrants attending public universities in Canada and the United States.

The first educational activity of the Association was to set up a summer conference for university students to help them think about Christian perspective in their studies. It was held just outside of Toronto in the town of Unionville on September 1–3, 1959. Three speakers, a Dutchman, a Canadian, and an American, were on the program. Sixty people attended the conference.

Dr. Hendrik van Riessen came from the Netherlands to speak on "The Christian Approach to Science." He talked about positivism as a non-Christian philosophy, about objectivity, religious neutrality, and secularization. Dr. Allan Farris of Knox College, Toronto, spoke on "The Relation of the Bible to History." He spoke about competitive understandings of history, including the Christian understanding; on Christ as the centre of history; and on the effects of sin in the world and the restoration of the world in Christ. Dr. H. Evan Runner from Calvin College in Grand Rapids, Michigan, spoke on "The Relation of the Bible to Learning." His stimulating address dealt with the challenge presented by the absence of God from secular learning, the synthesis of God's word with pagan ideas, the meaning of truth, and the choice before us of Christian understanding.

Peter Schouls, who later became chair of the Department of Philosophy at the University of Alberta and chaired the Institute's Board of Curators for many years, spoke at the Association's thirtieth anniversary of how he was affected by hearing van Riessen speak in 1959. A graduate student of philosophy at the University of Toronto at the time, Schouls said that for years there had been a struggle in his life between what he took to be the demands of objective "reason" and the claims of what he took to be subjective faith. "By the time I heard van Riessen's lecture," he said, "my faith was weak and cowering in the face of the imperial demands of reason. 'Reason' and 'faith' could never live happily together.

One of them would have to be triumphant. . . . Van Riessen's lecture was the beginning of a turnaround for me. . . . 'I am because I think' began to have a hard time of it; 'I am because I am responsible' was beginning to take over."

Following his lectures at the 1959 Unionville Conference, professor Van Riessen toured Canada, speaking on behalf of the Association, and in 1960 professor Zuidema of the Free University did the same, speaking in twenty-one communities.

That first conference was enormously exciting for many besides the students who attended, and a second conference was planned for the following year. Runner again stole the show with his penetrating insights and his infectious enthusiasm. His talk focused on scientism and Abraham Kuyper's concept of sphere sovereignty. Dr. W. Stanford Reid from McGill University in Montreal spoke on "Absolute Truth and the Relativism of History," and Dr. S. U. Zuidema came from the Netherlands to speak on "Pragmatism" and "Existential Communication."

The 1960 conference was attended by a larger group than the first year. The Association had come up with an excellent program, and student conferences were held every summer. Participants in western Canada then wanted to have their own conferences. In 1962, the first conference was held in Banff, Alberta, a conference that drew 300 people, mostly students. Later, a conference was added in British Columbia, then one in Pennsylvania, one in Michigan, and one in Iowa. These summer conferences gave Christian students a sense of excitement, an awareness that they did not need to leave their Christianity outside of their academic education. A list of the speakers for the early conferences held throughout North America is given in Appendix 2.

These student conferences continued into the 1970s. Some students kept coming to the annual conferences even after they graduated from university, were married, and had children. They were joined by older people who were eager to get new insights on higher learning and Christian living, so the character of the conferences gradually changed. The number of people attending grew into the hundreds each summer, and children became part of the mix. In the 1970s, there was a gradual decrease in the number of locations where conferences were held, but conferences in southern Ontario continued into the new millennium. In the 1980s and into the 1990s, some of the summer conferences drew more than a thousand people.

Glenn Andreas understood that spoken words could become lost, so following the first conference he published the speeches in book form. He had 2,500 copies of the books printed at a total cost of $2,300. There was great demand for the printed speeches, so each year a book of conference speeches was published. These books were known as the Christian Perspectives Series. They were enthusiastically received and were even sold throughout the world. The lectures in book form spread the ideas presented and promoted the work of the Association. A considerable following grew in many countries for the Association and the Institute, including many people who were not Dutch.

By 1965, the Association was receiving very positive and encouraging letters from, for example, a pastor of a Church of Christ congregation in Pennsylvania, as well as from distant places like Korea, Great Britain, Scotland, and New Zealand, all as a result of the Christian Perspectives Series.

Other Educational Services

As the kinds of people who came to the conferences broadened, interesting and important questions arose. A university works at academic learning with students who accept the discipline of academic study. If the

> **Glenn Andreas** was an American who became a lifelong, devoted friend of H. Evan Runner while the two were classmates at Wheaton College. Andreas was a member of a wealthy family and became president of a bank in Pella, Iowa. He used his money in generous support of the Institute and of Wedge Publishing Foundation, though at times he clearly used his money to the advantage of strictly Dooyeweerdian activities. Without his help and financial support, Wedge would have not been able to pursue its services in publishing books and *Vanguard* magazine. Andreas also worked with Paul Schrotenboer, Case Hoogendoorn, and others to set up and maintain the AACS Foundation, a charity that permitted American donors to receive tax credit for their donations to the Institute and related reformational Canadian causes.
>
>
>
> Andreas was vitally interested in how Reformed Christian people lived and worked. He followed Runner in holding to issues exactly as Herman Dooyeweerd articulated them, and he could be severely critical of activities that he did not consider to give a true reformational perspective. He was the major force behind the Institute's controversial policy in its early years that people applying for Institute membership would need their application to be supported by three signatures of existing members. He was a consummate strategist in meetings.
>
> —Gerald Vandezande

Association wanted to set up a university, what would it do with people who wanted to learn from its activities but did not necessarily have the ability or interest in learning from academic study? Should the Association try to enrich the understanding and the lives of such people?

The answers to those questions came, in part, from people whose donations made the Institute possible. They wanted some of the educational benefits the Institute could provide.

Thus, from the start the Association and the Institute it would establish aimed to build a depth of insight in the Christian community, a worldview that made clear the meaning of the conviction that God in Christ holds the whole world in his hands. The Association aimed to give Christian direction not only to academics but also to people without formal higher education and others not in academic life. Its unique structure allowed it to provide nonscholarly insight without compromising the strict academic work of the Institute, its university. Whether or not its people completely thought through this rationale as a solution to its problem, it did continue to serve nonacademic as well as academic seekers.

The Association changed its name in October 1968 to the Association for the Advancement of Christian Scholarship, which showed that academic learning was not its entire aim. The old name, Association for Reformed Scientific Studies, was dropped for three reasons. First was concern with the word *Reformed*—it was somewhat more restricted than *Christian* and was greatly misunderstood by people who connected it to reformatories. In addition, *Reformed* indicated the past tense, while the Institute would stress ongoing reformation. Second, the word *scientific* did not communicate well. It was probably a mistranslation of a Dutch word that means scholarship, but to Anglo-Saxons it indicated empirical studies of the physical world. Third, the Association was often referred to by its initials ARSS, which was associated with the British slang word *arse* that was pronounced in the same way but used as an expression for the part of the anatomy on which we sit.

During the first years, nonacademic activity was spoken of as "confessional" learning, but later it was spoken of as worldview education. The understanding was that everyone has a worldview, though not everyone is or has been engaged in academic activity. Our worldview, or confessional understanding, is made up of our ideals or philosophy of life. We all hold a range of intuitive attitudes about the people and life situations we encounter. Christians want to live lives guided by the Bible, but few of us are academic theologians. A confession of faith is a different kind of thing from a theological statement. A theological statement is academic, articulated with as much logical precision as can be brought to bear. But behind theology lies our attitudes, which are often held intuitively. Our lives can be enriched and made more purposeful from nonacademic learning as well as from academic study. In later years, the Institute became a world leader in the academic study of worldviews, which brings together intuitive beliefs and academic study.

In 1971, James Olthuis made the point in the Institute's newsletter *Perspective* that the Bible is a confessional book which should not be used as theological writing. He wrote:

> We believe that the Scriptures are a confessional book, and not a book of theology. Theology doesn't examine God; it examines one aspect of human experience. Theology as a science involves abstraction, while a confession of faith is an act which takes place with a person's whole being and is a faith confession which accepts whatever God does. When we confess our faith, we don't abstract, we confess before the face of the Lord integrally and totally, "This is my Saviour in whom I believe." In theology, on the other hand, you deal with confession in abstraction, and you're analyzing in order to understand better how the norm of God's Word holds for confession in general.

He added: "Many people don't distinguish their confession from their theology, and they think that anytime you try to relate the Scriptures or the Word of God, or Christ to anything, you're doing theology. And they think that if you start to change your theology or reform your theology, you're undermining faith in Jesus Christ."

FOCUS Student Clubs

Some of the Canadian university students who had attended the early Unionville conferences were so excited about the new insights set before them that they decided that once a year was not enough. They formed study groups in their universities, beginning in 1959 at the University of Toronto. They listened with close attention to the tape-recorded lectures given at the Unionville conferences, and they studied such similar written materials as they could get their hands on. Soon they organized themselves nationally under the general name of Federation of Christian University Societies, or FOCUS. They went so far as to start their own periodical. They wanted to own and develop the insights and convictions gained at the summer student conferences. They also wanted to promote a Christian witness in the various studies within the academic community.

Peter Schouls, who in his student days was a member of a FOCUS club, later said that they wanted to be able to accept "... the claim which the revelation of God in Jesus Christ makes upon the whole scholarly enterprise." The Association Board set up a committee to encourage the formation of these groups and give guidance to their development, and the Institute's Development Director, James Van Oosterom, affirmed that a study outline was needed for the FOCUS clubs with an emphasis on the foundations of Christian scholarship. The students, however, wanted to be independent and not subject to direction by well-meaning outsiders. The clubs continued throughout Canada for a number of years before they faded.

Incorporation

In 1961, the Association applied for incorporation, which was granted November 27 of that year. The signatories to the incorporation were Glenn Andreas, Rev. François Guillaume, Fred Masselink, Everett Kok, Rev. Dr. Remkes Kooistra, Rev. François Kouwenhoven, Peter Nienhuis, Rev. John Piersma, Dr. H. Evan Runner, Rev. Dr. Paul Schrotenboer, Rev. Alvin Venema, Roel Siebring, Peter Speelman, and Rev. Henry Van Andel. The objects stated were "To undertake or promote scripturally directed learning and scholarly enterprise and, in particular, to establish, control and develop a Christian university, and in these ways to equip men and women to bring the Word of God in all its power to bear upon

---

Rev. François Guillaume was one of the four people who took the first steps to found the Institute. In the early years, he defined the spiritual heart of the Institute. His preaching was described as passionate, prophetic, and powerful, shaped by his earlier incarceration in a Nazi concentration camp.

He was an outstanding leader and a dynamic figure who challenged people in Christian service. Along with other Dutch immigrant pastors to Canada like **Rev. Henry Van Andel** and **Rev. Dr. Remkes Kooistra**, he promoted a vision for communal Christian service in every aspect of life. Van Andel, whose wife was a daughter of Herman Dooyeweerd and who was a creative Dooyeweerdian thinker, was a progressive pastor who persuaded uneducated Christians to establish and build the Institute. Kooistra worked with great energy to help start the Institute. His advanced studies in sociology gave him an openly ecumenical approach to Christian higher learning. He chaired the Institute Board for a number of years in the 1960s.

—Gerald Vandezande

the whole of life."

The first Board, elected in 1956, worked with great energy and enthusiasm. There was much to do to begin the educational work, and soon the Board appointed an Executive Committee to meet each month. There was no paid staff member until January 1964, when Paul Schrotenboer started serving half-time as Executive Director, so the Board and its Executive Committee did everything in the early years. There was a great deal of discussion, organizing, and sometimes arguing. The meetings were long and frequent, and the minutes were very extensive. The Board meeting of October 1966, for instance, coming very close to the formal opening of the Institute, lasted four days, and its minutes are written in 237 articles, even though that by that time the Board was served by an Executive Committee and an Executive Director. No administrative matter was too small to be decided by the Board.

Newsletters

The first Unionville Conference in 1959 and the success of its lectures in book form catapulted the Association onto a world stage. The Board decided that a regular newsletter would be an important way to tell people far and near what it was doing and how plans for the start of an Institute were developing. In July 1960, the Board started publishing a quarterly newsletter written in turn by various Board members. Half of the first newsletter was written in Dutch and half in English. In 1963, this means of communication was upgraded to newspaper-size reports published each month in the weekly newspaper *Calvinist Contact*, which could be found in most Dutch Reformed homes in Canada. Editor and Association member Dirk Farenhorst generously made this avenue possible until 1967, when the Association started publishing its own newsletter, *Perspective*.

Around the same time, the bimonthly magazine *Vanguard* was started to proclaim a Christian worldview and to show how Christians were demonstrating in their lives that "all of life is religion." This helped develop an interest in "radical" Christian living, a way of living with roots in the Christian gospel with the message, to use the words of Dutch leader Abraham Kuyper, that "there is not a square inch in the world of which God does not say 'this is mine.'"

Membership and Identity

Membership in the Association was growing. In the 1960s, there were two classes of members. (The reason for this was the effort in

Philadelphia, Pennsylvania, to start a Christian university in the 1930s. That effort failed because the range of Christian viewpoints among the active participants was too broad for them to agree on specific plans of action.) The issue at stake was the control by members over the religious and philosophical direction of the Association and the Institute.

Glenn Andreas and Evan Runner, the Americans on the Board, wanted a more restricted, more focused Christian perspective. Further, they wanted the new university to develop on the foundation of "reformational" thinking as articulated in the Netherlands by Herman Dooyeweerd and his associates. Although very few of those interested in the Association would feel that these reformational ideas were not good, some of them felt that everyone who adhered to Calvinistic theology, whether they were "reformational" or not, should be able to find a place in helping to develop this Christian program. But the Board adopted the idea of the Americans, so in 1962 it required that all voting members not only needed to accept the Association's Educational Creed but also that each new voting member would need to be invited for membership by three current members of the Association as a person adhering to "reformational" ideas. Only after this nomination process did the Board vote on whether to accept the nominee to voting membership. Nonvoting members, called associate members, were those who simply adhered to the Educational Creed.

> **H. Evan Runner** was greatly influential in my academic development as a student at Calvin College. Runner's lectures in philosophy grabbed me. He would deliver them with much passion and conviction. His vision of a Christ-centered, scripturally directed approach to all of life set our hearts on fire. He taught us how the Greeks influenced Western culture and imbued it with a form of dualism that expressed itself especially in the nature-grace divide that could be found in so many expressions of Christianity, especially Roman Catholicism. He was more interested in shaping our minds, however, than in exposing us to other philosophers. Runner's passion also meant that he did not brook too much questioning. I remember asking a question in class; he indicated his displeasure by repeating a few times, "Of course, Witvoet thinks . . ." Not that I took it ill of him. He was a genuine child of God who was so caught up in his sense of mission that he did not always pay attention to interpersonal relations. I honour the memory of this faithful teacher and friend.
>
>
>
> —Bert Witvoet

This position became a matter of considerable tension within the Association as well as among some people who accepted reformational views but were not willing to become members because of the restricted Board membership. The idea of the institution run by an elite group was distasteful to them. That idea seemed contrary to Abraham Kuyper's strong embrace of the common people, expressed in Dutch as the *kleine luyden*. Under considerable public pressure, the Board dropped the provision for the two levels of membership in 1968. A significant reason for this was agreement with the view that the pledge of persons that they accepted the statements of belief expressed in the Constitution should be accepted in good faith.

One important person who rejected the leadership of Runner and restricted voting membership to people of "reformational" conviction was Peter Speelman, the original president and leader of the Association. Speelman made his views known to the Board orally and in letters. A central point for Speelman was that the new institution should be open to all persons who believed in Jesus Christ and the Bible and who held a Reformed Christian view of the world. He did not want the Institute to be centred in the Amsterdam philosophy introduced by Herman Dooyeweerd and his associates, which was advocated by Runner and others. When he saw that his views were not accepted, he wrote a lengthy public letter to Board and Association members in 1966. He argued that the Association was trying to build its work from the top down, not from the bottom up, that is, with elite leaders who did not necessarily accept the views of the ordinary pew sitter. Speelman saw this as a rejection of the Calvinistic idea of the office of all believers. He also objected to the policy of the Association promoting its work through its educational services rather than making direct appeals for support to all interested persons. Speelman's letter was published in *Calvinist Contact,* which upset the Board, although Speelman always insisted he did not know how his letter came to be published that way. Some people felt that Speelman was concerned that control of the Association was moving away from him and the people who started the movement and had now come to be in the hands of Runner and his academic followers.

The fears of Speelman and those who shared his views were bolstered in the mid-1960s when Evan Runner was heard to say that some of his former students, now studying at the Free University in Amsterdam, would soon be receiving their doctorates and would be ready for faculty positions at the Institute. In fact those fears, or blessings, depending on one's point of view, were to be realized when several of the first members appointed to the Institute faculty had indeed studied with Runner at Calvin College and later graduated from the Free University.

Membership in the Association slowly grew, impeded by the need for three supporting signatures for each new member. In 1963, there were 89 members, and in 1964, there were 148. In 1965, membership rose to 840 with 140 voting members and 700 associate members. In 1967, this doubled to 1,602 total members, 392 voting members and 1,210 associate members. In 1969, there were 2,500 members located in eight voting districts.

It should be noted that there was a general unspoken assumption that "membership" was a family matter. A "member" of the Association was understood to be a family, understood to be either a nuclear family with the husband and father as the representative or a single adult living alone. The family as the core unit of society, rather than the individual, characterized the covenantal social viewpoint of Dutch Reformed people. This viewpoint, however, was changing in the closing decades of the twentieth century with the rise of feminism and of divorce and the increase in the number of single adults.

Local Chapters

At an early point, a Dutch idea was adopted for members to be organized into local Chapters that brought together members in a given geographical area. Chapters were formed, starting in 1960, wherever ten or more members lived close enough together to meet periodically. The Association office prepared a sample constitution for the Chapters. In 1965, Executive Director Paul Schrotenboer developed four study outlines of material for discussion at Chapter meetings. They included such topics as the need for a reformation in scholarship, foundations for a Christian academic enterprise, the nature of the anticipated Institute, and what Christian learning could do for the people of God.

Chapters were seen as a good way to link the ongoing work of the Association with the individual members. The Association office would keep each Chapter informed of what the Board and staff were doing and respond to criticisms that might arise in the community. Chapter officers could do this more directly and personally than could be done from the head office. The Chapter board could also send to the office ideas and suggestions coming from the members at the grassroots level. Another important task of the Chapters was to maintain trust relationships between the Association and its members.

Community activities for Chapters included making arrangements for travelling lecturers of the Association, organizing summer conferences and study clubs for university students, recruiting new Association members, distributing literature, and conducting financial campaigns. Members were supposed to pay their annual dues to the Chapter, which would then send them to the head office. Chapters were also expected to promote the sale of Association-sponsored publications and *Vanguard* magazine.

In commenting on the value of Chapters, Board president Remkes Kooistra wrote in 1962:

> The ARSS is a movement which does not want to separate itself from the people. It can succeed only if it is rooted in the warm interest of the people of God. If the Association does indeed prove to be a blessing for all believers, including those who do not themselves take part in academic studies, we may expect that these believers will in turn become a blessing to all the inhabitants of our continent. This in brief is the service envisioned by the ARSS. Our main purpose is not the university, but to live in the fear of the Lord. A university is not an ivory tower for the scholar who keeps aloof from the common people, and even despises them because they are ignorant and are not able to understand the essence of life.

In 1962, there were eight Chapters, and in 1963, eleven Chapters. By 1967, the number rose to thirty-seven Chapters.

The idea and expectations of Chapters, however, proved to be too unrealistic and cumbersome. Immigrant people led busy lives. In 1967, the new Executive Director, Hendrik Hart, reported that by and large the Chapters were inactive, uninformed, and not doing what was hoped of them. Meetings were poorly attended, membership lists were not kept up to date, and dues were not being sent to the central office. In 1972, an eighteen-page Chapter Handbook was written to encourage Chapters to do what the Association Board hoped they would do. The administrative staff in Toronto became increasingly frustrated because it was required to communicate with the dispersed membership through the Chapters, many of which had ceased to exist. Gradually the expectations of Chapters were dropped and the structure abandoned. An exception was in Edmonton, where an elected Chapter board arranged certain functions, including a summer conference each year, until 2003. As the 1983 charter for ICS made no mention of Chapters, officially the Chapter structure died.

Women's Action for the AACS

Another distinctive idea from the Dutch history of the Free University became part of the Association in December 1959, and that was the role that women could play in the development of the Association. In those years, it was not very common for women to hold positions of Board leadership, and in the Dutch immigrant culture, married women often did not hold jobs outside of the home. A group of women met in Toronto and decided to contribute to the new movement in their own special way. They set up a committee called Women's Action for the ARSS, saying that "The Purpose is to help the ARSS financially to promote Christian Education on the University level." The women constructed a considerable number of small coin banks for families to place on their kitchen counter. Families were encouraged to put a coin, maybe just a penny, into these banks for the cause of ARSS. The women would then go around to the homes to collect the banks, meet as a committee, and contribute these monies to the Association. A photo with the article announcing the program identifies Mrs. Mulder from Brockville, Mrs. Vandezande from Woodstock, Mrs. Kooi and Mrs. Heemsbergen from Toronto, and Mrs. Lunshof from Drayton.

In February 1960, the Women's Action made its first contribution to the Association, slightly more than $100. In 1968, Mrs. G. Vandezande, Sr., reported that 1300 Penny-A-Day banks had been placed in homes. In 1970 Mrs. Kooi presented AACS with a cheque for $2,000, which was "the reward of a year's hard, diligent and faithful work by all the women supporters." Much of the money that came from the "penny banks" was used for office equipment for the Association.

Education for School Teachers

In February 1964, Executive Director Paul Schrotenboer announced arrangements had been made for the Association to offer a summer school for in-service Christian school teachers to be held in Hamilton from August 10–24. The courses offered were: Perspectives of Philosophy, by H. Evan Runner; Critique of Modern Pedagogics, by Remkes Kooistra; and Christian Teaching as an Office, by Paul Schrotenboer. The summer school was highly successful.

The Association offered summer courses for teachers from 1964 through 1968 in cooperation with the Ontario Alliance of Christian Schools, an organization started and supported initially by Dutch Reformed people in Ontario. In 1966, for example, four courses were offered in six weeks, with courses taught by Garrett Rozeboom of Dordt College, Maarten Vrieze of Trinity Christian College, and H. Evan Runner and Gordon Spykman of Calvin College. John Stronks of the Alliance was the administrator. Stronks said that the professors thoroughly enjoyed the teaching and the students were enthusiastic. Stronks reported that of the forty-six students who took courses in 1966, twenty percent had attended the summer session for teachers the previous summer, fifteen percent had no education beyond high school, sixty percent had recently completed teachers college, and half had no previous teaching experience. In those years, a teacher could be certified to teach in elementary schools in Ontario without having a university degree. A teacher needed one year of study beyond Grade 12 plus one year of study at a teachers college to be certified to teach in public schools, but teachers in non-public Christian schools did not need teacher certification.

In February 1967, the Association's new Executive Director Hendrik Hart reported that the Alliance favoured education for prospective Christian school teachers that would offer a broad liberal arts education with some special emphasis on educational courses, rather than a "mere technical training of a few years." They wanted this educational effort to be undertaken in cooperation with the Association.

But in September 1968, the Alliance informed the Association that it could no longer work with the Association on the summer school program for school teachers. The Alliance had found itself caught between the Association and its parent body, Christian Schools International (called the National Union of Christian Schools in the 1960s). CSI, based in Grand Rapids, Michigan, was not happy with the educational philosophy and methods of the Canadians nor with the Canadian work on new curricular materials that were different from those developed in Michigan. So it leaned on the Alliance to discontinue its working relation with the Association. Many Ontario teachers and school boards were not happy with the Alliance decision and wished to continue working with the Association.

Also in 1964, the Ontario Alliance of Christian Schools (OACS) set up a committee to explore setting up a Christian teachers college in Ontario. The Alliance was deeply concerned about what it saw as a tremendous shortage of qualified Christian teachers, which endangered the very existence of day schools serving Dutch Reformed residents of Ontario. Paul Schrotenboer met with the committee to assist with the discussions. In January 1966, Schrotenboer reported that since the Association agreed with the Alliance in favouring scripturally directed teacher education, the Association would support the Alliance's aim of starting a Christian teachers college.

In October 1967, Hendrik Hart prepared a working paper for

consultations between representatives of the Association and the Alliance about the cooperative development of an Education Department at the Institute. This development would mean that the Institute would undertake teacher education and that a separate teachers college for Christian school teachers would not be needed.

The paper started with these words:

> The intention of the proposed cooperation is the training of new staff members for the member schools of OACS, the further development of such staff members already employed, and work towards providing and implementing a Christian curriculum. . . . Although the proposed cooperation provisionally pertains only to the OACS and the ARSS, there are indications that other interested bodies may in the future be included in this venture.

The proposal for discussion states that "The ARSS agrees to develop an Education Department suited for the training of fully qualified Christian teachers, to develop a full Christian curriculum for both elementary and secondary education and to provide materials for use in such a curriculum." The Education Department would start with the appointment of Arnold De Graaff to the Education Department of the Institute.

But in 1970, the Alliance decided not to pursue starting a teachers college, partly because it could not see how it could be financed. In 1973, an unsigned report, probably written by Executive Director John Olthuis, raised the question of whether the Institute should start a teachers college separate from the Institute, and the Association decided to focus entirely on the Institute as a school for graduate-level foundational scholarship.

The Institute never did develop an undergraduate program to give prospective Christian school teachers the education they needed, though it did appoint De Graaff in 1970 to teach education as well as psychology at the Institute. While on the faculty of Trinity Christian College in the Chicago area, De Graaff had set up summer workshops in which experienced teachers prepared curricula for their teaching areas, and he continued this for some years in Toronto. This activity later became organized as the Curriculum Development Centre, which was supported by the Institute (see Chapter 10).

The Association supported teacher education in other ways as well. In the late 1960s, for example, Dr. Albert E. Greene Jr. asked the Association to provide teachers for an annual two-day teacher's conference he organized at Bellevue Christian School near Seattle. The Edmonton Chapter of the Association wanted six-week courses of a similar sort to those in Ontario and asked the Association to participate. The Association provided qualified teachers where it could in such cases.

In 1968, Hart reported that as part of a larger teaching program to offer courses in various Canadian cities, he was teaching a course in London, Ontario, and in Toronto for teachers, a course that was a slow exegetical study of John Dewey's book *Democracy and Education*. It was attended by about fifty teachers.

Early Relations with Calvin College

In 1964, Calvin College was indicating its intent to start a graduate program offering master's degrees in a number of academic areas. This looked like direct competition for the Institute's plans to start a graduate school. Further, a written report by Calvin's Graduate Studies Committee included a statement that the Association was going to become a rival rather than a colabourer in Calvin's plans to become a university. Each side seemed to have concerns about the other, so in April 1964, three leaders of the Association, Remkes Kooistra, Paul Schrotenboer, and Glenn Andreas, arranged a meeting in Grand Rapids with Calvin representatives.

The discussion showed some areas of disagreement between the two groups and their institutions. One area of difference was that Calvin was owned and controlled by the Christian Reformed Church. The Canadians rejected control of a school by a noneducational organization. But Calvin needed that arrangement for the financial and moral support of its work and was not willing to make a major move to develop a graduate program that was structurally separate from the church.

Another problem was the religious and philosophical base for the schools. Calvin was unhappy with the Institute's founding itself on its Educational Creed. Calvin's religious foundation was the creeds of the Christian Reformed Church. Calvin said it did not have insurmountable objections to the Educational Creed, but it did have concerns that this creed was hiding a fixed adherence to the Christian philosophy developed in Amsterdam by Dooyeweerd and Vollenhoven and their associates.

Calvin wanted its philosophy of education to be "representational," to represent the range of philosophical views held by Christian Reformed Church members. Calvin was able and willing to include faculty members who were Reformed in their theology and were sincerely interested in understanding their academic field in the light of its teachings, whatever philosophical view they might have.

The Institute wanted a sharper focus, namely, working with

reformational Christian philosophical ideas. The Institute opposed academic viewpoints like positivism, linguistic analysis, and humanism, but as Institute people saw it, Calvin did not seem sensitive enough to such viewpoints. The Institute was exclusive in that it wanted its faculty to work with the Dooyeweerdian viewpoint, though membership in the Association required only agreement with its creedal statements, which were not explicitly Dooyeweerdian.

The Canadian immigrants wanted to work with ideas on Christian scholarly work that had been developed in the Netherlands during the previous fifty years. Those developments were largely foreign to the Calvin people, who were more attuned to American developments, which had become increasingly secular in the area of fundamental thinking. One or both institutions would have needed to make major movement in foundational thinking to bring them together harmoniously.

Another reason for Calvin's showing a prickly skin to the Institute was simply that for almost a century, Calvin had been the only college run by members of the Christian Reformed Church, and it would not easily share its position of privilege. This first became clear when Calvin publicly opposed the start of Dordt College in Iowa by Christian Reformed people. Now, in a more muted way, it responded similarly to the start in Toronto of an alternative to Calvin's plans for graduate programs.

Communication between the two institutions carried on in a somewhat desultory way for the next few years. Association people complained that it was hard to get Calvin's reports and Board actions on the subject of its relations with the Institute. Finally, in November 1968, a committee of Calvin College reported to the Institute that it was recommending to its Board that Calvin "proceed to formulate its plan and program for a Christian university and graduate degree programs." It recommended that Calvin ask the Institute to "be dissuaded from following a parallel program." These recommendations, however, were not adopted at Calvin, and the plans for a Christian university at Calvin were dropped. As the years went by, Calvin became a willing partner of the graduate work of the Institute, especially under the leadership of Calvin's President Anthony Diekema.

It may be appropriate to identify major cultural differences between Americans who were descendants of earlier Dutch Calvinist immigrants and the new Dutch Canadian immigrants. Theologically, there were very few differences. But in the Netherlands, the Reformed religious culture was vibrant and dynamic, a rich culture that developed before the war. The American culture of Dutch Reformed people had developed in earlier years, and the excitement of building a Christian culture lost something as it moved across the ocean to the United States. There were indeed Dutch Americans for whom the vision of Abraham Kuyper was strong, but most of them worked hard to establish themselves in secure lives as they worshipped in Christian Reformed churches and sent their children to Christian day schools. The dynamism of claiming all of life for Christ lost some its verve in the large secular culture in which they found themselves. By the mid-1950s, it seemed that in many American Dutch locales the religious culture was living on the vision of past decades.

Consultation at Carleton University

In 1965, as the Association was developing its plans to start the Institute, it was invited to attend a Consultation of Christian Churches and Agencies Regarding University Work in Canada held in May at Carleton University, Ottawa. This gave the Association an opportunity to articulate its views on Christian higher education to a wide forum of Canadian Christians. Universities at that time saw religion as incidental to their work, unrelated to genuine scholarship. Religion might possibly be relevant to ethical matters, but otherwise it was strictly private and optional, though somewhat anachronistic and unscientific.

The Association's contribution to the meeting, evidently prepared and presented by Paul Schrotenboer, was strikingly different from this perspective. It presented the view that God's Word speaks about religion in a *comprehensive* way. The Scriptures are profoundly relevant to the academic work of Christians on the modern university campus. Academic work is not religiously neutral, as is generally held to be the case, and science is not really the source of truth. Although churches may have their different ways of relating to the university and its students, Christian scholarship is genuinely ecumenical, not divided along the lines of the denominations with all their divisions from each other.

The paper stated that scholars in its Association were "engaged in scientific, that is, analytical-synthetic academic investigation of the entire spectrum of structures and entities encountered, implicitly or explicitly, in human experience." It argued for "a truly Christian philosophical worldview which includes in its scope the entire world panorama."

The paper was presented at a conference where the chief activity of Christian churches on campus was university chaplaincies addressed to the hearts, devotional activities, and personal problems of students. The ministry of the Association was instead primarily addressed to the minds of Christian students, and thus it had a clear academic focus.

Although in some ways the conference was a disappointment to Institute people, it did introduce them to important Christian leaders like Wilbur Sutherland, who had a major Christian witness to people at the University of Toronto, and Eilert Frericks, a professor at that university. The Association became a member of this Consultation.

At the second conference of this Consultation in 1968, the Association was represented by John Vander Stelt, a Christian Reformed pastor who later became an Association staff member. In his report on the conference, Vander Stelt complained later that "Forces of liberalism, fundamentalist subjectivism, subtle relativism and annoying churchism were so strong at this conference among the majority of students, professors and clergymen that it becomes extremely difficult, at times even impossible, to create room for the normativity of God's Word." Just as at the first conference, he said that there appeared to be no basis for true dialogue and discussion.

Finances

At first, the Association had relatively few costs apart from mailings. Many costs of running the Association, like attendance at Board meetings, were absorbed by the Board members themselves. Once the basic structure of the Association was set in place, those who became Association members paid a membership fee of ten dollars a year, later raised to twenty-five.

When the first paid staff member, Paul Schrotenboer, started serving on a half-time basis in January 1964, there was a greater need for income.

> **Paul Schrotenboer** was a calm but passionate person with deep-down convictions. He was focused and had a central rootedness in the gospel. He had a special ability to keep complex issues simple and straightforward. His ability to hold firmly to a clear biblical path was touching. He didn't hesitate to speak his mind with gentleness in troubled situations, at which occasions
>
> he had a stabilizing effect. His well-reasoned voice kept sides together. He made major points in a subtle way, and he had a good sense of humour. He thought inclusively. He related well with both Dutch-born and American Christian Reformed pastors, who tended to have differing viewpoints. He championed "scripturally directed learning centred in Christ." He could broaden people's horizons.
>
> —Gerald Vandezande

Membership rose to 840 in 1965 and to 1,602 in 1967. The basic approach was to look for small donations from a large number of people. Income came from membership dues and donations solicited by letters. Often the rule of "faith economics" guided the Association.

For specific work on raising funds, visiting membership Chapters, and communicating directly with supporters, James Van Oosterom was appointed as Director of Development, starting his service in September 1966. He was expected to be "on the road" to get new members, work with Association Chapters, and solicit donations. He talked with many Christian Reformed pastors in southern Ontario about the Association. At one time or another, most of them had had serious questions about how the ideals of the Association were to be made concrete. Almost all of them agreed that the principles and ideas of Association were good, but they had problems with the persons and personalities of the people representing the movement. He said that about eighty percent of the complaints were about persons and personalities, so that the Association had a distasteful image to these pastors. Their complaints all seemed to be directed at what they perceived to be a "boss" image. Instances of rancour and mistrust were never forgotten. However, most of these people were of the opinion that the work of Paul Schrotenboer and his conciliatory ways were very important to the continued survival of Association. Changes to the constitution in 1966 seemed very good to the pastors, and many were willing to reappraise the matter of their personal and public support of the Association

Van Oosterom served effectively for one year, at which time he left to study at Calvin Seminary in Michigan. He was followed in 1967 by two Directors of Development, Fred Cupido for western Canada and John Vander Stelt for eastern Canada. Both of them served for one year, at which time Cupido left for graduate study at the Free University in Amsterdam and Vander Stelt left to accept a faculty appointment at Dordt College in Iowa. When they left in the summer of 1968, John Hultink was appointed as International Director of Development.

A "400 Club" was set up in 1967 to get four hundred people to commit one dollar a month to cover payments on the first mortgage for the purchase of the first Institute building on 141 Lyndhurst Street. By March 1968, a total of fifty-nine members had contributed $340.50 to the fund. Under Hultink's leadership in the eight months prior to July 1969, the Association received 709 applications for membership.

A Reforming Institution

The founders of the Institute were breaking new ground at every turn. For the major activities, this was a necessity. There have always been many freestanding Christian colleges and universities in the United States, but that was not true in Canada, nor was it the case in the Netherlands. The structure of higher education in Canada is British, which means that all schools of higher education, except for seminaries and Bible colleges, can exist only as a "royalty" given by the government, that is, by the Crown through the legislature.

In the late 1960s, both Regent College, founded in Vancouver, and the Institute for Christian Studies started as Christian graduate schools. Each needed to feel its way into curricula and patterns of research. The Institute also experimented with governance structures. Its reason for existence, its curriculum, and its governance were new in Canada. Not many people—from other universities or from the government of Ontario—understood the Institute, so it was difficult for universities to relate structurally to the Institute and for it to obtain a charter from the government.

Added to this uniqueness was the Institute's financial structure. Who ever heard of a graduate school that did not receive grants from the government and received only small amounts of money from churches and student tuition fees? Was it possible for a graduate school to exist whose only significant income arises from free-will donations?

Furthermore, the Institute's staff and Board members did not understand the cultural climate in Canada, and the staff resisted learning about governance, curriculum, and pedagogy from other institutions. The result has been a certain amount of stumbling that, especially in the early years, hurt the Institute's development.

An important question that has arisen from the Institute's experience is whether establishing a Christian graduate school it is really a responsible Christian activity. Many people have doubted that it is. But the founders of the Association and of the Institute were convinced with all their heart that it was the right thing to do, however impractical it may have seemed. They believed that if God wanted them to do such a thing, then he would provide the means for his people to do it.

2

Setting Up the Institute

The years from 1956 to the mid-1960s were years of preparation in the development of the Institute for Christian Studies. Important work was being done, like putting in place foundational documents such as the Educational Creed, conducting summer conferences for students, publishing books, organizing university student clubs, forming members into Chapters, and appointing a half-time Executive Director.

All this activity pointed to something much larger. The aim was to start a school, even a university, and all sorts of ideas about what kind of school it should be were floating around. But how was this new university to be started in an unfamiliar country? In 1964, the Board appointed a committee of three of its members with doctoral degrees, Remkes Kooistra, Paul Schrotenboer, and Evan Runner, to prepare a report that would show the way.

The twenty-page report turned out to be a landmark paper that galvanized the Association's members, a paper that summarized why an Institute was needed and what it could do. It was called "Place and Task of an Institute of Reformed Scientific Studies." The chief writer was Runner, a very passionate professor of the history of philosophy at Calvin College.

In bold print, the report stated: "The ARSS knows that in the continuing present crisis of our world it must bring home to the hearts and minds of this student generation the claim which the revelation of God in Jesus Christ makes upon the whole scientific and scholarly enterprise. . . ." It noted that higher education, unlike the church, had never had a reformation, and quoted Henri Marrou: "A Christian upbringing was something superimposed on a humanistic education that had not previously been subject to the requirements of the Christian religion." The point was that the Institute should avoid the dichotomistic viewpoint of nature and grace as it had developed in earlier centuries. The report called for people giving leadership to the Institute to have philosophically controlling ideas that are biblical, "an inner reformation of scholarship." What was needed was a Christian mind, a Christian structure of thought.

The writers stated that an "institute" would be a good form for the new school to have. An institute is well known in educational circles and has the advantage of being a very general name that can refer to any organization for the promotion of learning, the arts, the sciences, or skills. It offered the flexibility needed at that early stage of development. It would give scholars the best way to develop the kind of Christian mind they were seeking, which the authors felt did exist at the time of the report.

As a model of how such an institute could function, the report pointed out Victoria University, which is federated with the University of Toronto. Federation gives Victoria students access to university libraries and university courses. It has two colleges, Victoria College, which is the arts college, and Emmanuel University, which is the theological college and seminary. The writers noted that the Association could build the Institute, and even a relatively small faculty "could include within it the nucleus of a future law faculty, a faculty of medicine, a faculty of theology, or a teachers college."

The teaching of philosophy was to be given central place in the institute. As a general academic field, according to the report:

> philosophy is concerned with the totality of all aspects of created reality and aims to give a theoretical insight into the whole coherence of our temporal world. The study of philosophy should thus help all Christian students in the fulfillment of their more specialized tasks, and equip them to evaluate the systems of ideas which they encounter in their studies. It will also enable them to form a proper view of the place of their particular studies in the total framework of a Christian theoretical enterprise within the whole of human life before the face of God.

Theology was not chosen as the academic focus of the Institute's foundational and interdisciplinary studies because in philosophy, not theology, are found the basic religious questions of the academic disciplines. It is not helpful to have a "theology of history" or "theological aesthetics" or "a theological cultural history," as Calvin Seerveld later put it. Rather, he said, "Scripturally directed learning requires that all faculty members need to be academically versed in theology, need to have the Bible as their mother tongue," so that God's written word directs the academic studies of God's creation.

Seen from a much later historical perspective, the 1964 "Place and Task" report seems not only enthusiastic and optimistic but even triumphalistic. Yet at the time, its vision and practicality had a catalytic effect in rallying people to work together to build an exciting and God-honouring Institute.

The document asked the Board to recommend to the members that such an Institute be set up in the Toronto area to open in September 1967. The report and its recommendations were adopted by the Board in February 1965 and by the members of the Association in October 1965.

The next year, a committee chaired by Harry Vander Laan recommended to the Board that the primary emphasis of the Institute should be on graduate work. It also recommended a location in Toronto, an affiliation with an Ontario university, and the use of the library facilities at the University of Toronto. The recommendations, adopted in 1965, included affirmation of the opening of the Institute in September 1967, which was indeed when the Institute started.

Staffing

Vision and big plans need legs to make them work. Already in the early 1960s, the Board was eager to get an institution set up and operating. But they needed money and staff. In February 1962, the Board offered a "tentative appointment" to Bernard Zylstra, hoping it could raise $10,000 to pay his salary and expenses. There was considerable difference of opinion on the Board about this appointment, and some confusion, since some Board members thought an appointment to Zylstra meant that an appointment would not be made to Dutch professor Hendrik van Riessen, whom they very much wished to appoint. But van Riessen indicated that he would not consider an appointment to be the first person to be hired because he did not wish to be involved in administrative or fund-raising activities.

Bernard Zylstra

Later in 1962, the Board appointed a special Finance Committee to recommend an alternative plan of action. Committee members were Board members John Piersma, Glenn Andreas, and Alvin Venema. In a twenty-five-page report, the committee made the bold recommendation that three people be appointed full-time to start the Institute: Evan Runner, Hendrik van Riessen, and Bernard Zylstra.

The committee prepared a three-year budget to show the feasibility of its recommendations. It looked forward to significant income from "quotas" (expected donation support) for higher education from Christian Reformed churches for the year 1967, the first year the Institute would operate. Quota income would contribute $63,500 to a total income of $120,000. Expenses were projected to be $84,200 for the year, with a surplus of income over expenses of $35,800. It was expected that the Association would be able to rent suitable space for its program for $6,000 for the year.

The committee had recommended Zylstra "for the purpose of getting our house in order so as to make physically and financially possible the appointments of Runner and van Riessen." It was expected that Zylstra could begin work for the Association in January 1965 and prepare the way for the opening of the Institute in September 1966 with van Riessen and Runner as the initial faculty. The presumption was that soon thereafter, Zylstra, with his new doctoral degree, would follow as a member of the faculty.

These recommendations also raised a great deal of controversy among Board members and were not adopted by the Board. Instead, it appointed Paul Schrotenboer to a half-time position as Executive Director, starting January 1, 1964. Schrotenboer lived in St. Catharines, Ontario, and worked the other half of his time as Executive Director of the Reformed Ecumenical Synod (now called the Reformed Ecumenical Council), an international ecumenical association. He did exceptional work in laying a solid foundation for the Institute.

Schrotenboer served three years in this position, to the end of 1966, when he accepted the position of Executive Director of the Ecumenical Synod on a full-time basis and established its office in Grand Rapids, Michigan. In August 1966, Hendrik Hart arrived with an appointment to prepare for the opening of the Institute. He became the Executive Director on a short-term basis when Schrotenboer left, serving until June 1967. Next, John Olthuis became Executive Director half-time and served until March 1974. When the Institute opened in September 1967, Hart became its first faculty member.

Developing a Structure

In October 1966, a committee of people with doctoral degrees, headed by Harry Vander Laan, presented a report structuring the entire organization. The committee set up a very complex structure, with heavy involvement of the few thousand members of the Association. The report recommended that the faculty should not only give Christian Perspective courses for undergraduate students on university campuses, but should spend a large fraction of its time and effort in research, publication, and supervision of the research of Institute graduate students. The primary duties of faculty members, said the report, should be to teach and engage in research and publication. "Upon request, members of the staff may also be engaged in providing services, for example, to student clubs, teaching organizations, the Christian Labour Association, Citizens for Public Justice, and the like."

That was a pretty heavy load, even for exceptionally gifted people. It was too heavy, of course, and the toll began to tell in the early years. The Institute tried to be all things to all people, and clearly that would not work. After the Institute had been operating for a few years, realism slowly set in and the faculty work load was changed.

Supervising the Academic Work

In October 1966, the Board approved a committee recommendation that "the primary emphasis of the Institute should be on graduate work." But how was the Board to supervise and give direction to this advanced academic work if many Board members did not have a university education? The answer came from the Dutch experience. The Free University was controlled by an association, but it recognized that its Board would not be made up solely of academically qualified persons holding advanced degrees. So the university set up a Board of Curators to supervise the academic work and advise the Board on faculty appointments and academic policies.

The Institute did the same. A Board of Curators was appointed to consist of between five and nine members of the Association qualified to make judgments in academic matters. Each member served a five-year term and could be reappointed any number of times. The Curators interviewed all candidates for faculty positions upon recommendation of the faculty and recommended faculty appointments to the Board of Trustees. Faculty appointments and termination of appointments could only be made by the Trustees. The Curators decided educational policy, including the structure and direction of curricular development, and supervised the implementation of educational policy in consultation with the faculty.

That kind of structure necessitated very good communication between the two boards, so a Board of Governors was set up "conduct all the affairs of the Institute." Its membership consisted of all members of the Board of Curators and all members of the Executive Committee (first called the Board of Directors) of the Trustees. But trying to hold together the governance of an institution with persons from all over the large nation of Canada became very complicated. After a very few meetings, the Board of Governors was declared unnecessary and the Board of Trustees related directly with the curators in approving academic matters.

Locating the Institute

Canada is a very large country, and maintaining contact throughout its distant borders is always a problem. Western Canadians felt that they were seriously underserved in regards to Christian higher education, and in 1966 Association members living in Alberta made a strong case that the Institute should be located in Edmonton. One of the weighty reasons they gave for a western location was that the Alberta provincial government was much more open to providing funding for independent colleges and universities than was the Ontario government. The region was much more receptive to new and creative schools than is Ontario, they argued.

The Association Board considered this at length, but in February 1967 decided to start the Institute in Toronto. Most of the Board members of the Association lived in Ontario, and they assumed that the Institute would be located near Toronto. They said that Toronto was more strategic and its location more central. In addition, larger numbers of Reformed Christians lived in Ontario than in Alberta.

Western Canadians don't give up easily, however, and in early 1967, Albertans were making initial plans for a Christian undergraduate college of their own. The Association Board became concerned that a college in Alberta, even if it were limited to education for the first years beyond high school, would cost enough money to jeopardize the starting of the Institute. So Executive Director Hendrik Hart went to Alberta and met with those moving to start the college, urging them not to do it. The Albertans were not much impressed with Hart's plea, and they decided to move ahead. But serious planning did not take place in Alberta until 1972, and The King's University College was not able to open until 1979. But the merits of locating in Alberta rose again in 1990 when the Institute seriously considered moving to Edmonton.

In Ontario, there was a real need to find a location for classrooms and offices. When Paul Schrotenboer ended his service as Executive Director and moved to Michigan, the office moved temporarily from his home, which was now in Hamilton, to the home of Gerald Vandezande in Toronto. That's where Executive Director Hart worked, starting in August 1966.

A Board committee to find a location said that the ideal location would be on a plot of land of fifty to seventy-five acres north of the Toronto city limits. A building could be constructed there suitable for classrooms and offices, as close to York University as possible. But the Board preferred a location within Toronto.

A building soon came up for sale at 141 Lyndhurst Avenue, an ideal location in midtown Toronto near Bathurst and St. Clair avenues. It was a large and stately house in a good residential area, and the realtor was confident that zoning to permit a small school to start in the building would be no problem. So the Association bought the building for $83,117, and Hart and the office staff moved in during May 1967. To help with finances, Hart and his family occupied the second floor of the house. Now the Institute had a highly visible location, and the building was dedicated amid much celebration in October 1967.

Academic-Religious Direction

During the later 1960s, excitement about the Institute was rising, although opposition was vigorously expressed at every turn. Each Dutch immigrant who related to the Association felt that this movement in higher education was part of the religious heritage of his family. Many people took personal responsibility for building the Institute, just as they did for building their churches and Christian schools. And everyone felt

---

Gerald Vandezande has an intense biblical vision and is good at initiating things. He has wide personal contacts with persons outside the Dutch immigrant and Reformed circles, including journalists, political figures, and leaders of all stripes. He understood the yearnings of "God's little people" and could articulate persuasively the Institute's vision in terms they understood. As originating coleader of the Christian Labour Association of Canada, he knew how to struggle with the reigning spirits of the age. The home of Gerald and his wife Wynne in Rexdale was a meeting centre for old-timers and newcomers alike who were intent upon having the Christian faith  show its pertinence for being a living witness in society at large. Later, with Citizens for Public Justice, Gerald continued tirelessly to serve the Lord in supporting the poor. He knows how to focus complicated matters into the crucial point of taking a normative direction. His communication skills and leadership quality were of vital importance to the Institute during the years it was besieged by critics on every side. Gerald was crucial in persisting and helping the Institute achieve a government charter to validate the Institute's academic work with the deserving legal approval. Gerald knows how to keep his eye on our Lord and get things done on earth.

free to speak a word of criticism. For one thing, if the Institute was a way they were building Dutch Reformed Canada, who was this American who seemed to be taking it away from them?

The American in question was H. Evan Runner. He was born in Pennsylvania and graduated from Wheaton College, where he was a classmate and close friend of Glenn Andreas. Then he studied at Westminster Theological Seminary under Cornelius Van Til, who pointed him to Dutch neo-Calvinism. From there, he studied at the Theological School in Kampen, the Netherlands. During World War II, he studied with Werner Jaeger at Harvard University, and then returned to the Netherlands to complete his doctorate at the Free University in the history of philosophy. He taught philosophy at Calvin College from 1951 until his retirement in 1981.

At Calvin College, Runner inspired many Dutch Canadian students as well as many Americans. He passionately urged students headed for graduate school and even for seminary to study philosophy at the Free University, where a major cadre of leaders filled with "reformational" ideas was developing. In addition to his formal classes, he started the Groen Club for discussions on the implications and applications of reformational philosophy to all of life. Runner's work was central to the academic formation of early Institute professors Hart, Olthuis, Zylstra, De Graaff, Seerveld, and Wolters. Runner's view was that all scholarly concepts already have religious ideas built into them. The only question is: what religion? His central theme, repeated over and over, was "All of life is religion."

In the end, Runner and his vision for Christian scholarship set the vision for the Institute, over early objections that this Christian foundation for academic life was too narrow, as it was built on one particular philosophy. The response of certain Institute people was that this philosophy was a very useful tool that provided the way to deal with basic Christian issues in scholarship, to be used until something better came along. As the years went by, it became clear that the Institute ultimately did not follow with blinkered vision this philosophy, developed at the Free University by Dooyeweerd and his associates, but refined and reshaped it as they worked with it in relation to the thinking of other scholars and in application to the needs of today. In fact, the Institute's disagreement with certain points in Dooyeweerd's philosophy upset Evan Runner in his later years.

Reformational Philosophy

Because this philosophical systematics has been the basis for the development of the work of the Institute, we should briefly summarize its basic ideas. In addition to the brief nonacademic treatment below, there are many academic books that give more complete descriptions. For our purposes, I make use especially of an unpublished paper by Brian Walsh and Jonathan Chaplin, both former Institute students and later Institute professors, entitled "Dooyeweerd's Contribution to a Christian Philosophical Paradigm." Another source for this section is Jacob Klapwijk's article "The Struggle for a Christian Philosophy: Another Look at Dooyeweerd," which appeared in the February 1980 issue of *The Reformed Journal*.

Herman Dooyeweerd saw philosophy as the foundation to all other scholarship. It provides methodo-logical criteria by which theories are judged: what evidence is admissible, what constitutes a true conclusion, and what is the nature of demonstration. Philosophy describes the boundaries of disciplines and the relation of the disciplines to each other. Philosophy entails a view of the relations of scholarship to all other aspects of life.

Dooyeweerd stood solidly in the tradition of Abraham Kuyper, John Calvin, and Augustine. A central theme in his thinking was the idea of sphere sovereignty, articulated by Guillaume Groen Van Prinsterer and Kuyper. Kuyper held that different social and academic structures each had their own unique authority which is not subject to other structures. Different social structures did not develop pragmatically, but their distinctives were rooted in the kingship of Christ.

Dooyeweerd affirmed that everything that exists is creaturely, having been created by God. All created things have been perverted and misdirected by the fall into sin, and everything is within reach of redemption in Jesus Christ. With this idea, Dooyeweerd rejected two-realm theories of the spiritual and the natural.

The cosmic scope of redemption is the religious force behind the development of a distinctive Christian philosophy. Kuyper and Dooyeweerd spoke of the "antithesis" to mean that the forces of Satan want to claim all things for him, while God as creator claims every square inch as his.

God rules his world by his law, which Dooyeweerd said is the boundary between God and his creation. Everything, including philosophical theories themselves, is subject to and exists only in response to a law that holds for the entirety of created reality. According to Dooyeweerd, the structuredness of all reality is rooted in God's law, a law that establishes the orderedness and coherence of the entire creation.

God didn't just say, "Let there be trees," he also said, "Let trees grow and bear fruit." The relation between creation and God's law is foundational to Dooyeweerd's philosophy. He worked to help avoid worshipping the creature rather than the creator. He understood our situation in a world with sin by saying that God structured everything rightly, though the direction of human response by sinful people may not always be in accordance with his structured design.

Dooyeweerd opposed reductionism, in which an explanation for a thing is given outside of the sphere in which God created it. So that everything could be understood in its own terms of reference, he articulated a modal system to account for how things function.

Dooyeweerd's thinking clearly has Kantian overtones, but his conclusion is opposite to that of Kant. Kant critiqued pure reason by means of reason, but that approach was in opposition to Dooyeweerd's idea. Dooyeweerd used a transcendental critique that was directed to experience and the presuppositions underlying it. He severely criticized the pretended autonomy of theoretical thought. He refused to consider theory as a closed system based only on logical laws and empirical data. All thinking, he said, has religious pretheoretical presuppositions and motivations. He considered philosophy to be theoretical, built on a worldview, not negating worldviews, as other philosophers insisted.

Reason is not purely objective, he stated, but is embedded in other dimensions of life. It's not possible to build a philosophy rooted in the self-sufficiency of human reason, he said, for the Bible tells us that out of the heart are the issues of life. All philosophical systems are ultimately and inevitably rooted in religious belief.

The Association and the Institute were set up on in accordance with Dooyeweerd's conviction that one must say "no" to all pretensions of the autonomy of the human person and academic thought. The Institute wanted "to bow humbly before the sovereign work of God in creation and redemption." It was committed to be free from external institutions like church and government, free in its direct and complete submission to Christ and the Scriptures.

Walsh and Chaplin say that it is not surprising that some people "exaggerated Dooyeweerd's significance, sometimes to the point of implying that no other attempt at Christian philosophizing was truly Christian.... He often moved too quickly from confessional foundations to philosophical specifics, implying that only his own theoretical formulations were compatible with such a confessional foundation. But

Dooyeweerd did seek to stress that philosophy remains an expression of faith and never its object." Walsh and Chaplin conclude:

> Dooyeweerd's philosophy is serviceable when it is taken as a distinctively Christian, yet unavoidably fallible attempt to develop a Christian philosophical paradigm. When viewed in this way, Dooyeweerd's work could prove to be a significant contribution to Christian philosophy, to all Christian scholarly activity, and to Christian cultural witness in its widest sense.

In 1985, Institute professor C. T. McIntire assessed three phases in the Institute's use of Dooyeweerd's thought, writing the chapter "Herman Dooyeweerd in North America" in the book *Reformed Theology in America,* edited by David F. Wells. In the first phase, in the 1950s and 1960s, the Institute people chiefly translated Dutch scholarship into English, brought Dutch scholars to North America, and promoted Dooyeweerd's thought. Dooyeweerd himself visited Toronto in 1958 and again in 1970. In the second phase, to the late 1970s, the Institute developed into a serious academic community, beginning to become independent from Dooyeweerd, yet continuing in his academic tradition. In this phase, the Institute opened up differences between conservative and progressive emphases among the broad group of scholars who related to Dooyeweerd's thought. The Institute scholarship of the third phase, since the late 1970s, has in general continued the tradition of Christian thought identified with Dooyeweerd and his associate D. H. T. Vollenhoven while being in conversation with contemporary scholarship within the academic world at large.

McIntire noted that the prevailing North American traditions of Reformed theology and analytic philosophy were unsympathetic to Dooyeweerd's thought. He added that the generation after Dooyeweerd successfully made the transition to viable, innovative scholarship in the context of the North American community as a whole. He called Dooyeweerd "the most creative philosopher in the Reformed tradition thus far in the twentieth century."

Dooyeweerd himself said he did not write about theology but about philosophy informed by Christian insights. He wrote about the general structure of the world and human existence. He said that religion is not a distinct department of life or scholarship, and we can do nothing that is separable from religion. He developed his modal theory as a scholarly movement from Abraham Kuyper's notion of sphere sovereignty.

McIntire expressed his appraisal of Dooyeweerd's contribution to scholarship this way:

What may continue and be of value to others is not Dooyeweerd's system or his specific formulations, but a type of approach to scholarship. That approach may perhaps be summarized in this way: the impulse to explore reality empirically and theoretically, so that the irreducible diversity yet the coherent integration of reality is respected, that the insights of the Christian religion are intrinsic to scholarship in full discourse with the academic world, and that the results are of service to God and to all people.

The Counterculture

The summary given above of the underlying philosophy of the new Institute might be attractive to the minds of Christian scholars, but how about to the general public, people who may not have a high school diploma and may have only a loose grip on the English language? It is these people, after all, who will need to support the Institute through prayer and financial means.

Persuasion is only effective if it speaks to the religious hearts of people. The following paragraphs come from a brochure titled "The Basis of ARSS—The Power of God's Word" from the mid-1960s:

> The ARSS is different. It differs from other institutions of higher learning in many ways. There is none that is perhaps smaller, for all it has is a constitution and a small shelf of books. There is none that is bigger in its ideas, for it envisages exercising dominion in the name of Christ over the whole domain of academic enterprise and leading every academic thought captive to Christ. How the ARSS differs is indicated by its basis.
>
> It differs from modern secular institutions of higher learning in that it says "no" to all pretensions of autonomy of man and his science and bows humbly before the sovereign work of God in creation and redemption.
>
> It differs from church-related colleges and universities in its immediate creedal tie-in with the Holy Scriptures without recourse to the confessions of the church or the control or supervision of church bodies. The ARSS is free from other societal structures, free from external pressures. Its freedom consists in its direct and complete submission to Christ and the Scriptures. It honours the creation structure which accords the university a place alongside (not under) church and state.
>
> The ARSS differs from many independent Christian institutions for higher learning in that it conceives its task in scholarship as far more than the combination of scholarship and Christian persons in the same institution. It has set for its goal Christian scholarship. This must indeed be done by Christian men and women of academic achievement, but the Christian influence may not come to rest upon the person, but

should carry through—in fact direct and permeate—the teaching.

The ARSS is studiously trying to avoid withdrawing any part of the process of learning and teaching from the directive power of the Scriptures and the Christian faith. It has committed itself to a total submission of mind and heart, both in attitude and in function, to the Lord God. This is expressed in its confession that life in its entirety is religion. This means that human life is a response action. It is not original but derived. It is the human response to God's confrontation of him in Scripture and in the Law that holds for all created reality. Since all of human life consists of this religious response, scholarly study also unfolds itself as service either of the one true God or of an idol.

The ARSS is convinced that religion is both totalitarian and antithetical. It encompasses the whole of life, for everywhere God confronts humans with his Word, his Law and his handiwork. And since there are two kinds of responsive beings among humans, believing and unbelieving, there are necessarily two kinds of scholarship. Scholarly study accordingly becomes the service either of the one true God or that which humans have erected to take God's place.

The difference of the ARSS by which it distinguishes itself from most other academic institutions is its recognition of the Power of the Word of God. Christ, the Word of God incarnate and the Scriptures, the Word of God written, together make up the initiating, creating, governing, redeeming action of God to which people are forced to respond, either in obedient service, or in pretended autonomy. The power of this Word has revealed to us that life is religion, that the world and they who dwell in it are the Lord's, that everywhere we go, God is there, that the Law of God, since the day God gave people his assignment to rule the creation in his name, establishes and maintains order and regularity in nature and places upon humans the responsibility to obey.

This statement was given to Dutch immigrants in all walks of life. They were working to build a new culture for themselves and for Canada. Further, this was the 1960s and counterculture was in the air. Young people were asking all kinds of serious questions about society and the meaning of life, and they weren't just accepting the timeworn answers of those in power. There were sit-ins and communes and very unconservative lifestyles thrown in the face of everyone.

The ferment of the young was especially clear in higher education. The standard ways, the old ways, were being rejected. Rochdale College, on Bloor Street near the University of Toronto, opened in 1968 in a brand-new eighteen-storey building in walking distance from the Institute. The building included housing as well as classroom space. Its promotional literature, carrying a similar tone to that of some later Institute literature, included the following paragraphs:

> Rochdale College is opening up new directions in higher education. Members decide on the form and content of their own education, and accept responsibility for the governing of the college as a whole.
>
> Education at Rochdale is directed towards the re-opening of fundamental questions: What is important? What is the best way of learning it? How does academic knowledge relate to other kinds of knowledge?
>
> To encourage this kind of questioning, the college has set aside some widely-accepted notions about education. There are no pre-established courses; members develop courses and projects to meet their interests and needs. There are no institutional exams—members are encouraged to rediscover the exam as a pedagogical tool, not a means of certification. There are no degrees or other inducements held out to members. There is only one class of membership at the college: people are recognized as teachers on the basis of whether or not they can teach. In short, there is no reason for members to learn apart from their own desire, kindled and sustained by the rest of the community. The principle is that a man learns best when he first discovers what it is he wants to learn and how he wants to learn it.

If the Institute was crazy, it was not alone. But the Institute has survived longer than did Rochdale College.

There is a sense in which the attitude of "counterculture" fits comfortably in the Dutch Reformed psyche. Dutch Reformed people have always held firmly to the idea that being Reformed is not only an activity of reformers like John Calvin and his colleagues, but that it also means "always reforming." Progressive Dutch Reformed people are always examining accepted ideas and institutions to see whether they can be reformed today according to today's understanding of the Bible and Christian living. They are not mainline people but rather people always ready to critique the main line. They do not accept public schools because those schools usually do not understand that religion pervades all of life. Mainline churches always need reform, and so do politics and everything else. This mind-set is, for example, in contrast to that of the predominant religious groups in Canada. Mainline Canadian churches don't withdraw from public schools or major political parties—they stand at the centre of such institutions. But Dutch Reformed people don't stand in the centre. They are at the edge, arguing for reform.

Rev. Henry Van Andel identified the vision of the Institute in a sermon he preached in November 1981 at the twenty-fifth anniversary of the founding of the Association. He preached on the text 1 Corinthians

1:25, where Paul contrasts Greek wisdom and the wisdom of God. The Greeks looked for wisdom, but failed to find God through their wisdom. Paul contrasts wisdom and folly, saying that Christ crucified was folly to the Greeks. The ancient Greek way of self-salvation by way of reasoning was a typical feature of the sinful nature of the human heart. The worldly wisdom that was propagated rejected salvation through the crucified Christ. But the so-called foolishness of God is wiser than the wisdom of men. It has often been stated that the Christian faith and true scientific research could not be combined. Yet the Institute worked at scholarship in the light of the world that is to come. Christ's kingship is all-inclusive.

Chicago Consultations

Anticipating the opening of the Institute in September 1967, new Executive Director Hendrik Hart called for a meeting of people from Dordt College and Trinity Christian College. This meeting of representatives of these three postsecondary schools was held on the Trinity campus in the southwest Chicago area for two days in June 1967. Hart asked for the meeting so that college officials could share information and plan activities among postsecondary schools related to the Christian Reformed Church that, unlike Calvin College, were freestanding and not controlled by the church.

The schools expressed their desire to work together in a basic spirit of Christian unity. The representatives of each school hoped that they could work with cooperation rather than competition in areas like fund-raising and student recruitment. They also hoped that the schools could each embrace enough of the Amsterdam philosophy as to profit from joint conferences, lecture tours, research, and the sharing of academic materials. Joint publications were encouraged.

There was a very good spirit at the meeting, but some were concerned at what seemed to be an effort to position the three institutions in opposition to Calvin College.

One fruit of the conference was Trinity's hosting of academic conferences between the Christmas and New Year's holidays for three or four years. The conferences encouraged this kind of consultation and the presentation and discussion of academic papers and were attended by persons from Calvin College as well as from the other institutions. The first conference was held January 2 and 3, 1969, with C. Thomas McIntire, Maarten Vrieze, Bernard Zylstra, and H. Evan Runner as speakers.

Institute for Advanced Christian Studies

In 1966, Carl F. H. Henry and others started the Institute for Advanced Christian Studies with the help of the Lilly Endowment. Its literature stated that "The Institute was established to foster consultations, research, and writing by evangelical scholars. Underlying this purpose are two convictions: (1) that the Christian world view needs wider enunciation in the face of a sweeping contemporary secularism; (2) that the Bible needs to be applied as the guide to faith and practice on all fronts in today's problems."

This Institute sought to carry on its work through wide support from interested Christians. It was not identified with any Christian denomination, and its scholars were chosen without regard to church affiliation. It gave grants to established Christian scholars for research projects and publication. It did not give grants to students for study toward advanced degrees. It maintained a mailing address in Chicago, but had no office and no paid employees. People at Toronto's Institute for Christian Studies maintained cordial relations with this Institute, and at times attended its conferences. It ceased to exist in the early 1980s.

Financial Development

Excitement about the Institute was rising, and the membership in the Association was growing, from 840 members in 1965 to 2,055 in 1968.

> **John Olthuis** has what one might refer to as a slow but steady approach to life. You don't hurry him. Maybe it's his northern Alberta origins that endowed him with this unwavering and calm demeanour. As such, he is a formidable opponent when he argues a case in law, as he has done so many times on behalf of native peoples. I have always admired John for his insistence that the Christian life should express itself in an unwavering struggle for justice on behalf of those who have been oppressed.
>
>
>
> His dedication and hard work for the Institute can not be overstated. He was an exemplary strategist who kept his focus on the big picture, but he was also very good at important details. I once told him why I wanted to resign as a member of the Board of Directors at the Institute. I was quite busy and felt that additional work might interfere with my need to come from the centre of my being. John looked at me with his big eyes, and after a little pause, he said, "Wouldn't we all like to do that."
>
> —Bert Witvoet

Setting Up The Institute

The Association started sending out its bimonthly newsletter *Perspective* in 1967, and *Vanguard* magazine was whipping up the need to break out of the old mould. In 1967, C. Thomas McIntire gave an address on "The Forgotten Art of World-Shaking" at the summer Association conference. It was a rousing speech lamenting the passivity of most Christians and their organizations, and it called for a radical approach centred in starting the Institute. The winds of counterculture were blowing.

But Executive Director John Olthuis had concerns about finances. Expenses in 1965 were only $14,835, but they would greatly increase from then on. With the start of the Institute, the Association would need about $100,000 income each year, requiring the dues of four thousand members at $25 a year. He wondered whether the Association had the faith to undertake that responsibility.

As the time was nearing for the Institute's start in 1967, Executive Director Hart supervised sending a Christmas card and letter to 12,000 addresses, asking people to donate in support of the Institute. About 500 responses were received, with total donations of $1,983. The mailing was a failure in terms of money received, said Hart, but it was a public relations success.

The Association did not have a clear idea about raising money to support its plans. In 1966, the Executive Committee drafted a position description for a Director of Development that made no mention of direct fund-raising. As late as 1973, the Board did not have a staff member charged with fund-raising but was instead trying unsuccessfully to appoint a Director of Financial Planning, for which the position description again did not include fund-raising. Association people did not know how to raise money for their activity, and overconfidence in their faith vision kept them from getting advice from those who knew how to do it.

At the same time, criticisms of the Association and its proposed Institute were holding back the needed financial support. For example, people were very angry about needing three signatures of support from existing members to become a full member of the Association. Peter Speelman, a highly respected leader, continued to be a very public thorn in the side of the Association. And there was vocal criticism of how the Institute to be founded on a certain philosophy. People who want a tight-knit community to do something bold will never lack for objectors.

3

The Institute Opens

The official opening of the Institute was celebrated on October 6 and 7, 1967. Five hundred people gathered from many parts of North America for the events, which started in the Second Christian Reformed Church of Toronto. Present were representatives from Calvin College and Seminary, Dordt College, Trinity Christian College, Westminster Theological Seminary, the Free University in Amsterdam, and the Potchefstroom (South Africa) University for Christian Higher Education.

The choirs of Leendert Kooy sang with their accustomed exuberance. One of the four founders, Rev. François Guillaume, gave the meditative and inspirational address. "People say we should have waited longer to start the Institute," he said, "but people will always express concern about timing, especially if they don't want you to do what you are doing." He concluded by saying, "From tomorrow, the Lord willing, our Institute will get to work. Our humble prayer goes up to him that he may use it for many years to come, that it may stand firmly based upon his Word, and that it may never, never deviate from the laws and ordinances God has given for all of life, also for the field of higher education."

Calvin Seerveld came from Trinity Christian College in Chicago to give the charge to the students. He included this statement,

> Students cannot by scientific searching find God or find life, liberty or happiness or get wisdom and understanding. Wisdom, which is the pearl of great price, cannot be gotten by Christian scholarship either. Wisdom is God-given rather than humanly achieved, completely a blessing. Scientists and philosophers are made by accredited universities and institutes of higher learning, but only God can make people wise and outfit them with understanding.

Board member Rev. François Kouwenhoven led a celebratory prayer of thanksgiving.

The next day H. Evan Runner of Calvin College gave the official Institute opening address under the title "Point-Counterpoint." He said that the Institute was starting at a time when Western culture was in the grip of humanism and that Christianity was in a crisis that began with the Renaissance. In his characteristically forthright manner, Runner asserted that the Institute was engaged in a battle of spirits, the spirit of light against the spirit of darkness. He felt that the Kingdom of God was descending to Toronto as God moved among his dedicated servants who were preparing to bring unimagined blessing through higher education to the entire world. Runner's address deeply moved the audience and was followed by a litany of dedication of the Institute to the glory of almighty God.

Later in the day, Hendrik Hart, the first professor at the Institute, gave his inaugural address on "The Spiritual Unity of Christian Scholarship," which placed the Institute within the larger community as well as the academic community. He said that secular universities lack unity because they do not have the unifying gift of God's truth. The philosophy of Dooyeweerd and Vollenhoven was the only available tool at present that could account on a theoretical level for what Christian scholars confess in their hearts.

The exciting two-day celebration and dedication was capped by a banquet at which congratulations from many academic institutions throughout the world were read. Those who attended these events prayed that Christian students would be guided by Christian scholars who would gather together to work to understand what God's Word means not only for their particular field of study but also for contemporary Western society.

It was noted that the Institute started 450 years after the Protestant Reformation began with Martin Luther's presentation of his ninety-five theses and one hundred years after Canada became a nation. This was seen as a great religious and political portent moving the Institute to a special place in God's Kingdom.

The Academic Beginnings

A gigantic leap of faith connected this celebrative opening of the Institute to the reality of the situation. The Institute consisted of one professor, a small administrative staff, and a house. What was the one professor going to do?

That professor, Hendrik Hart, put the Institute on the road. In the first year, he gave five series of lectures and taught five courses to 125 students in twelve locations all over Canada. He taught university students and also the general public. His travels had nothing to do with academic credits toward university degrees. Rather, an academic seed was being sown in all who would receive it.

At the home base, the Board was recruiting more professors. It struck gold with the addition to the faculty of two more of Runner's students, James Olthuis and Bernard Zylstra, who had just finished their doctoral degrees at the Free University. Olthuis specialized in ethics and philosophical theology and Zylstra in legal and political theory.

The plan was that in the second year of the Institute the three professors would tour Canada as teachers for the Institute. Eight courses would be taught in twenty-five locations throughout Canada. In eight locations, the courses were directed to university students; in thirteen places, for the general public; and in four places, for Christian school teachers.

Eleven public courses were actually offered, with an estimated attendance of 250. About 130 teachers regularly attended lectures addressed to their professional situation. Overall, however, the response was less than expected, and Jack Vos, secretary of the Board of Curators, reported that "Of those who attended, we cannot always speak of a disciplined participation which includes faithful attendance and preparation. The causes for low attendance appear to be lack of education, cost, apathy and inadequate promotion on our part. For the university students one must consider that the present student generation is not particularly receptive to leadership."

In his report to the trustees, Vos also wrote,

> Both the current and the proposed program for the West are not conducive to developing the academic program which the Board of Trustees has assigned to the Curators. The West, as well as other parts of the North American continent, does point up the need for Reformed leadership in all cultural areas. We therefore request the Trustees to tackle this as a problem of the Association, not of the Institute, and suggest as a possible solution an international Christian social action seminar to be developed in conjunction with the Institute staff."

The reason for this, Vos added, is that

> The specific goal of the Institute must be clearly delineated. In past meetings the Board of Trustees has agreed that the work ought to be geared to the graduate students while not ignoring the need of the undergraduates. The Institute program can be developed in two directions, for there are two pressing needs. On the one hand there is a dearth of leadership in the Christian community. On the other hand there is a dearth of Christian scholarship. Should the Institute develop

so as to provide as much immediate leadership as possible? Or should we concentrate on the development of Christian scholarship? The Curators, in discussion with the staff, are of the opinion that the Institute has the *specific* and *limited* calling of developing Christian scholarship. The main emphasis must be on scholarly work. At the same time such development must not take place in *isolation* from the Christian community. For that reason we also agree that "research, to be responsible, must be directed to an audience." Nor can the setting of priorities be divorced from the most pressing needs of various sectors of the Christian community.

Given this accent on the development of Christian scholarship, the Institute clearly has to become a properly operating *centre*. Only then can we attract full-time students. Major gaps in the instruction during the academic year would make it irresponsible for us to recommend that students register for a full-time program at the Institute. The concept of mobility must be redefined so as to allow for the viable operation of an academic centre.

The Trustees received this recommendation at its meeting in March 1969, and after "long discussion" decided that indeed "The Institute must develop as an academic centre now, and that the mobility of the Institute must on that account be drastically reduced from the Institute program of 1968–69." It further decided that instead of faculty-taught courses all over Canada, it would set up a series of "social action" seminars in which the speakers would be other than the Institute faculty, except perhaps in some areas close to Toronto. So the Association set up the annual Discovery Lecture Series, which brought lectures to as many as twenty-two places each year. The first Discovery Lectures were to be on the theme Explorations in Contemporary Living with ten different speakers, including professors from Reformed Christian undergraduate colleges as well as Institute faculty members.

As a result, starting in 1969, the Institute faculty stayed in Toronto. Zylstra, as chair of the faculty, reported to the Trustees that the Institute had ninety part-time students and thirteen full-time students. Of the full-time students, eight were from the United States, seven had major interests outside of the academic areas taught at the Institute, four did not have a background in a Dutch Reformed church, and only two did not have a college degree. Registration in the Institute's courses was as follows:

    11 in Anthropology (Hart and Olthuis)
    41 in Theory of Education (De Graaff and Hart)
    23 in Curriculum Workshop (De Graaff)

11 in Political Theory (Zylstra)
14 in Ethics I and II (Olthuis)
30 in Systematic Philosophy I and II (Hart)
20 in Systematic Philosophy III and IV (Hart, Olthuis, and Zylstra)
13 in Theology, Ethics and Hermeneutics (Olthuis and Hart)
14 in Industrial Relations (Zylstra).

The focus of the Institute was already on full-time students, some of whom were considering staying for the next year. The faculty felt it needed to emphasize having full-time students at the graduate school. The Board also asked the faculty to consider the place and the degree of priority that ought to be given to theology in relation to an overall balanced development of the Institute, especially in view of possible interest by students of theology.

The faculty prepared and distributed the Institute's first *Academic Bulletin* for the year 1969–1970. It gave information on the history of the Institute, what it stood for, and how it saw its work in Christian higher education, stating, "The Institute is geared to those students who are committed to developing a Christian frame of reference without concern for accreditation and to those who have already attained degrees."

Four professors were named in the *Bulletin*, including Arnold De Graaff, who taught part-time in 1969 and started full-time in September 1970. It listed the courses offered with a course description for each. It said that the Institute would give letters of standing for course work completed, and grant Certificates and Titles for work accomplished at the graduate level.

Space for a School

In 1969, more than one hundred students, part-time and full-time, descended on the house at 141 Lyndhurst Avenue that served as the school building. The building was bursting at its seams.

Furthermore, there was a misunderstanding when the Institute bought and moved into the building. It was not true, as the realtor had led them to believe, that zoning could be arranged for a school to operate in this residential area. The problem was heightened by the fact that John Yaremko, the next door neighbour, was a cabinet minister in the Ontario government and was the government official who had signed the Association's Charter giving the Institute the authority to exist. The students descended on the building in droves; in truth, many of them found the illegality of their location quite acceptable and even exciting, part of the counterculture.

When a class was in session, all the curtains were drawn to prevent neighbours from looking in. But with twenty-five cars parked around the house and large numbers of young people coming and going daily, the neighbours knew that the busyness was not just a family reunion.

The city inspector thus was often called in to investigate. He accepted the explanation that the Institute honestly thought it could legitimately occupy the house as a school, so he applied "gentle persuasion" for the Institute to find a solution. In the meanwhile, he would phone the Institute twenty-four hours before coming so the staff could make the building look like a normal home. When he arrived, office equipment was hidden in the coal bin and some of the students had temporarily moved beds to the ground floor from upstairs where the Harts lived with their two young children.

Obviously, the house was too crowded to serve the growing Institute, so the Board started looking for a larger place to move to. In 1971, a supporter offered to pay half the cost of the building at 229 College Street, right across the street from the University of Toronto campus. The Association sold its property at 141 Lyndhurst in December 1971 and bought the six-storey building on College Street for $550,000. John Olthuis reflected on the move this way:

> The move from 141 Lyndhurst, the quiet residential area, to 229 College, a bustling, ethnically diverse area bordering on the University of Toronto campus, symbolizes the conscious effort of the AACS/ICS community to be a contributing presence in the centre of the cultural stream in North America. This move marks a significant point in the fifteen-year pilgrimage of the Association which began in the studies and living rooms of predominately Dutch-born ministers and others of the Christian Reformed Church.

The building at 229 College Street has an interesting history. It is located on part of a 100-acre grant of land by the crown to Mr. Peter Russell, a farmer. In 1811, he sold the property to Robert Baldwin, who later sold eighteen acres of it to John Ross. Ross built his estate mansion at what is now 229 College Street. Around 1910, the lodge, The International Order of Odd Fellows, bought the property, tore down the mansion, and build the current building, which was completed in 1918. The Odd Fellows built a large concert hall on the main floor, where performances were major Toronto cultural attractions for many years. Bowling alleys and club rooms were built in the basement.

The Odd Fellows used only the fourth floor and rented out the rest of the building. In the 1960s and early 1970s, the Toronto Public Library was the major tenant. In 1972, the library received permission to build a large new library building at a different location. The Odd Fellows were concerned that the loss of this tenant would give them financial troubles, so they decided to sell the building.

The building was a godsend for the Institute because of its ideal location and the flexibility in the use of space. In addition, the rapidly rising market value for the property in the 1980s gave the Institute the equity to borrow money to cover its annual operating deficits. For several years, the Institute itself used only the fourth floor of the building.

4

Growth and Turbulence in the Early 1970s

Building the Faculty

The next step in developing the Institute was building its faculty. In the process, there were a number of well-qualified applicants, but not all of those appointed, like Bob Goudzwaard and H. Evan Runner, were able to join the faculty.

For the two academic years from 1968 to 1970, the faculty consisted of the three professors, Hendrik Hart, James Olthuis, and Bernard Zylstra. In 1970, Arnold De Graaff joined the faculty full-time, having taught part-time the previous year. He received his doctoral degree from the Free University for studies combining education and psychology, and his appointment at the Institute spanned both fields. De Graaff had taught psychology at Trinity Christian College in Illinois for three years after receiving his doctoral degree.

In 1970, the Institute announced that Dr. Bob Goudzwaard had accepted an appointment to teach economics at the Institute to start in 1971. Goudzwaard had taught at the Free University and was also a member of the Dutch parliament. He resigned his seat in the parliament, but when he and his family took medical exams as part of their application for living in Canada, they discovered that their son had a medical problem that would not permit him to immigrate to Canada. This was a major blow to the Goudzwaards and to the Institute, but over the years, Goudzwaard made very many valuable contributions to the academic program of the Institute.

In 1972, the Institute announced that it offered an appointment to Dr. H. Evan Runner to teach the history of philosophy full-time at the Institute, to start in July 1974. He had been teaching philosophy at the Institute part-time for four years from 1971 to 1974, coming from Calvin College to Toronto to teach on alternate weekends. He accepted the appointment in December 1972, but the following year he raised questions about the arrangements and, in early 1974, said he would not be able to move to the Institute full-time.

In 1972, Calvin Seerveld accepted the Institute's appointment for research and teaching in aesthetics, or philosophy of art, at the Institute. Seerveld held degrees from Calvin College and the University of Michigan, together with a Ph.D. from the Free University in Amsterdam.

In 1973, C. Thomas McIntire became Senior Member in History and Historiography at the Institute after two years of study to complete his doctoral degree. He had previously taught at Shelton College and Trinity Christian College.

In December 1972, Albert Wolters was added to the Association staff as Director of Programs and Special Events. He had graduated from Calvin College and the Free University in Amsterdam. When Evan Runner declined his appointment to the Institute in 1974, Wolters became Senior Member in the History of Philosophy.

In 1976, Sander Griffioen started three years of service in Economics at the Institute, having recently completed his doctorate at the Free University in social philosophy with an emphasis on economics. His work at the Institute was fruitful, though he had rather few students because faculty and students at undergraduate Christian colleges were slow to recognize his credentials in economics.

In 1977, George Vandervelde opened the field of Systematic Theology, in his first year replacing James Olthuis, who was on sabbatical leave. Vandervelde had recently completed his doctoral work at the Free University. His emphases were on the person and work of the Holy Spirit, christology, eschatology, and Roman Catholic theology.

Some years later Bert Witvoet, in the 25th anniversary issue of the Institute's newsletter *Perspective,* wrote that the early professors were all quite young, in their early thirties. They had just come from being university students and did not always sense the difference between a student society and the general society. They carried some student attitudes into the important role of spokespersons for a community-based association.

The new professors, said Witvoet, came straight from graduate school and saw themselves as prophets. Witvoet reported that "One woman recalled how professor Bernard Zylstra took one of his characteristic stances in front of an audience, leaned over, looked her straight in the face, pointed his finger at her and thundered, 'I am talking about people like you housewives.' She almost withered under his forceful, well-meant, prophetic proclamation. This manner of address both gained and lost adherents. Some people were aroused to obedience; others to wrath."

Public Relations Gains and Loses

The starting of the Institute was a wonderful time to tell the great news of the school to people far and near. It was also a very necessary time to raise money, since expenses had now shot up. In the calendar year 1967, the Association's income was $36,010, almost enough to meet the year's expenses of $40,460. But in the following year, expenses rose to $82,000.

Raising Money. As mentioned previously, in the summer of 1967, John Vander Stelt and Fred Cupido were hired for a year each to make as many personal contacts as they could among Dutch immigrants in Canada and raise as much money as they could, Vander Stelt in eastern Canada and Cupido in the west. Raising the money was an uphill struggle. Not only were the immigrants rather poor, but people who resist giving away their money can find all kinds of reasons to criticize the work of those asking for the money. There were indeed enough reasons to criticize.

Following the opening of the Institute, John Olthuis recommended in March 1968 a shift in promotional emphasis from directly approaching people for financial and prayer support of the Association and the Institute to "promotion through Institute services." The Institute professors could now be visiting many areas to give speeches, thereby serving people and motivating them to contribute financial support. The Association staff would consist of Olthuis as half-time Executive Director, a full-time Director of Development, and secretarial staff.

In October 1969, Trustee Peter Schouls reported that the Northern Alberta Regional Council in Alberta had asked students in its area to contribute to the Institute one day's pay from their summer jobs, which many had agreed to do. During the previous year, Schouls had given a series of ten lectures with the general theme "Understanding our Times" which were each attended by seventy to one hundred people. He was planning another lecture series for the coming year.

After Vander Stelt and Cupido had served their year for the Association, the Board employed John Hultink as full-time International Director of Development starting August 1, 1968. A member of a Dutch immigrant family, Hultink had worked half-time in Development for the Association during the previous year in Grand Rapids, Michigan, as he completed his studies at Calvin College.

In 1972 the Association Board allowed Hultink to leave its employ to set up Wedge Publishing Foundation as the publisher of reformational books and of the periodical *Vanguard*. Harry Houtman, who had served as Associate Director of Development beginning September 1, 1971, replaced Hultink as Director of Development. At the same time, Sylvan Gerritsma was appointed for one year as Associate Director of Development for western Canada and midwestern and western United States, and James Visser was appointed part-time as Assistant Development Director for western Canada, serving from November 1971 to March 1972. John Horner served as half-time Eastern United States Development Agent from summer 1972 until June 1973.

"Chaos on the Campus." As a single person, Hultink was able to spend weeks at a time in western Canada and other places outside of Toronto. He had boundless energy and sharp insight, passion and clear vision for action centred on God's Kingdom. He was focused on what the situation should be and what it could be. He was an excited person who could excite others to implement a vision. He appealed to uprooted people who did not have a great deal to lose if established institutions were attacked. He was radical in every sense, and sometimes showed a streak of wildness that could be over the top. But his vision for Christian higher education was excellent, and his dedication and commitment were an inspiration. He knew and could say the right things with passion, but his volatility sometimes had a downside.

Hultink prepared an effective one-page flyer titled "Chaos on the Campus" as an aid to student recruitment. It showed how university students are confronted with many conflicting non-Christian philosophical viewpoints in their studies. The resulting confusion and weakening of Christian faith become major problems for the Christian student and for his or her family and a loss for the Christian community. The brochure listed some examples, such as a biology professor assuming a naturalistic and evolutionary view that would lead all thinking about the natural world. History would probably be taught from a materialistic point of view, sociology from a Marxist perspective. The ethics professor might well be a pragmatist for whom ethical action is not a matter of faithfulness but of expediency. The brochure ended with the question addressed to parents: "Can your sons and daughters at high school, college and university fit the pieces of the puzzle together to form a Christian vision of life?" In five courses, it noted, there might be five different visions of life tugging away for the student's allegiance. The conclusion was: "In the educational system, and particularly in the college and university, the real problem is that of forming a thinking community because the members of that community cannot think together. They do not share the same view of life."

In December 1970, John Hultink wrote an internal memo to the Board of Trustees on his Development plans. He saw the Association gradually moving away from the Christian Reformed Church, which he described as a ghetto, and moving toward evangelical Christianity.

The Primacy of the Word of God. In the early years of teaching and public speaking, the first professors would make reference to three forms of the Word of God. Those forms were taken to be the Bible, Jesus as the Word incarnate, and God's revelation in his creation. Conservative Reformed people, including a number of pastors, were upset by this because they perceived that this weakened the unique and authoritative place given to the Bible. They took this as confirmation that people could not trust the soundness of the Institute's Christian teaching. The controversy over this perception continued for several years.

In 1977, James Olthuis articulated the Institute's position on the Word of God as follows:

> Creation can only be understood in relation to God's Word which brought creation into being and which continues to uphold it. It is this Word for creation, as God's dynamic plan for creation which is incarnated in Jesus Christ and which is inscripturated in the Scriptures. God's Word may not, as in evangelical Christian circles, be limited to the Scriptures. . . . God's Word dynamically structures creation, is experienced in terms of creation—even though it may not be identified with creation—and is the very condition for its existence.
>
> God's Word in the Bible is completely in tune with God's Word for creation. The Bible is a redemptive re-publication in human words of God's Word for creation, a Word which calls us to recognize that redemption from sin is not "flight from creation" but restoration to a life of love and freedom in the creation. Jesus Christ as the Word Incarnate is understood to be not only both the mediator of redemption but also the mediator of creation. Redemption is cosmic in scope and design, not limited to soul-salvation.

John Hultink wrote an effective article "The Word of God and the ARSS" which publicly helped clarify the Association's position. Around the same time, Paul Schrotenboer wrote an article "What Is the Bible?" and Trustee Gordon Spykman wrote "Moralism and the Bible." The three articles were bound together into a booklet that received wide

> **Jan de Koning** was steeped in the reformational perspective before he came to Canada from his native Holland. In that sense, he was ahead of most of the "young Turks" who characterized the early movement known as ARSS. Jan and his wife, Jane, had been influenced by Dutch theologian Klaas Schilder, and thus belonged to the "Vrijgemaakte Kerk," known in Canada as the Canadian Reformed Church. But Jan and Jane switched to the Christian Reformed Church when they felt that the Kuyperian worldview they cherished did not fit very well into the church-centred views of the more conservative Canadian Reformed Church.
>
>
>
> Jan has been an elder in the Willowdale Christian Reformed Church and has served several times as a member of the Board and the Executive Committee of the organization that continued to morph from ARSS to AACS to ICS. Both Jan and Jane were faithful and cheerful attendees at most ICS conferences.
>
> —Bert Witvoet

distribution.

An important argument in the Institute's favour on this issue was a statement by Trustee Jan de Koning that professor Klaas Schilder, a Dutch theologian highly regarded by conservative Dutch immigrants, publicly affirmed his support of this understanding of the Word of God. Before long this view was included in statements of faith drawn up by various ministries of the Christian Reformed Church.

Christian Schools and Christian Churches. In a memo to the Board of Trustees in October 1969, Executive Director John Olthuis pointed to "the disastrous situation we now have in Christian schools and Christian churches." He saw Christian schools as largely ineffective and said that in spite of the existence of thousands of Christian churches and millions of Christians, ". . . yet as a cultural force Christianity is all but impotent. . . . The Christian church functions as a place for world flight and fantasy, as God's world is a tea break from life in the Devil's world." He urged Christian university professors to seek appointment at secular universities in Toronto and vicinity so that they could become part of the Institute team.

In May 1969, the church council of the Second Christian Reformed church of Toronto, pastored by Rev. John Byker, wrote a letter to all its members saying that it had decided ". . . not to continue to support the AACS or the Christian Labour Association of Canada financially or by promoting these organizations in any way." It complained of ". . . the continuing pressure, power struggle and subsequent tension and disunity within the church," which it said these organizations caused. The leaders in the church wrote that it ". . . does not believe that what is being manifested by the said organizations is in line with the historic Christian faith which this church ought to be committed to promoting." The church leaders were not willing to discuss the matter with the Association Board to identify what lay behind these actions. The Association replied by saying that the charges were "empty and unsubstantiated." Byker appealed his case to the Synod of the Christian Reformed Church, its highest judicial body. It appointed a committee to visit Toronto, which found largely in favour of the Institute. The controversy continued throughout the Christian Reformed Church for two or three years.

In 1970, a major split occurred at Toronto District High School at a time when Hendrik Hart was chair of the Education Committee of the school. The trouble was sparked when Bert Witvoet, a known supporter of the Association and teacher of English literature at the school, assigned to one of his classes the reading and discussion of Pierre Salinger's book *Catcher in the Rye*. Special protestors of this assignment were local Christian Reformed pastors John Byker and Harry Van Dyken. Support of Witvoet by friends of the Institute was used by these pastors and their supporters to hurt the Institute as well as Witvoet himself.

A Director of Communication. In 1970, the Association decided it needed to upgrade its tools of communication and add staff in that area. It appointed Robert Carvill as Director of Communications to work half-time to broaden the outreach of the Association and the Institute. He also served half-time as unpaid editor of *Vanguard* magazine. Carvill had been an Institute student the previous year, and earlier he had worked at Trinity College in Deerfield, Illinois. Carvill became editor of the Association's new bimonthly newsletter *Perspective,* and he dealt with the large volume

> **Robert Carvill** was an excellent journalist, a person who had flair and kept the pot boiling. He was a very good editor for the journal *Vanguard,* which reached many Christian college and university students at the time of the counterculture. In the 1960s, he shared the view that "we can change the world." He was a non-Dutch person of non-Reformed background who accepted the vision of the Institute and deeply wanted to export it to evangelical Christians. After his untimely death from cancer, each year the Institute designated one of its newly published books in tribute to him.

of correspondence the Association was receiving. He also looked forward to strong sales of Association and Institute books through the new Association-related publisher called Wedge Publishing Foundation. A few months after his appointment, he wrote in an internal memo that he did not seek controversy for the Association but said that controversy will come if the Association and the Institute were making a contribution.

Carvill and Hultink worked closely together in promotion. A major splash that they made was a bold student recruitment advertisement showing the Institute as a House of Subversion, a term that originated in an article about the Institute in the leading newspaper of Windsor, Ontario. The text of the ad read like this:

> Are you going to grad school? Try the House of Subversion.
>
> That's right. We're interested in subversives. Subversives who want to shake the foundations of their disciplines in the cause of Christian reformation. If you're original, brilliant, not too worried about security, looking for a mind-blowing graduate career and an unusual degree, we're looking for you.
>
> We are subverting the American university structure. We don't have million dollar buildings. We use other universities' libraries and classrooms. We don't pay graduate students to study. We aren't scholarly imperialists. We've stopped worshipping the Ph.D. We give guerrilla credentials.
>
> We don't want tame sheep in our walls. If you are a world-shaker in theoretical research, we might consider you. If you like European-trained professors whose lectures sizzle with prophetic insight, you might consider us. Write us: ICS, 141 Lyndhurst Ave., Toronto 4, Ontario, Canada. THE INSTITUTE FOR CHRISTIAN STUDIES: A Community of Christian Scholars Shaking the Foundations. Join us.

Carvill noted that this ad needed to be followed closely by a House of Healing approach. Calvin Seerveld responded to this campaign by saying that "subversive activity" and "being on the cutting edge" are not biblically rooted metaphors for followers of Christ to adopt. Christian scholarship is not counterespionage, he said, but is giving away faith, love, and hope in concrete deeds of hard-won theoretical insight which will be radically different from the accepted patterns of much North American life."

In June 1973, the Association announced that both Robert Carvill and Peter Steen, a vigorous Institute supporter, had been diagnosed as having cancer. Carvill died the following summer at age 31. The Robert Lee Carvill Memorial Book Fund was set up in 1985, financed by donations specifically given for the fund. Each year the interest money of the Fund became available to the Association for the publication of a book on a subject most closely related to Carvill's priorities for Christian higher education, a book that then became the Carvill Memorial Book for the year.

Sunday Services. In 1969, Sunday morning worship services began to be held at Hart House on the University of Toronto campus, located not far from the Institute. Campus pastor Morris Greidanus led the services. Many Institute students and others close to the Institute began attending, and attendance grew rapidly. After a few years, the worship services were moved to the basement in St. Matthew's Anglican Church in the east end of Toronto. Most of the people attending the services were active in the Institute program.

Because some of the practices in the services were at variance from those approved by the Christian Reformed Church, the decision was made to separate the worship services from the campus ministry. It become a somewhat maverick independent Christian Reformed congregation, which came to be named St. Matthew's-in-the-Basement. As young members married, had families, and moved away, the membership became too small to continue operation, and it disbanded in 1987.

In the late 1970s a number of families, including those of some Institute professors, left their participation in the Christian Reformed Church and became members of the Bloor Street United Church in Toronto. This added ammunition to those who felt the Institute was departing from traditional Reformed values.

Out of Concern for the Church

The first book published by Wedge Publishing Foundation came out in 1970 with the title *Out of Concern for the Church*. It contained a series of talks given by young Institute leaders John Olthuis, Hendrik Hart, Calvin Seerveld, Bernard Zylstra, and James Olthuis. Full of counterculture energy, these men were giving talks at various public meetings expressing their concern about the church, especially the Christian Reformed Church. The book's Preface says, "The church in all of her forms . . . has failed to disturb modern society with the prophetic Word of judgment or healing because to an alarming degree the church has become an expression of modern society. . . . [T]he institutional church, in failing to preach the Word of God in its central sense, has become both internally sick and externally irrelevant."

The book was a shocker, created an uproar, and soon became a best seller.

> **Marinus Koole** was a Board member who helped hire me as a teacher at Hamilton District Christian High School in 1960. When I applied for the editorship of *Calvinist Contact* in 1982, Marinus Koole was a member of the Board that interviewed me. When I became the chairperson of the Board of Beacon Christian Schools, Marinus had been the chair before me. When I became chair of the council of Jubilee Fellowship Christian Reformed Church, I realized that Marinus had been the chair of this council, too. I couldn't take any steps without running into Marinus. His footprints either crossed my path or I had to step into them, more or less like a junior apprentice.
>
> Marinus could be a little gruff. He didn't have much patience for whiners or "losers." Having experienced difficult times himself during World War II in Holland and having struggled himself during the early immigrant years in Canada, he expected others to be strong. He could be tough and pragmatic. But above all, Marinus had the strength and conviction to be a leader. He was, at heart, a generous and kind man. He knew when to help people, and help them he did. And who can count the hours he took from his time at work and the miles he drove to further the cause of church and school? He was a man of high Christian principles.
>
> There was a time when Marinus was referred to as the Pope of Niagara. No wonder. Wherever Niagara peninsula people of Reformed persuasion got together to establish a Christian Reformed church or a Christian school, you could almost count on Marinus being at the centre of that effort. He was also a regular member of the Executive Committee and the Board of Trustees of the Institute. He was a sturdy saint from the Dutch province of Zeeland, with his golden earring—not a trendy hippy emblem but a token of respect for his forefathers, who also wore earrings in Zeeland. We thank God for the man who would say "Amen" louder than anyone else in church, because he meant it and because he had a big chest that was meant for booming out his faith. He was wise and centred, and his white wavy hair reminded you of the foaming waves around Zeeland. His sturdy frame reflected what the people of Zeeland mean when they look up to their provincial logo: "Luctor et Emergo": "I struggle and I overcome."
>
> —Bert Witvoet

The Response. In the December 3, 1970, issue of *Calvinist Contact*, the Rev. Dr. Louis Praamsma bemoaned the fact that in his church community, the Christian Reformed Church, there was ". . . a kind of radicalism among us that, in my view, in some of its than reformational." Praamsma was offended by the following statements, which he quoted from the book:

John A. Olthuis: "Churches in North America own over one hundred and twenty billion dollars worth of real estate. . . . Perhaps we should sell some of our church buildings, worship in rented halls and pool our resources to take a stand for Jesus Christ in those areas of American culture where its spiritual direction is today determined: the schools, the universities, the arts, politics and industry."

Hendrik Hart: "The church is dead, or at best unconscious; sleeping, or comfortably drowsy in the warm air of its safe traditions. . . . If forty-five million believers really *believed*, we would have a lot of mustard seed. All we have now is a lot of mustard to make the North American hotdog more palatable."

Calvin G. Seerveld: "My modest proposal for reforming the Christian Reformed Church in North America is this: Close Calvin Seminary. Disband all denominational boards and standing committees. Strip yourself of ministerial status; and let the ruling elders in the congregations designate as instructors in the Word whomever can bring the Word of Life from the Scriptures and is practicing a daily walk of prayers and fasting in the spirit of the Gospels."

Bernard Zylstra: "It is quite clear that the conservative evangelical wing of the Protestant churches has come to a standstill, defending ever more vehemently a status quo position. Christ's judgment of the Pharisees is to the point here: 'You have a fine way of rejecting the commandments of God in order to keep your tradition.'"

James H. Olthuis: "It is clear that the interests of the New Testament were as wide as the normal affairs of life, and certainly not limited to cultic exercises. Thus one cannot say that what the Scriptures say about the 'church' only refers to the institutional church."

Praamsma says he "was more or less stunned by the deafening sounds of these explosive words clothed in the garment of modest proposals." But he was also shocked to read Hart's words under the heading "The Church Is Dead" that the sleeping, comfortable church will "seek refuge not in the obedient response to the call of the Gospel, but to a verbalized, doctrinal, theological faith—a brain-faith, a mouth-faith, a paper-faith Church."

Praamsma was not impressed with the Association's posture of "a new Christian radicalism." But to the Association, "radical" meant going down to the roots of a thing, not being content always to work at a surface level. That, they said, was the way of reformation.

Praamsma's evaluation of the book was shared by many but not all. The book demanded attention, and both the book and the Institute received it. The attitudes expressed could be found among the writings of others, not all of them Christian, in accordance with the culture of the time. Many people were offended by the book, but many younger people in that time of criticism of cultural institutions became strongly attracted to the Institute.

A year or two later, Wedge published a sequel to this book, written by most of the same authors, called *Will All the King's Men . . .* , which dealt with the same subject but had a much more positive and constructive tone. It called for Christian reform of church and culture. That book, however, did not receive such wide notice as *Out of Concern*.

A Statement of Consensus. By 1971, public dissension over the Association and the Institute grew to the point that the health of the Christian Reformed Church in Canada was an issue. In April 1971, the leaders of the weekly newspaper *Calvinist Contact* invited a wide group of CRC leaders to a private two-day conference that included people who actively supported the Association and those who opposed it and its ideas. About fifty-five leaders in the CRC in Canada were invited, in addition to the members of the paper's Editorial Committee. Rev. Jacob Geuzebroek chaired the meeting.

The conference was a success beyond everyone's expectations. The editor of *Calvinist Contact*, Dick Farenhorst, wrote later:

> Many people, including several who participated in the conference, thought that even a limited achievement would be impossible. The Spirit of the Lord moved among those present and brought them to a conclusion, which was considered impossible at the beginning of the meetings." A "Statement of Consensus" was drawn up at the close of the meeting and given wide publicity. Included in the Statement was: "In a discussion on the concept of 'The Word of God' it was agreed that the infallible Word of Scripture is the only source of our knowledge of Christ, the incarnate Word and of the proclamation of the Word of the Gospel. The term 'creation-word' occasioned some debate. Its meaning, as expressed in the discussion, included the Word by which the Creator calls His world into being, the Word by which He holds His creation together, and the Word as it functions for and in the structures of creation. With reference to this last-mentioned usage there was agreement that no one should speak of this creation-word in isolation from the written word, or in isolation from Christ crucified.

Quotes Out Of Context. In 1973 a striking and effective booklet called *Quotes Out Of Context* was produced for the Institute by graphic artist Willem Hart. In eye-catching colour and with unusual size it presented quotations on their view of Christian study in their disciplines by H. Evan Runner, James Olthuis, Arnold De Graaff, Hendrik Hart, Bernard

Zylstra, Calvin Seerveld, and C. Thomas McIntire. Winning an award for its design, the booklet was widely distributed.

Influence and Opposition

The Association went through some rather severe storms in 1971, John Olthuis reported to the Board of Trustees. In January, a full page ad in *Calvinist Contact* accused the Association and the Institute of driving "wedges" (clearly referring to Wedge Publishing Foundation) of all kinds between churches and their agencies. The issues at Second Toronto CRC and disagreements at Toronto District Christian High School mentioned earlier created major problems. The leaders of that church sent across North America long letters about the Association as a heretical institution that was determined to destroy Christian Reformed congregations. Important newspapers like the *Toronto Star* and the *Globe and Mail* carried inaccurate and hurtful articles about the Association. A "Committee of Concerned Laymen" was started in Aylmer, Ontario, as a centre of opposition to the Association. Verbal slugging matches occurred between CRC conservatives and Association radicals.

During the turmoil, a few hundred "conservatives" resigned from the Association, including twenty-one pastors. At the same time, however, a few hundred people joined the Association. It was said that the Association grew most when it opposed and was opposed by parts of the Dutch immigrant community.

In late 1970, Hultink reported to the Trustees that the influence and effect of the Association were growing among churches, Christian schools, professors, and university students, and that opposition to the Association was also increasing. Some critics felt that the Association people were dominating schools and churches. Especially severe criticisms were coming from very small denominations like the Free Reformed and Canadian Reformed churches.

The Association and its Institute were pushing a whole new understanding of the Christian faith in relation to society, including its institutions and even the church and Christian schools. They were pushing for a dynamic understanding of the gospel in all its ramifications and were trying hard to rally Christian people. But they were running into the "comfortable pew" syndrome. This included the attitude in the United States that now, in 1973, Reformed Christianity had indeed already been applied to all realms of life, so that a new reform was not needed.

The Institute came to think that its failure to rally thousands of people to its cause was related to the naiveté of Association supporters. There was indeed a much higher development of Christian reformational insight in the Netherlands by the time of World War II than there was among the Dutch immigrants in the United States of one or two generations earlier. In part, that is seen from the fact that the Association could not rally the support of American Dutch Reformed Christians as it thought it could. Because the visionaries of the Association did not understand the secular mind-set of most Christians, both in the United States and in Canada, they did not succeed as they had hoped.

There was the danger that by responding to all the criticisms brought against the Association it would be swamped and not be able to carry on its work effectively. The Trustees adopted a policy, upon the recommendation of John Hultink, not to reply in general to attacks against the Association.

The Board Looks to the Future

The Association followed a clear blueprint, "The Place and Task of an Institute for Christian Studies," when it started the Institute in 1967. But by 1970, the Institute was in its third year and there were calls for the Association to move in various different directions to work at Christian reformation in higher education. The "Place and Task" document could no longer serve as a guide.

The Committees. In 1971 the Board of Trustees appointed a new "Place and Task" committee, consisting of Peter Schouls, philosophy professor at the University of Alberta, along with staff members John Olthuis, Robert Carvill, and James Olthuis. The committee reported in late 1971 and again in March 1972. The committee aimed to produce a book, using in part scholarly documents already at hand. The book would consist of five parts: biblically normed graduate education, biblical foundations, the academic task, the role of the Institute, and conclusions that would include a communal challenge. Writers would be persons on the Institute faculty or people very close to the Institute. It soon became clear, however, that an academic person was needed to pull such a book together, but all such people at the Institute were already overloaded.

In October 1971, the Board of Trustees appointed John Olthuis and Peter Schouls to recommend what the future role of the Association should be. Since Schouls lived in Edmonton, he and Olthuis found it unrealistic to meet together. Schouls prepared a twelve-page paper giving his ideas, to which Olthuis replied with his own twelve-page paper in basic agreement. Schouls recommended a broadly based public education program to supplement the work of the Institute as it tried to reach as many people as possible in different walks of life with good educational insights.

In November 1971, the Board of Trustees appointed another committee, this one to study trends in higher education. Its members were Barbara Carvill, Adrian Guldemond, J. William Kamphuis, and Louis Tamminga. At its meeting in September 1972, the committee considered a report from John Olthuis on trends in higher education that commented on the status of colleges whose graduates came to study at the Institute. The report noted that the Association had been approached to consider seriously starting an undergraduate Christian college alongside the Institute. Reaching out to the Christian community educationally would be more effective with a Christian college "free from the traditional structural rigidity, which through a system of fundamental core courses

> I knew **Peter Schouls** from the days I studied for a master's degree at the University of Toronto. Peter was studying philosophy, and we met at a Calvinistic students' group led by François Kouwenhoven, an Old Testament scholar. Schouls was a student leader for Institute development while at the University of Toronto in the 1960s. He accepted the Institute's reformational philosophy while he was learning all about analytic philosophy at the university.
>
> Peter and Jeannette came out of the very conservative Free Reformed Church. It didn't surprise me that they left that church; they were some of the most light-hearted, fun-loving people of faith I knew.
>
> Peter was appointed to the philosophy department at the University of Alberta, and he was highly valued by the reformational community in Edmonton. Clarence Visser, a strong supporter of reformational thinking, once scolded Peter for kayaking to the Visser potato farm by himself on the fast-flowing Saskatchewan River. According to Clarence, Peter was too valuable to the community to risk his life that way! For many years during the growth of the Institute, Peter chaired the Board of Curators, which later became the Senate. He was a gifted academic leader at the Institute and a solid champion of the faculty during peaceful and turbulent times.
>
>
>
> Schouls very much wanted the Institute's philosophy to be accepted as good philosophy by university philosophy departments and by secular philosophers. He was methodical and highly focused. Over the years, he became highly regarded by Canadian philosophers.
>
> —Bert Witvoet

would make education at the college level available to students as well as people from a variety of walks of life, and therefore would have to be structured very flexibly." The committee also received a serious request to start a teachers college.

Some committee members did not favour moving in this direction, however. In May 1973, the Board of Trustees decided "to suspend the work of the Trends Committee, with the understanding that later we will have more clarity on the state of development within the Institute."

A New Master Plan. Already in October 1972, the Board of Trustees mandated John Olthuis "to begin to devise a master plan for the Reformational community in North America to meet its challenge in the seventies and eighties." This plan was to contain a critical review of the Association's past, its achievements, and its failures, as well as a proposed program of community services for the years ahead. It asked Olthuis to free himself, as soon as responsibly possible, from his daily Association activities to be able to take up the task outlined. He was to take a month for reflection and then six months to carry out his task and to present his report to the October 1973 meeting of the Board of Trustees.

Olthuis reported that in addition to the many positive results achieved by the Association, its outreach also led to many misunderstandings and misinterpretations. He said that the Association

> ... must acknowledge some measure of responsibility for those misunderstandings. In the early years of the Institute its people were sometimes forced, even in areas outside their immediate competence, to introduce ideas that were in the early stages of development. Certain ideas were introduced before they were fully developed. Institute people assumed a context of trust in which ideas could be shared at various stages of development. But often the community was not ready for the introduction of these beginning ideas. The fact is that unless you are working in a situation of trust, the less ready a community is to entertain a new idea and the more fully that idea must be developed and explained before it is introduced to that community. Our attempts suffered because we assumed a trust relationship that was not present and the "trust" was consequently further undermined by the ideas introduced. This situation was further complicated by enthusiastic Association supporters who replied to criticism about Association "ideas" by putting the "finishing touches" to those ideas. In many instances those "finishing touches" are not shared by the Association/Institute, but they get a life of their own as Association ideas.

A Transition. In 1973, the Board of Trustees faced the fact that the prime supporting community of the Institute, the Christian Reformed Church, did not in general have the vision and focus of ministry to provide the strength that the Association expected of it. Much of the CRC in Canada had been alienated by the Institute. How could the Association and the Institute relate to the church and its members with mutual support? How could it appeal to churches and their members in view of sharp criticism of the churches?

To help solve this dilemma, the Board appointed a Guidelines Committee. It consisted of three pastors, Louis Tamminga as chair, Alvin Venema, and Klaas Hart, and two nonpastors, Michael van Wijk and Mirth Vos.

The committee had heard some voices within the Association saying that the time might have come for people sharing a common understanding of the Word of God and of living reformationally to leave the denominations of which they were members and form a new church. But the committee wasted no time in rejecting that idea. It stated that Association members should not be fringe members of their churches but rather be full contributing participants who were willing to learn even from a church that was not entirely what they wished it to be. It emphasized that no "ideal" church existed. Adherents of the vision of the Association should not retreat from congregational life into an elitist fellowship.

The report from the Guidelines Committee asked, "How does the Association now proceed? Can it offer critical analyses and at the same time demonstrate empathy with churches and church members? Fundamental to the Association/ICS's projection of such an attitude must be a recognizable modesty when it offers genuine guidance in areas of the church's concern." It said that sloganeering is easy, but implementation in an increasingly complex world is very hard.

The committee said that the Association and the Institute needed to be very empathetic toward the CRC, and not be as fiercely critical of it as it had been. It stated,

> With the benefit of hindsight, the Association community can agree that it has over-rated both the clarity of the *Pro Rege* vision and the ability or inability of the CRC to carry out this vision in its performance as church. A great amount of frustration has been the result. . . . It is time for the Association to turn aside from speaking as if it has been called to bring light to the darkness of the present church scene, bolstering itself with biblical examples which in effect equate today's church to the apostate church of the Old Testament prophets or the Jewish church

of Jesus' day. The desire to be prophetic is in danger of acquiring an Elijah complex.

This report was the response of the Board of Trustees and other supporting members to certain uncontrolled countercultural expressions in the recent past by staff members. It was a signal that the wind would now be blowing from a somewhat different direction. A transition was taking place.

Faculty member Bernard Zylstra agreed in a response to the Guidelines Report written in May 1974 that the Association had not been sufficiently working in a context of historical continuity. "You need to reform what actually exists, not work from some idealized picture," he said. "We need to be reforming, not revolutionary. We should acquaint ourselves with the present Canadian situation. Our academic freedom has not always been accompanied by social responsibility."

5

The Professors and their Courses

The first *Academic Bulletin* of the Institute, dated 1969–1970, said that the Institute

> . . . intends to bring together persons who can relate the problematics of individual sciences to an overarching, unifying outlook on reality. At this early stage of its existence, therefore, the expansion of the Institute will lie in the appointment of persons who can explicate the fundamentals of their particular area of specialization in terms of a total Christian life-view. In that way a genuinely Christian free university can be developed.
>
> Scripturally-normed learning is a communal challenge and responsibility for the body of Christ. The Institute is meant to be a centre where scholarly communion in Christ can grow and flourish. Teamwork must be the watermark for this project. The call to join such a team goes out, not to teachers and students who are incidentally also Christians, but to persons who in concert yearn for a learning that is of one piece with Christian conviction. This call goes out to believers who wish to offer up also their academic work as living sacrifices to the Lord. Since an authentic community of learning is only possible when a communally-held world-and-life-view is translated into a commonly used theoretic model, the Institute gives primal place to the study of philosophy—the interdisciplinary science par excellence which provides the background, integration, and unity of conception essential for the proper placing and functioning of the special sciences.
>
> The forms and shapes that this undertaking will assume cannot be predetermined. Here ingenuity in resourcefulness must shine. There will be discussions and seminars, with and without student participation; sustained research; student guidance, both formal and informal; original publications; translations—in short, a research-teaching rhythm will develop conducive to the best interests of all concerned. Students can thus look forward to joining a community in which the emphasis will be on the formation of a team of Christian scholars. Although students will be expected to rely on their own initiative, to a large extent, as the situation allows they will be given the optimum of personal attention. A student will be free to attend and participate in as many or as few activities as he or she desires.

While the Institute was in the process of getting started, the rhetoric describing the aims of its program seemed unachievable. The Institute was going to show how the Christian faith could illuminate all academic study as had not ever been done in North America. Its vision was pictured in sharp contrast to the best that North American colleges and universities were doing to date. The Christian faith would not be something added to religiously neutral study, an application brought as an afterthought. Faith was to be the water and fibre of the growing plant itself, the very constitution of all academic thought. From this would come leadership to all Christians and to Canada itself.

The question is whether the real Institute could achieve anything near this utopian vision. A look at the academic program as it developed will show whether there was substance to the vision. After discussing the teaching and research program, we will look at some of the tangible activities that reached outside the classroom.

Systematic Philosophy with Hendrik Hart

The Institute's first professor, Hendrik Hart, was born in the Netherlands and immigrated to Canada with his family when he was eighteen. He graduated from Calvin College and the Free University of Amsterdam.

Hart's teaching and research centred on the core issue of reason in Western culture. His colleague and lifelong friend James Olthuis expressed it this way in 2001, when Hart retired after thirty-five years of work at the Institute: "For Henk, philosophizing finds its ground not in the so-called certainties of reason, but in experienced confidence and the hope of faith. Indeed, this feature is so crucial for him that I believe that it marks out the two persistent themes in his life as a philosopher: that inordinate regard for rationality can be the death of both faith and reason, and the urgent need to recover faith as trust. Doing philosophy for Henk is a spiritual exercise, a passion, rooted in his faith and streaming from his faith."

Hart was concerned about how forms of orthodoxy could degenerate into doctrinalism and legalism. He saw that reason could even displace Christ and the Holy Spirit. He argued that knowledge and truth cannot be limited to rational-conceptual cognition. Over time, he became concerned that the reformational thinking might be too rational in its thinking about truth, tradition, and order.

A pillar of Hart's teaching in the early years was his course on the thinking of Herman Dooyeweerd. In the course, he and the students would read together, line by line, one hundred pages in Dooyeweerd's book *A*

New Critique of Theoretical Thought. All problems, unclarities, objections, disagreements, and possible meanings would be closely scrutinized, both through commentary by Hart and other faculty members and through discussion by all participants.

An aim of the course was to help students gain experience in the reading of a crucial philosophical text written with the religious-philosophical viewpoint of the Institute. Successful participation in the course would mean that, having learned to interpret the section or sections covered in class, each student would be able to interpret any other section of the work's three volumes with equal ease and confidence.

Students were required to prepare thoroughly for each class by studying intensively the section to be covered that day. During the year, each student needed to read systematically through all three volumes of the *New Critique,* so as to take a turn being responsible for reading sections aloud in class and raising difficulties. Students also became acquainted with the treatment of a major Dooyeweerdian problem as dealt with by a scholar in a different intellectual tradition. And they each wrote a paper comparing Dooyeweerd's treatment of a theme with that of some other thinker.

For some years, Hart also taught a course on epistemology. In 1979, he described the course as asking students to come to grips with contemporary developments in the perception of knowledge, logic, theory, and science. The dominant viewpoint in philosophy at the time was positivism, the idea that philosophy needed to be studied as a science. Students in the course needed to understand why positivism was being challenged and what alternatives were being offered. The course examined the positivist viewpoint and its roots, with current criticism that had been offered by Kierkegaard, Dewey, and Wolterstorff, with the ideas of Polanyi and Radnitzky as alternatives. Serious attention was given to biblical perspectives on knowledge and truth, along with discussion of a paper "Theses on Science and Revelation" cowritten by Hart and Olthuis.

In addition to his teaching, Hart served as a thesis supervisor and director of the doctoral program. After serving as part-time Registrar for a number of years, Hart was appointed to a three-year term as Academic Dean in 1997.

On Hart's retirement, his former students Ronald A. Kuipers and Janet C. Wesselius edited a Festschrift, published in 2002, in recognition of his services entitled *Philosophy as Responsibility: A Celebration of Hendrik Hart's Contribution to the Discipline.*

Philosophical Theology with James Olthuis

The Institute bases its academic study on philosophy with Christian insight, so the study of theology must also be very close to its core. Thus, one its first three professors was a theologian, James Olthuis.

Olthuis grew up in Edmonton, Alberta, graduated from Calvin College and Calvin Seminary, and then received his doctorate from the Free University in Amsterdam. His entire teaching career was spent at the Institute. His academic field was philosophical theology, and he was the only theologian on the Institute faculty until 1977, when he was joined by George Vandervelde.

The question was how to teach and do research in philosophical theology that used the abilities of Olthuis and that advanced the ministry of the Institute. Olthuis said that he understood his discipline as seeking to promote conversations between theology as the academic study of faith and the surrounding academic areas like hermeneutics, philosophical anthropology, and psychology. He said that a scripturally directed understanding of the world required and included, among much else, both the development of views of personhood, of biblical interpretation, and of faith, as well as the implications and practical outworking of these views in daily life.

In the early years, Olthuis emphasized the concept of "certitudinal hermeneutics" as the best approach to understanding biblical authority. In 1974, he wrote, "We believe that the Scriptures are a confessional book, not a book of theology. Theology doesn't examine God, it examines one aspect of human experience. Theology as a science involves abstraction. A confession of faith is an act which takes place with a person's whole being. . . ."

Olthuis said that the Bible is our authority for all of life, a book of certainty whose focus is on ultimates or end-questions. It addresses the human heart in ordinary language with a dimension and richness that has meaning beyond being a rule book for living or being a rational textbook. The Bible is a book at the level of personal confession and the frequent intentional multiple meanings of passages suggest that what different readers bring to a text may appropriately lead to alternate interpretations of specific passages.

He added in 1986, "Since the underlying purpose of the Bible is to present its life-giving message to build our faith, it is at that level that the ultimate meaning and certainly of the Bible must be read. Therefore a faithful hermeneutic of the Bible will be *pastoral*, that is, appropriate to its redemptive and edifying purpose."

Underlying the work of Olthuis is the conviction that the world in which we live is God's creation and is not religiously neutral. He always had a strong sense of obligation to his students because they made special sacrifices to study at the Institute.

Olthuis saw at least five interrelated questions to help him identify where he needed to give his attention in philosophical theology: What has the possibility of being most pastorally redemptive in this broken world? What lies within his academic competence and the resources of the reformational tradition? What excites and motivates him? What are the needs and desires of students who come to the Institute? What issues and ideas in this field are timely for study today?

Olthuis saw urgent issues coming together in one overriding question: How does a person of faith live in this modern/postmodern world, and how is faith developed in a person? These questions surface in many guises. If reason is dethroned as a god, new openings will appear in academic discourse for revelation and mystery. If subjectivity is often a distorting mirror, and nonprejudice is impossible, we need to rethink claims to objectivity. The role of grand ideas may not include marginalizing people, so life experience, the tendency to domination, and the ultimate questions of life are raised once again with new urgency.

Olthuis was excited by the new opportunities he saw in this time of the demise of Enlightenment rationality. He said that the reformational tradition has always questioned the autonomy of theoretical thought without ending in scepticism and nihilism. It has stressed the nonindependence of the human self without thereby denying human agency. It has not only recognized the radicality of evil but also the possibilities of repentance, forgiveness, and renewal in the suffering love and grace of God. It has also stressed the importance of theory in serving to alleviate the suffering in the world and in promoting justice.

Olthuis thus chose to concentrate on three interrelated topics: If you begin with an ontology of love, what does it mean to be a gifted and called human agent (philosophical anthropology); to be an interpreting agent led by faith (hermeneutics); and to be an interrelating agent of faith and feeling (interpersonal relations and psychology)? He said that of first importance to him was to work on the development of an ontology of love in the face of the postmodern challenge.

Olthuis taught a course in theological anthropology and psychology that explored and developed a biblically inspired, holistic, multidimensional, relational, and developmental view of what it means to be human. He alternated this with a course in philosophical theology that featured hermeneutics and led student thinking of the ideas of contemporary theologians. In 1983, he taught a course that dealt broadly with creation, fall, and redemption, dealing especially with issues of creation and the problem of evil.

Olthuis always had the largest number of Institute students working on their theses under his supervision, about thirty-five percent of those completing degrees at the Institute. In 1993, he was elected president of the Canadian Theological Society. For many years, he worked one day a week as a psychotherapist. He was valued for his writing and speaking that reached a nonacademic as well as an academic audience.

On his retirement, his former students James K. A. Smith and Henry I. Venema prepared a Festschrift for him with the title *The Hermeneutics of Charity: Interpretation, Selfhood and Postmodern Faith*, published in 2004.

Political Theory with Bernard Zylstra

Bernard Zylstra joined the Institute faculty in 1968, one of the three professors who started the school in Toronto. As a child, he immigrated with his parents to Grand Rapids, Michigan. He graduated from Calvin College and Calvin Seminary and received a degree in law at the University of Michigan. He received his doctorate from the Free University under the supervision of Herman Dooyeweerd, which was rare because Dooyeweerd accepted very few students. He served as Director of the Institute of Philosophy at the Free University from 1966 to 1968.

Zylstra worked to link the political philosophy of Dooyeweerd and the Amsterdam School to contemporary trends of political liberalism, and he worked at the interface between religion and the political order. He was good at situating reformational thought in its cultural context.
In 1969, the Christian Action Foundation requested that the "Institute initiate a programme of research in the political field, focusing special attention on the Canadian political scene in order to better understand the forces which have shaped the philosophies underlying Canadian political life today." Zylstra responded with a letter to the Board of Curators in which he stated:

> I am of the opinion that at this time the teaching and research program in the area of political and legal theory within the Institute should not be specifically directed to the Canadian political scene. I believe that my academic task lies in the development of a *general* theory of the state in terms of a Christian conception of social structures. This involves:

(1) The delineation of the *internal structural elements* of the state. By this I mean a normative description of the empirical modal dimensions of the state. Here I hope to gain deeper insight into the way in which the body politic is imbedded in the entire creation order.

(2) A treatment of the *variable forms* that states may assume at different stages of the historical unfolding process in the light of the Christian view of man. Special attention can here be given to the phenomenon of parliamentary government in the western democracies and to the philosophies that support or reject this form of government.

(3) An analysis of the *changing task of states* in terms of their *external* modal structure. This demands new insight into the implementation of public justice in all of the non-political spheres of life. New advances by reformational political and legal scholarship are necessary here if a genuine alternative to *laissez-faire* and socialistic conceptions of the state is to be developed.

During his sabbatical leave in 1976–1977, Zylstra worked on the philosophic underpinnings of behaviourist trends and of systems trends in political theory, focusing especially on themes of modernization, value, ideology, and belief systems. He studied Daniel Bell (a traditional liberal) and George Grant (a neo-classicist). He was interested in writing on justice, law, and the political order. He travelled twice to South Africa, first with Bob Goudzwaard and the second time with both James Skillen and Goudzwaard. He met and was the last person to interview Steve Biko in South Africa in July 1977, not long before Biko's death in prison, and his writing about that interview drew wide attention in Canada and the Netherlands.

In 1979, Zylstra reported to the Board of Curators that his emphases in teaching and research were (1) classical political theory, emphasizing Hobbes, Locke, and Marx; (2) contemporary political theory; (3) trends in Christian political thought; and (4) reformational political thought, with an emphasis on Dooyeweerd and his school. His special interests were the crisis of liberalism as a political philosophy, especially as manifested in Canada and the United States, dealing with the phenomena of empire, the mediating structures of society, and the problems of the welfare state.

Zylstra's chief areas of research and teaching at the Institute were modern political thought, with a focus on liberalism and Marxism; contemporary political theory, with a focus on neoclassical thought (Hannah Arendt, Eric Vogelin, and George Grant); Christian political thought, with a focus on consociational theory in neo-Calvinism (Abraham Kuyper, and Herman Dooyeweerd) and the liberation theology of Gutiérrez and José Miranda.

Zylstra regularly taught two courses at the Institute. His course on Systematic Political Theory focused on the dependence of sociopolitical theory upon a theory of reality. Themes chosen to illustrate this dependence were love, justice, power, and social structure. The intent of this reflection was to develop a normative theory of justice as related to a general theory of the state. He also taught History of Political Thought, focusing on the origins, paths of development, and present trends in behavioural and systems analysis in social and political thought. He paid attention to the concept of value, the fact-value dichotomy, and the notions of behaviour.

For his sabbatical leave in 1983, Zylstra studied the crisis of the welfare state, noting how the role of the government has gradually changed in Western nations. In addition to government's responsibility to protect human rights and dispense justice, it is now expected to guarantee the material welfare of its citizens. Relief of the poor now includes welfare, unemployment insurance, old age pensions, Medicare, day care, and more. Zylstra concluded that individuals as well as governments have the responsibility to take care of these needs. But ultimately the crisis of the welfare state is a spiritual crisis that asks us whether we exist to love God and our neighbour or to advance our own material happiness. This study was part of Zylstra's broader interest in assessing liberalism as a democratic political ideology.

Between 1970 and 1977, Zylstra advised all his political theory students to finish their studies at the Institute but then to get a master's degree at the University of Toronto. He did not then have confidence in the strength of the Institute program that he led. Starting in 1980, however, with Paul Marshall beginning to teach political theory part-time and then becoming full-time in 1982, Zylstra did urge Institute students to get their Master of Philosophy degrees in political theory from the Institute itself.

In 1985, Zylstra was diagnosed as having an inoperable cancer, and he died on March 4, 1986, at age fifty-one. In October 1985, the Institute paid special tribute to Zylstra with a dinner and program that acknowledged his contributions to the Institute. Albert Wolters called Zylstra a man of "contagious vision," a speaker who was able to electrify an audience. Yet he was a man of fundamental simplicity. A memorial scholarship was set up in tribute to his unique service to the Institute.

After his death, his former students Jonathan Chaplin and Paul A. Marshall prepared a posthumous Festschrift for Zylstra in 1994 titled *Political Theory and Christian Vision: Essays in Memory of Bernard Zylstra.*

Psychology with Arnold De Graaff

Arnold De Graaff started work in psychology at the Institute on a part-time basis in 1969, taking a full-time position in 1970. He had graduated from Calvin College and Calvin Seminary and received a doctorate from the Free University in Amsterdam for studies in church education. His doctoral studies included extra work in the area of psychology. Before moving to the Institute, he taught psychology at Trinity Christian College in Palos Heights, Illinois.

De Graaff defined psychology as a "discipline that investigates the dimension of human sensitivity (sense perception, feelings, emotions) in its integration with all other dimensions." The Institute's interdisciplinary program in the foundations of psychology focused on the religious and philosophical foundations of psychology. Different schools of psychology were examined in the light of the underlying views of human nature. Particular attention was given to research dealing with human sensitivity and psychotherapy. His courses for first-year students dealt with developmental, educational, and cognitive psychology, and topics for the second year included anthropological models, theories of psychotherapy, and counselling with regard to a person's faith life. The program built explicitly on ICS courses in biblical and philosophical foundations. The emphasis throughout was on student development of a biblically founded anthropological and psychological working model that allows for the integration of the wealth of psychological data available.

This program fit well with the general program and emphasis of the Institute, as De Graaff specialized in the analysis of the philosophical presuppositions inherent in the major theories of the various disciplines and in the development of a distinctively Christian philosophical framework for theorizing in the various fields of investigation. Like Zylstra, De Graaff did not recommend that his students work to receive their master's degree from the Institute.

At the same time, De Graaff continued to work on curriculum development in Christian schools, which led in 1974 to the Board's restriction that he limit his work on education to one-fifth of his time. From 1976 to 1980, he mostly worked half-time at the Institute with the other half of his time being spent on outside work as a psychotherapist. His services to the Institute ended in 1980.

Aesthetics with Calvin Seerveld

Calvin Seerveld received a Bachelor of Arts from Calvin College, a Master of Arts from the University of Michigan in comparative literature, and a Ph.D. in philosophy and comparative literature from the Free University in Amsterdam. He taught at Belhaven College in Mississippi and at Trinity Christian College in Illinois before coming to the Institute in 1972.

The focus of his teaching and research was on the turning points over the centuries in understanding art and theories in art. Most particularly, his interest was on the systematic study of the history of art, philosophy, literature, and music that arose between 1715 and 1850, the period that set the aesthetic issues of our day. Seerveld was particularly interested in the writing of Immanuel Kant, especially his *Critiques,* writings that for the first time gave aesthetics a place of its own in the realm of serious philosophy.

Seerveld's teaching at the Institute centred in the history of aesthetics and on the methodology of art history, for which he made use of a version of the methodology for the study of history developed by his professor at the Free University, Dirk Vollenhoven. Seerveld saw certain basic types of misconceptions of the world shown in paintings, such as the sexual, the heroic, and the other-worldly. He regarded as close to a reformational spirit "the troubled cosmic" perspective that sees the world as a place in which sin and misery are evident and in need of compassionate attention. He saw this spirit in Rembrandt's later work and in Rouault. An expression of this spirit in music is evident in Bach's music, which is basically composed in a Rococo spirit. Seerveld wanted people to see the important place of the aesthetic dimension of their lives, to build up and protect Christians against evil artistic influences, and to show them the avenue for artistic praise. His intense work over the years with the Bible's Wisdom Literature was aimed to enable Christians to see how literary critique can open up Scripture reading.

In his wide-ranging public lectures throughout North America, Seerveld especially enjoyed meeting Christian art professors and students who became aware that the artistic activity they were busy with indeed had biblical foundations. They delighted in hearing that they and others should see their artwork as being important as a Christian testimony, that their work had a solid Christian rationale.

He aimed his teaching and research to help future art teachers give redemptive structure to their teaching of survey courses in art history, and he hoped to reform traditional, humanist categories of art history and show how art is implanted in the life of a culture. He also wanted to present a deepening of aesthetic theory by showing how faith perspective affects the truth or falsity of artwork and, in general, to give leadership in aesthetic matters, including matters of style, taste, and imaginative education.

Seerveld found it distressing that work in university philosophy departments has been so highly theoretical that there has been little contact between art and philosophy departments. He urged a reorientation in the thinking of philosophers and artists, to open a bridge between them.

Seerveld always had a strong interest in how theoretical ideas on aesthetics are tested in the verse and music of congregational singing. He worked on the differences between a hymn and a psalm set to music and on criteria for different kinds of church songs. Many of his translated versions of psalms and other part of the Bible are printed in his books, along with his versifications of many psalms. Recently, Eerdmans Publishing Company published his translations of many of the Psalms under the title *Voicing God's Psalms*.

Upon his retirement in 1995, two of Seerveld's former students, Lambert Zuidervaart and Henry Luttikhuizen prepared a Festschrift for Seerveld titled *Pledges of Jubilee: Essays on the Arts and Culture, in Honour of Calvin G. Seerveld*.

History with C. Thomas McIntire

C. Thomas McIntire graduated from Shelton College and Faith Theological Seminary, and received his Ph.D. from the University of Pennsylvania. Before coming to the Institute, he taught at Shelton College and at Trinity Christian College.

McIntire started his teaching and research at the Institute in 1973 fully aware that work in history at the Institute at the master's degree level could not duplicate the work of a history department at a university nor the work in church history at a seminary. He specialized in the foundational questions that underlie and surround all historical study and are relevant to achieving historical understanding and awareness of the ongoing process of history. His work focused on the points at which history, philosophy, and religion interpenetrate. At all times, he was concerned to understand history from a Christian perspective and to develop a Christian view of history.

McIntire worked with students to build up an understanding of history and historiography that depend on the central insights of the Christian faith. The program examined the human process of making and unmaking culture as ongoing work for positive cultural life or the distortion of life. One course was "Four Views of History: Christian, Hindu, Liberal and Marxist," which explored how people in all cultures have some view of history to help them understand the course of their lives. He also taught a course on the history of secularization. He did not work substantially with Dooyeweerd's ideas, stating that Dooyeweerd's philosophy of history was extremely fertile but did not altogether deal with issues vital to historians.

In 1982, McIntire was cross-appointed as professor at Trinity College, University of Toronto. Starting January 1983, he taught a course at Trinity, the first course to be taught at the university by an Institute professor. He was also appointed to the Advanced Degrees faculty of the Toronto School of Theology. In the fall of 1983, he had no new history students, and the course he taught at the Institute consisted entirely of students registered at the university and the university's Toronto School of Theology. McIntire resigned his position at the Institute in 1984 to teach full-time at Trinity, and the Institute did not subsequently appoint someone to teach history. When he left the Institute, he was appointed Adjunct Senior Member at the Institute, which enabled him to serve as a mentor for Institute students interested in history.

History of Philosophy with Albert Wolters

In 1974, when Evan Runner decided not to come to teach full-time at the Institute, Albert Wolters was selected for the position in the history of philosophy. Wolters was the obvious choice because he was already on the Association staff in educational outreach and had all the right credentials: graduate of Calvin College and the Free University, graduate study of the history of philosophy, and a strong commitment to reformational philosophy.

Wolters' teaching and research had two main emphases. One was the intellectual background and early development of reformational philosophy in the Netherlands in the twentieth century. The other was the early interaction between neo-Platonism and Christianity, especially as this centres in the thought of Plotinus and Augustine. What unified these two emphases was the problem of the assimilation of pagan and humanistic philosophical schemes into the tradition of Christian reflection. His work therefore moved on the borderline between philosophy and theology and paid special attention to the way philosophical thought-patterns, especially neo-Platonic patterns, have had a structuring impact on the Christian intellectual history of the West.

During a sabbatical leave in Amsterdam in 1981–1982 paid by the Dutch government, Wolters studied in depth the background and history of early reformational philosophy, particularly the early understanding of the relation between philosophy and worldview. He found that the first professors of philosophy at the Free University did not have a systematic philosophy worked out, and in fact, none of them were philosophers by training. But they all had a clear understanding of a Calvinistic worldview, though they didn't know precisely what that meant for their philosophy. It was left to the next generation of professors, Dirk Vollenhoven and Herman Dooyeweerd, to work out a systematic philosophy. The whole problem of the relationship between worldview and philosophy was initially posed by German philosophers, said Wolters, so the categories and terms of reference were very contemporary and were hotly debated by German philosophers. Vollenhoven and Dooyeweerd insisted that worldview is essentially religious and an integral factor in one's philosophy. A person's worldview, therefore, underlies all the person's other academic or philosophic work. On the Institute faculty, Wolters and Zylstra were the ones who conducted research on Dutch academic thinking.

The other part of Wolters' academic interest was in the works of Plotinus and his fifteenth-century exponent, Marsilio Ficino, who translated the works of Plotinus in 1486. Plotinus, a Greek philosopher who lived in the third century A.D., had a strong influence on early Christian thinking. His research required Wolters to do detective-like searches in European academic libraries where he even found Ficino's personal copy of the works of Plotinus, with Ficino's handwritten notes in the margin.

Wolters had a major effect on Christian worldview teaching at the Institute, culminating in his worldview book *Creation Regained*. He also taught the core course Philosophical Foundations for some years. In 1984, Wolters resigned from the Institute to move to Redeemer College to teach theology. He always had a strong interest in theology and he had some advanced education in that field. Wolters taught philosophy half-time at the Institute in 1984–1985. In 1985, William Rowe took the position in history of philosophy at the Institute, which he held until 1990 when he accepted a professorship at Scranton University in Pennsylvania.

Economic Theory with Sander Griffioen

In 1976, Sander Griffioen arrived at the Institute for research and teaching in the area of economics. He was a Dutch national who had just received his doctorate in social philosophy from the Free University, and therefore was known personally by the first Institute professors. His degree program had special emphasis on economic philosophy. He came with a commitment to serve at the Institute for three years.

Griffioen taught two courses. One was the history of socioeconomic thought under the general theme of "Reformation and Revolution." He worked with several lines in the history of Christian social thought, its biblical roots, developments in the Middle Ages, the period of the Reformation, and recent Christian social thought, including the modern movements of liberalism and socialism. The course also dealt with key ideas in the history of economic thought, continuing the work that A. B. Cramp and Bob Goudzwaard gave in previous Institute seminars on economics. He gave special attention to the "end" of the Keynesian era.

His second course focused on problems of economic theory and economic systems. It investigated and evaluated the contributions of Christian scholars to economic theory, done in the context of the current crisis in economic thought. It also dealt with the economic systems of totalitarian regimes, the structure of "the Western system," and the possibility of a genuine Christian witness in the midst of economic life.

Griffioen's service was fruitful at the Institute, though he had rather few students because students and faculty at undergraduate colleges were slow to recognize his credentials in economics and may not have been interested in economic theory. When he left the Institute in 1979, another appointment to this position in economics was not made, though various courses and conferences in economics were held through the years.

Systematic Theology with George Vandervelde

George Vandervelde came to the Institute faculty in 1977, when James Olthuis was leaving for a sabbatical year of research. Vandervelde's academic credentials are no surprise: Calvin College, Calvin Seminary, and a doctorate in theology at the Free University. His doctoral research was on aspects of Roman Catholic theology.

His early emphasis in Institute teaching was on Roman Catholic theology along with the fields of soteriology, Christology, eschatology, and foundational theology. In 1981, Vandervelde set a pattern of alternating courses on Christology and on eschatology, in both courses focusing on reformational theology in those areas and in dialogue with the Roman Catholic and evangelical/fundamentalist traditions. He also taught the Institute's Biblical Foundations course for some years.

In Catholic Christology, he worked on the basic issue of the meaning of grace and redemption in Jesus Christ in relationship to creation and culture. Christology was chosen because it is a crucial area in contemporary systematic and historical theology and because it involves several other doctrines, such as the doctrine of God, the nature of revelation, soteriology, and eschatology.

Vandervelde's work on eschatology focused on the relation and interaction between non-Christian sources of hope and a biblical view of the future as reflected in various theologies. Of major interest was the significance of human activity in the present time for the "future world." How is God's presence in Christ at the end of the world related to his presence now? This question was explored by comparing trends in contemporary Christian theology with the themes in secular futurology.

Vandervelde's research included study of various models of church structure to clarify a number of issues that included identifying church structures that facilitate or hamper the full realization of the priesthood of all believers. He also worked on the relation of a normative or christological church versus a pneumatic approach that is more experiential. His work embraced a keen interest in church unity in divergent cultures.

He also studied the major themes of the person and work of the Holy Spirit and organized a major conference, which led to the book *The Spirit—Renewing and Empowering Presence,* which he edited in 1989. In 1992–1993, he made a special study of native spirituality and native self-government in Canada as part of an interdisciplinary seminar. His work in the mid-nineties on "gospel and culture" fit well the central focus of the Institute and led him to work to elucidate the concept of *koinonia* to relieve a dispute of the World Council of Churches on contextualization of the gospel in distinction from more classical approaches.

His studies on the nature of the church led him to membership on the Interchurch Relations Committee of the Christian Reformed Church and to service and leadership in the Faith and Order activities of the World Council of Churches. He was president of the North American Academy of Ecumenists.

In 1988, Vandervelde was invited to attend and address the Special Assembly of Bishops of the Roman Catholic Church held in Rome. He challenged the Catholic church to press forward on ecumenism, quoting Pope John Paul II's statement that ecumenism "stands at the very heart of Christ's mission." Implicit was Vandervelde's concern that the Catholic church avoid discriminatory pressure on Protestant Christian groups in countries where Catholics are strong. During the sessions, Vandervelde had a brief personal conversation with the pope.

At times, Vandervelde's courses needed to be cancelled because of a shortage of students registering to take them. For a time he had some uneasiness about his presence on a faculty of philosophers, and in 1984 he chose to serve on the Institute faculty half-time to explore how he could participate in local church ministry. In 1986, he returned to full-time service at the Institute. In 1992, he was cross-appointed as a professor at Wycliffe College of the University of Toronto.

On his retirement, Michael W. Goheen and Margaret O'Hara prepared a Festschrift for Vandervelde titled *That the World May Believe: Essays on Mission and Unity in Honour of George Vandervelde,* published in 2006.

Political Theory with Paul Marshall

Paul Marshall, a Briton with a master's degree in geology, first came to the Institute in 1971 as a student. After a few years of study at the Institute, he moved to York University in Toronto, where he received both a master's degree and a Ph.D. in political theory. He then worked for Citizens for Public Justice (CPJ), which was located in the Institute building. When Bernard Zylstra became chair of the Institute's academic work and could no longer work full-time at research and teaching, Marshall started teaching at the Institute part-time, at which time he also wrote a thesis and received the Institute's master's degree under Zylstra's supervision. Marshall continued to work one day a week for CPJ through 1984–1985. In 1984, he published his ground-breaking book *Thine Is the Kingdom,* which gave a basic perspective of a Christian view of politics.

In 1982, Marshall was appointed full-time to the faculty. In a sense, his appointment turned a corner in the source of faculty appointments, which now found Institute graduates, not Free University graduates, as new appointees to the Institute faculty.

In 1988, Marshall reported to the Senate that for his course on Contemporary Christian Political Theory, meaning theory of government, state, and the law, he discovered that there was not much work of any quality on that subject apart from that written by Roman Catholics. Mostly he was finding a "theology of politics" and various ethical appraisals of overall social structure. He had hoped for more. In 1983–1984, he taught a course called Political Theory in the Reformation, with a focus on theories of toleration. His research emphasis was on post-fifteenth century English political thought, on toleration and especially on the Christian theory of human rights.

In July 1985, Marshall was appointed Academic Vice-President while Clifford Pitt was President, a position he held until August 1987. He left the Institute in 1998 to become Senior Fellow in the Center for Religious Freedom at Freedom House in Washington, D.C.

Clifford Pitt

Educational Philosophy with Harry Fernhout

Apart from the work Arnold De Graaff did on school curriculum in the 1970s, no one served on the Institute faculty in the field of education until Harry Fernhout was appointed to be Senior Member in Educational Philosophy in 1985. A Canadian citizen, Fernhout graduated from Dordt College in Iowa and was in the first group of Institute graduates to receive Master of Philosophy degrees in 1975. He then worked some years developing school curriculum in Old Testament biblical studies at the Curriculum Development Centre, located in the Institute building. He received his doctorate in 1986 from the Ontario Institute for Studies in Education of the University of Toronto. His dissertation was titled "Moral Autonomy and Faith Commitment: Conflict or Integrality." His research followed closely the thinking of Lawrence Kohlberg, the leading scholar in that field, and Kohlberg was one of the examiners who participated in his final oral examination.

Fernhout's teaching and research at the Institute centred on the development of faith and on moral development in children In the fall of 1985, he taught a course in the evening to teachers on "Moral Values" Education: A Christian Critique. His teaching also included the evaluation of contemporary Christian ideas of the philosophy of education.

In 1987, Fernhout succeeded Paul Marshall as Academic Vice-President of the Institute, and in 1989, he was appointed President.

Educational Philosophy with Ken Badley

Ken Badley started his service in Educational Philosophy at the Institute in 1992. He had received master's degrees from the University of Regina and from Regent College and a Ph.D. from the University of British Columbia. He had taught for nine years at Canadian Bible College in Regina.

Badley's special interest was in the integration of education with the Christian faith, with an emphasis on the moral dimension of life, and on the meaning of teaching as a calling or vocation. He linked education to wider issues like indoctrination, pluralism, and the curriculum priorities faced by Christian teachers. Badley had a strong interest in Reformed educational thought, and he had broad contacts with evangelical Christians in Canada.

Badley became Academic Vice-President at the Institute in 1994 and also served as Acting President of the Institute for six months while Fernhout was on sabbatical leave. In conjunction with Harro van Brummelen and Gordon Smith, Badley set up regular national conferences at which Canadian professors could share experiences in the development of teaching their subject matter integrated with Christian insight. After Badley served for four years, he left the Institute in 1996.

Educational Philosophy with Doug Blomberg

Doug Blomberg came from Australia to study at the Institute for a year in the mid-1970s. He holds a bachelor's degree and a Ph.D. from the University of Sydney and a master's degree and an Ed.D. from Monash University in Australia. For many years, he was a leader in the Christian school movement in Australia. He taught at the Institute for the year 1997–1998, and after that taught half of each year for three years. In January 2003, he started serving full-time as Professor of Education.

Blomberg views education as an interdisciplinary subject, especially combining philosophy, history, and religion, serving as a testing ground for philosophical discourse. His focus is on biblical wisdom as a paradigm for Christian teaching. In addition, he works on understanding the practice of teaching and learning. He especially works with the fact that schools relate with pluralism, religious communities, parents, government, and issues faced by non-public schools. He has a keen interest in a biblical view of knowing.

Blomberg sees the possibility of a deep resonance between the ancient notion of wisdom and some tendencies of postmodernism. His Ph.D. dissertation is titled "The Development of Curriculum with Relation to the Philosophy of the Cosmonomic Idea," and his Doctor of Education dissertation is "Wisdom and Curriculum: Christian Schooling after Postmodernity." "Wisdom," he says, "is more a process than a body of doctrine. It is a way of living. A further irony is that 'a way of living' is also (called in Latin) 'curriculum.'"

Christian Worldview Studies with Brian Walsh

In 1988, Brian Walsh was appointed Senior Member in Worldview Studies, serving as Director of the Institute's Christian Worldview Studies program. After receiving a master's degree from the Institute, he became

Director of the Institute's ministry of teaching Christian worldview and Christian perspective courses on campuses of secular universities. After receiving a Ph.D. in Religious Studies from McGill University and being Christian Reformed campus chaplain at Brock University, he returned to the Institute in Worldview Studies.

Walsh and the Institute wanted to help people with a bachelor's degree who sought advanced Christian education but were not planning academic careers. The program was started as a response to the realities of the culture within which the Institute does its work and in which the church exists. Walsh believed with others that Western culture was in decline, so a vital question was how the Institute could respond to this and what responsibilities and dangers Christian action faces. Walsh's insight was that Christians generally offer a fragmented and privatized gospel that is essentially irrelevant to social-cultural life. Religion is treated as a consumer choice, as a product to be advertised, bought, and consumed. He saw that religion should have a transforming place in culture. Our worldview must not be limited to a vision of the world in general but become a vision for the real world in which we live today. Our present sociocultural situation cries out for redirection. Worldview studies must adopt an "integral and radical vision," said Walsh.

The program was designed to help people develop Christian wisdom, to help them deal with the split they encounter between their Christian faith and the secular world in which they live and work. This program flowed from the Institute's more academic program, building on biblical and philosophical foundations. It was set up, for example, to help people aiming to serve in medical professions go beyond working only with the human body, to develop a holistic, multidimensional approach to health in the light of the biblical notion of shalom. Seerveld's work in aesthetics would help Christian musicians and visual artists. Christians headed for careers in business would receive help in thinking through the nature of the business enterprise and how a business should be subject to the norm of stewardship rather than focus centrally on belief in profit. With Walsh's leadership, the program gained high visibility and led to considerable sensitivity to the importance of a person's worldview among evangelical Christians.

In 1993, the Institute received a modification in its charter permitting it to offer the degree of Master of Worldview Studies. It was publicly stated that the program ". . . is designed to help professionals develop a Christian approach to their vocations so that their relationship with God is not only personally engaging but culturally relevant as well. The program is directed to people in various professions who already have an undergraduate degree but want to develop their Christian perspective in their work."

A special fruit of Walsh's worldview leadership at the Institute was the book he wrote with Institute doctoral student J. Richard Middleton, *The Transforming Vision: Shaping a Christian World View*. Walsh continued in this position until the end of 1995, when he became campus chaplain for the Christian Reformed Church at the University of Toronto.

History of Philosophy with Robert Sweetman

After Albert Wolters and later William Rowe left teaching the philosophy of history at the Institute, Eduardo Echeverria was appointed to the position for one year. Then the Institute appointed Robert Sweetman, who joined the faculty in 1991. He was a graduate of Calvin College, had received a Ph.D. from the Pontifical Institute for Medieval Studies at the University of Toronto, and had taught history for several years at Calvin College. Sweetman is not a philosopher but a medieval historian whose study of the history of philosophy puts him in a good position to contextualize philosophical thought within its temporal setting. He was appointed to the H. Evan Runner Chair in the History of Philosophy when that position opened in 2004.

Sweetman works with the Institute's mission in using historical writings to address the religious character of theoretical practice. Working from medieval documents, his writings address the spiritually directed understanding of the world. He is able to place Refomational philosophy and its founders within their historical context in Protestantism and within Dutch neo-Calvinism. He has also examined the complex historiographical legacy of Dirk Vollenhoven that has been used by some Institute professors.

Besides the foundational course in Reformational Philosophy, courses he has taught include "Spiritual Exercise as Christian Philosophy from Augustine to Bonaventura" and "Aristotle, Aquinas and Scholastic Approaches to Philosophy."

Biblical Studies and Hermeneutics with Sylvia Keesmaat

Sylvia Keesmaat started teaching at the Institute in 1994, becoming the first person at the Institute to teach Biblical Studies and Hermeneutics. She was graduated from Redeemer University College and received a master's degree from McMaster University and a Ph.D. from Oxford University. She held that biblical studies are only faithful to the Scriptures when they bear fruit for the Christian community and that biblical studies need to be communal and not individualistic. She taught the Institute's Biblical Foundations course as well as "Paul and the Crisis of Worldview—Paul's Interpretation of his Scripture and Tradition" and "Creation and Exodus in the Biblical Tradition." After giving birth to two children, she taught part-time at the Institute for two years and resigned her position in 2004. She continued as an Adjunct Professor at the Institute.

Political Theory with Jonathan Chaplin

Chaplin grew up in England and received the degree B.A. (Hons.) at Pembroke College, Oxford University. He studied at the Institute in 1980, receiving its Master of Philosophical Foundations degree. He returned to England to receive a Ph.D. in political theory at the London School of Economics and Political Science, then taught at the university level in England for eleven years. He came to the Institute faculty in 1999.

Chaplin's research interests lay in social justice and in Christian scholarship in its service, as well as in Christian political theory, especially in theories of the state. He had a keen interest in pluralist political theory, including theories of civil society, association, and cultural pluralism. He studied deeply the political thought of Herman Dooyeweerd, and he held the Herman Dooyeweerd Chair in Political Theory and Social Philosophy at the Institute from 2004 to 2006. Courses he taught included "Christianity and Constitutional Government," "Liberalism and Cultural Pluralism," and "State and Civil Society in Christian Perspective." Chaplin served as Academic Dean and also as Acting President of the Institute. He left ICS in 2006 to become Director of the Institute for Christian Ethics at Tyndale House in England.

Philosophical Aesthetics with Adrienne Dengerink Chaplin

Of Dutch origins, Adrienne Dengerink Chaplin received a bachelor's in philosophy from the Free University in Amsterdam and a degree in violin at the Sweelink Conservatory in Amsterdam. She studied at the Institute in the early 1980s for two years while also meeting and marrying fellow ICS student Jonathan Chaplin. She received a Ph.D. from the Free University and joined the ICS faculty in 1999.

She was very active in academic and professional aesthetics organizations, including being president of the Canadian Society for Aesthetics. Her special research interests lay in art and religion; the history of aesthetics, art, and embodiment; the philosophy of music; and the question of meaning in art. Her doctoral dissertation at the Free University in Amsterdam has the title "Art, Mind and Body: The Problem of Meaning in the Cognitive Aesthetics of Susanne K. Langer." She explored the relation between art and knowledge and the bodily nature of art and prereflective experience. Her teaching at the Institute included such courses as "Music, Meaning and Understanding," "Contours of Contemporary Aesthetics," and "Art, Faith and Postmodern Culture." She left the Institute at the end of 2006.

Systematic Philosophy and Lambert Zuidervaart

Lambert Zuidervaart came to the faculty of the Institute in 2002 after two decades of teaching at Calvin College. A native of California, his undergraduate degree is from Dordt College in Iowa. He was in the first group to receive the Master of Philosophy degree from the Institute in 1975, and he was the first Institute graduate to receive a Ph.D. from the Free University in Amsterdam. Upon graduation, he took a teaching position at The King's University College in Edmonton.

Zuidervaart's teaching and research are centred on the nature of theories of knowledge and on social philosophy. He also aims to understand how far art is embedded in the major structures of society, working toward an interdisciplinary social philosophy of art. He has been active for years on integrating his theoretical work with the practical work and experience of others. One of his main goals is to knit together philosophy as a rigorous, demanding discipline and philosophy as a practice contributing to the understanding of society and human flourishing. He is hoping that his work will generate insights to organizations and movements that work for justice and shalom. His book *Artistic Truth* was published in 2004, to be followed by a book on *Art in Public*.

Zuidervaart served as Academic Dean at the Institute during 2003–2004, using his previous experience to give special assistance in the preparation of materials that enabled the Institute to receive a highly favourable review from the Post-Secondary Education Quality Assessment Board and a great improvement in its degree-granting powers from the government of Ontario.

In 2003, he was cross-appointed as professor in the Philosophy Department of the University of Toronto.

Theology and Nicholas Ansell

Nicholas Ansell's origins are in England, where he received his undergraduate degree, which he followed by enrolling at the Institute for the master's degree. He holds a Ph.D. from the Free University in conjunction with doctoral study at the Institute. From 2001 to 2003, he taught theology at The King's University College in Edmonton. He joined the Institute faculty in 2004.

Among the courses he teaches are Biblical Foundations, which explores the biblical writings from start to finish and works at discerning appropriate hermeneutical methods in a way that has significance for life and for academic study, and a course on the nature of evil.

Philosophy of Religion and Ronald Kuipers

Ronald Kuipers grew up in Edmonton and studied at the University of Alberta and also at The King's College, from which he received his bachelor's degree. He received his Ph.D. in the joint ICS–Free University program and joined the ICS faculty in 2005. In his first year, he taught "Pragmatism and Religion: Dewey, Stout and Rorty" and "Community, Faith and Justice: Hannah Arendt and Religious Critique."

Kuipers always approaches his work from existential issues, particularly around questions of faith. One of the main issues that interests him is uncovering the religious background of secular debate. He is working with recent developments in philosophy that have led to what some people are calling a "postsecular turn," where secular philosophers are turning to religious texts and traditions to help develop their theoretical work. He hopes his work will make a contribution not just to academic debates but also as a "resource" for the wider community.

There is much more to be said about the professors and their courses, both about the professors briefly identified above and others who have served on the faculty. For example, there are William Rowe, Eduardo Echeverria, Vaden House, Carroll Guen Hart, and others. The stories of these appointees and those yet to come will need to be told in a different place.

6

The Broader Context for Academic Courses

Courses taught by excellent professors are the heart of a university degree program, but there always needs to be a supporting context for this instruction and research activity. At the Institute, this context is complex, and it varied as years went by, as would be expected of a pioneering institution.

Academic Structure

When Hart, Olthuis, and Zylstra started teaching together at Lyndhurst Avenue in Toronto in 1969, each taught such courses as they wished to a range of students eager to experience the excitement of a breakthrough in Christian insight. Students from widely diverse backgrounds absorbed what they could and what they wished to receive, and they did outside reading as it suited them. Oral class presentations were required of each student in the courses. Research papers were required for each course, which some students completed and others did not. There were no time deadlines for the completion of research papers for courses and no examinations: tests and exams have never been given at the Institute except for oral exams for students who were defending their theses for degrees. No records of student achievement were kept in the early days. In the early 1970s, when students asked for a transcript of courses taken, the transcript was made up largely from the professor's memory of what the student had achieved. Not until 1975 did the Institute set up a formal system for keeping records of student work.

An *Academic Bulletin* for the year 1969–1970 said that "the Institute will grant Certificates and Titles for work accomplished at the graduate and undergraduate level.... The precise requirements for these Certificates and Titles will be announced in the near future." A year or two later, it offered a Certificate in Christian Studies for one year of study; a Certificate of Philosophy, which became a master's degree in

1975; and an Advanced Certificate in Philosophy, the equivalent of the doctor's degree.

The one-year Certificate in Christian Studies was aimed to introduce the student to a systematic understanding of a Christian philosophical and biblical perspective, together with some experience in working with that Christian perspective in an academic area of emphasis.

The 1969–1970 *Academic Bulletin* was written by Bernard Zylstra and included this statement: "The constitution of the Association commits its members to work toward a Christian university. Such a university is to be seen primarily as a body of Christian scholars working communally to bring a biblical perspective to bear on the universal emphasis of academic endeavour. . . . In view of the limited financial and scholarly resources of the evangelical community in North America, the AACS is not striving for a university with a vast array of buildings, libraries and laboratories. Instead, it intends to bring together persons who can relate the problematics of individual sciences to an overarching, unifying outlook on reality."

After these first few years, a common way of teaching was for the professor to describe to the students the research he was currently working on, and together the professor and the students would carry the research forward. The idea was that students could learn best at this level by watching the professor conduct research, with some student contribution, and in that way the students could learn how to do their own research. This approach was based on the idea that advanced study should be rooted in research and be done communally by experienced and developing scholars working together. This unstructured approach was aimed toward a degree given in the early years of counterculture excitement, but soon the students wondered where it would all lead. They could not be students forever and they would need jobs where formal degrees were required. After a few years, the method of instruction moved closer to that of usual graduate school seminars.

In 1973, a clear curriculum was established that required students to complete nine units of study for a program similar to a master's degree program. Each unit consisted of a year-long course or its equivalent, and students would take three courses each year. In 1975, when it became clear that the Institute could not become affiliated with a Canadian university nor receive a legislative charter to grant degrees, the Institute decided to grant its own Master of Philosophy degree, having found that it was not illegal to do so. But some students did not complete programs because they did not think that studying three years for an unrecognized degree was worthwhile for them. At times students were not finishing courses because firm deadlines were often not in place, and master's degree theses were becoming too long, sometimes three hundred to five hundred pages. So a curriculum review committee was appointed which in 1979 reduced the requirements to two years of study. The new program, which continues to this day, is:

Year 1
Unit 1. Philosophical Foundations
Unit 2. Biblical-Theological Foundations
Unit 3. Seminar in major area
Unit 4. Guided readings in major area

Year 2
Unit 5. Interdisciplinary Seminar
Unit 6. Seminar in major area
Units 7 and 8. Thesis and Examination
Summer: Thesis, if not completed earlier

Students were now expected to take four units each year, including the thesis units. In 1979, the Institute stated its aims for the Master of Philosophy degree: insight into and a working understanding of a communal Christian philosophical perspective, experience in interdisciplinary study on a foundational plane, academic competence in working critically on foundational problems in a major area, and experience of some research on a question or problem having foundational import.

Master's degree theses were expected to be 75 to 150 pages, with an upper limit of 200 pages. The Institute faculty standard was that the master's thesis should be the equivalent length of three to five academic articles. In one instance, an outside thesis examiner at the University of Toronto said that the thesis he was to review could be slid under the door of his office if he were not there, but no Institute thesis was ever small enough to fit under an office door. A doctoral thesis was expected to fill two hundred to four hundred pages, "equivalent to a book."

Doctoral Program

From the start, the Institute aimed to offer a doctoral degree. It had faculty members qualified to be mentors for Ph.D. students, but its faculty was considered too small to carry a full Ph.D. program by itself. The most likely university to help was the Free University in Amsterdam.

The Institute's first professors received their own doctorates from the Free University, and many close links remained, especially to the university's Philosophy Department. Several of the university's professors lectured for the Institute throughout Canada in the early years. Yet starting a doctoral program at a new Institute that would be supported and approved by a foreign university was very difficult.

When he received the M. Phil. degree from the Institute in 1975, Lambert Zuidervaart said that he would like to be the first candidate for the Institute's doctoral degree. He started doctoral study at the Institute, but it was thought that his program would advance better in Amsterdam. He soon moved to Berlin for two years of research and for the writing of his dissertation. He received a Ph.D. from the Free University in 1981 under the joint academic supervision of Calvin Seerveld of the Institute and Johan van der Hoeven of the Free University.

The Institute had a Ph.D. program on paper and had even accepted three students into the program. But in 1978, the Board of Curators decided that it really didn't have the academic resources to follow through on the program and dropped it, agreeing that somehow the Institute would take care of the three students who had entered the program. Also in 1978, however, the heads of the Free University, Calvin College, and the Institute met and decided to establish a tripartite relationship for mutual academic development. The first step that was taken was that the Free University would work with the Institute to develop a Ph.D. program in which the studies would take place in Toronto at the Institute but the final oral exam, which is the defence of thesis, would take place in Amsterdam and the degree would be awarded by the Free University. Hendrik Hart worked very hard to set up the program with the Free University, and in 1980 it was in place. The first student to complete that program with this arrangement was Vaden House, who received a Ph.D. in 1988.

The doctoral program is intended for people whose vocational goal is a life of scholarship and teaching philosophy or the philosophy of a particular field of study. The aim is to help develop scholars who can become independent and contributing members of the academic community, competent to teach others, knowledgeable in philosophy, and ready to advance Christian insight into learning.

Doctoral study is designed to take four years of full-time study after the student receives a master's degree from the Institute. The first two years require study in Toronto, which culminates in a comprehensive examination. This is followed by at least two years of research and the writing of a dissertation under the joint supervision of an Institute professor and a Free University professor. The student is able to draw on the academic resources of both institutions.

The joint Ph.D. program had the effect of affiliating the Institute with the Free University, originally a private Christian university, which later became part of the Dutch government's secular university system. The Philosophy Department, however, is staffed largely by adherents of Abraham Kuyper's Christian worldview, so the Institute feels very comfortable with its religious views.

The Foundations Courses

Two courses are required of all students in degree programs, Biblical Foundations and Philosophical Foundations. In developing the Foundations courses, the faculty worked to make clear the irreducible diversity of all of reality but also its coherent oneness. It emphasized that the insights of the Christian religion are intrinsic to scholarship, that scholarship needs to be in direct communication with the existing academic world, and that faithful results bring praise to God and service to all of God's people.

Instruction and research at the Institute have their historical context in reformational philosophy, earlier called the Philosophy of the Law Idea. Since not all students entering the Institute have experience with this philosophy in their undergraduate education, the faculty decided in 1977 to teach a one- or two-week special course on the foundations of philosophy before regular classes began in September. All new students are required to take this course, which at first was dubbed "boot camp," or more formally as Prologue. At first, the course was taught by Hendrik Hart, with various other faculty members brought in for special lectures. Later, Albert Wolters was in charge of the course, followed by William Rowe, and in more recent years, Robert Sweetman.

When taught by Wolters, Philosophical Foundations had three parts: (1) an introductory series of lectures linking a Calvinistic worldview with the distinctive features of reformational philosophizing, together with an initial orientation to the history of philosophy, (2) an exposition of some primary features of the philosophy of Dooyeweerd, especially as these relate to its worldview distinctives, and (3) a relating of the basic features of reformational philosophy to specific problems in a variety of academic disciplines.

The course description now reads:

Religion, Life and Society: Reformational Philosophy – (Required of all students working for the Master of Arts degree)

An exploration of central issues in philosophy, as addressed by Herman Dooyeweerd, Dirk Vollenhoven, and the "Amsterdam School" of neoCalvinian thought. The course tests the relevance of this tradition for recent developments in Western philosophy. Special attention is given to critiques of foundationalism, metaphysics, and modernity within reformational philosophy and in other schools of thought.

In the early years, the Biblical Foundations course was team taught, with most of the faculty participating by leading the class for a few weeks on a particular biblical subject area. Students, however, said that the course taught this way sometimes lacked coherence. Later, the course was taught for a number of years by George Vandervelde. He designed the course to help the participants read and understand the Bible as the authoritative foundation for our calling in the world and specifically for our calling in the area of academics. This course also consisted of three parts: (1) the nature, authority, and interpretation of Scriptures, (2) the key biblical themes of creation, fall, redemption, and covenant, and (3) variant interpretations of selected biblical passages.

The current course description reads:

Biblical Foundations – (Required of all students studying for a master's degree)

Exploring the biblical story from start to finish, with an emphasis on the story of God and the way in which the biblical story is intertwined with that of humanity and the world. We will also attempt to discern appropriate hermeneutical methods for reading this story in a way which has significance for both present day life and for the academic enterprise.

A third Foundations course, Worldview Foundations, is required of all students working for the degree Master of Worldview Studies. Its description reads:

In this course we will begin to locate the reformational tradition as part of the larger Reformed tradition, in its continuities and distinctiveness. We will also examine some characteristic features of this tradition, particularly those that inform our view of God's world and our attempts to live out all aspects of our calling in all dimensions of God's world. We will examine the role of philosophy within a reformational worldview and also look at some of its larger contours in a variety of Christian organizations.

Over the years, there have appeared two additional emphases in the academic work at the Institute and in the public activities of its faculty. One has been a special concern for people who might be called "the other," people who do not fit within the mainstream of society, who are voiceless and generally are discriminated against. The other emphasis has been on the study of postmodernism and how to deal with that way of thinking in relation to the convictions of the Christian. These two emphases show up in various ways that are not often noticed, such as in the Institute courses, in the writings of Institute people and in various kinds of societal activity.

Issues Research

In the early 1970s, the educational contours of the Institute's work were not firmly set, and different people wanted it to branch out into different directions. After all, the whole world needed to be brought under the reign of Christ. Some members of the Institute faculty felt that the Institute could offer some professional training programs at the graduate level in addition to its foundational research. De Graaff and Olthuis, for instance, hoped the Institute could start a master's degree program to prepare people for psychotherapeutic counselling in a way that would avoid the complete secularism of existing programs. But in 1974, the Board of Trustees decided against that kind of program as well as against a more practically oriented master's degree.

By that time, the Institute had largely moved away from the atmosphere of counterculture, and the faculty was now focused on theoretical academic research. But some faculty and Board members were concerned that a basic dream for the Institute and its Association was being forgotten, namely, the wish to build Christian leadership to deal with the burning issues of the day. Faculty members could work on aspects of the practical problems of our culture as well as on foundational issues, it was said. Maybe the Institute was simply becoming an ivory tower. There was talk of the need for "translation" of the Institute's foundational insights to the practical world.

Accordingly, in October 1976, the Board of Curators endorsed the idea of an Issues Research Centre and asked the Board of Trustees to establish it. The Trustees appointed a committee of seven persons to study the matter. The committee recommended to the Board that it reaffirm the building of a centre for Christian academic scholarship as the Institute's central mission and highest priority. Included in this would be a program of studies in which a student in one year could complete work for a Certificate in Christian Studies that emphasized "the fruitful application of biblical and philosophical principles to the dynamics of contemporary culture." The committee also recommended that the second priority of the Association be a university campus ministry in which Institute graduate students would teach non-credit courses with reformational Christian insight applied in the courses. This would give the Institute increased visibility, identify prospective Institute students, and give Institute students some employment and experience in actually using the insight they were gaining.

The committee further observed that the Association and the Institute were ill-equipped to bring about a general reformation of life in North America. It did, however, encourage Institute faculty members to participate in summer conferences, public lectures, and short-term nonacademic courses for the public. The committee also recommended that an Issues Research Centre not be established.

The Board adopted the committee's recommendations. This action was a step toward identifying the limits of what the institution would be able to do, in contrast to what some of its people might wish it to do.

Hart's Worldview Program

The Institute's one-year program awarding the Certificate in Christian Studies did not serve students well in providing perspective for their vocations. With such a small faculty, special courses could not be offered to serve this need, so students took the Biblical Foundations and Philosophical Foundations along with all other students, as well as one or two other courses of some interest to them. From this, however, students could hardly gain a Christian worldview to apply to the nonacademic work they wished to do.

In the year 1978–1979, Hendrik Hart offered to set aside one year of his teaching and research to lead a creative course for such people. Intended as a leadership training program, the aim was to provide a learning experience that could be meaningful for each person's life. The focus was on providing a strong foundational sensitivity out of which the person could move toward service to Christ in any area of life.

The year's course brought together a biblical foundation, a focus on the worldview framework, and a cultural orientation. Insights were presented in terms of life experience to foster a more integrated learning process. The basic requirement for admission was a bachelor's degree from a college or university.

The year's program went extremely well. Six persons were admitted to the program, each with a very different background and expectations.

In each week of the course, there were three class sessions of three hours each. The academic year was divided into three parts of nine weeks each, with each of them including biblical foundations, philosophical foundations, and areas of special interest. In addition, each student had one hour a week of consultation with Hart or another faculty member on a individual basis. For each nine-week block, each student chose a project for a special paper or other kind of product. The final three weeks of the year were reserved entirely for reading, writing, and consultations.

Of the six students in the program, only Sue, an American, came directly after graduation from college. She was a creative writer who wanted to work out some intellectual problems she was finding in her writing. Magdalena was a South African computer specialist with experience teaching math to school children. She wanted to work on some scientific and political problems she had bumped up against. Terry came from Montreal with a degree in physical education and two years of church work wanting to deepen his Christian worldview before further study to become a pastoral counsellor. Barb took a leave of absence from her job in a nursing home for the aged to sort through in a Christian way some basic problems in the way society treats the aged. John, a Canadian engineer who came from three years of development relief work in Bangladesh, wanted to find a way to relate theology and social analysis so as to find an approach to direct change in complex interwoven social situations. Marj was a singer and Christian songwriter who wanted to enlarge the kinds of songs she wrote but felt she needed help from Christians to give her direction and support.

These six people found this to be a very exciting year. The six students created a splendid team and were very supportive of one another. They learned much about themselves, about their faith, and about making their faith count in the world. Hart reported that the growth of each one in insight, maturity, confidence, and leadership was remarkable. It was also an excellent learning experience for Hart, who learned to talk philosophy in a nontheoretical way, free from jargon. Hart summed up the year's experience this way: "It was a tough but valuable experience to think deeply about a Christian way of life and then apply the insights gained to practical life situations. You find out a lot about yourself. Students who are best served by this program would be those who find themselves vaguely unhappy with their prospects, but not quite able to figure out what is wrong."

For the second year, only three students registered for the course. Two of them came from Australia, Marty and Jan, a couple who had worked hard with others to build the Australian system of Christian day schools. Hart worked out for them a special program to join significantly in other Institute courses while he worked part-time with them, feeling that his full-time investment in the program could not be justified. This special program was not offered again after that.

The Interdisciplinary Seminar

Even before the Institute started, it was clear that the thinking of the professors and the outlook for its graduate students would need to be interdisciplinary.

But interdisciplinary teaching and research are very difficult. For one thing, nearly everyone's advanced education has taken place in one discipline, that is, in one academic field. The result is that the academic thinking of nearly every scholar is disciplinary, not interdisciplinary. Further, interdisciplinary work in humanities and social sciences requires drawing on worldview insights to make connections between disciplines. This means that scholars doing interdisciplinary work must have closely similar philosophical directions as well as ways of working that can be brought together. The result is that interdisciplinary work turns out to be a deeply religious activity because the issues one confronts tend to be clearly religious.

One consequence of this tendency is that universities generally do not undertake interdisciplinary work except where closely similar academic fields join together. There probably is no other place in the world where half-a-dozen scholars from a diverse range of academic subject areas are trying to do interdisciplinary work. The Institute's special vision of a faculty with compatible religious and worldview commitments has claimed from the start that it has what is needed for important interdisciplinary work.

At first, the interdisciplinary work at the Institute consisted of two faculty members, like James Olthuis and Arnold De Graaff, working together. But the real aim was to have a larger group of people from diverse fields engaged in research together in what came to be called the Interdisciplinary Seminar. Already in 1975, Calvin Seerveld reported to the Board of Curators that "Each Senior Member wants carte blanche to do his own dedicated thing. We need to be encouraged to humble our personal choices into an integrated team that highlights our strengths, corrects our weaknesses, and gains the exponential force of truly communal study, perhaps planning our books that way." Seerveld also reported that in the early interdisciplinary seminar on systematic philosophy and aesthetics, there was "assumed a background of Hart's systematic philosophy seminar or its equivalent, and Hart, Seerveld and Wolters proceeded often to enter into a triangle of debate which left the Junior Members more auditing spectators rather than bona fide talking participants." That approach was not very satisfying for the students. It turns out that interdisciplinary study is something scholars as well as students need to learn how to do,.

Seerveld's summer course in 1977 was a signal point in showing a community of scholarship at work. Institute aesthetics students Lambert Zuidervaart and Barbara Carvill gave presentations, as did Thomas McIntire. Nicholas Wolterstorff held a one-day session that Hendrik Hart attended. Sander Griffioen attended the course discussion on Hegel. Aesthetics students Peter Enneson and Mark Okkema had structured tasks that contributed to the discussions. There were lectures by University of Toronto professors Geoffrey Payzant and Cyrus Hamlin and by The King's University College professor Kobie Kloppers.

After some experimental work, the Interdisciplinary Seminar was set up to engage the Institute in the study of a limited problem that would build on and update its rich intellectual tradition and facilitate contributions from special fields of knowledge. It could therefore provide a modest, Christian signpost in the cultural world of scholarship that challenged its secular positions. As the seminar is now structured, a foundational topic is chosen that is considered to be of special cultural importance to the current scholarly scene on matters of interest to both philosophers and nonphilosophers.

The seminar provides a scheduled interaction of faculty members that forces them to think together on the same topic, assisted by advanced graduate students, which is crucial for developing genuinely communal Christian scholarship. Faculty members as well as students are expected to produce a finished paper each year as their contribution to the seminar, and the aim of the seminar is to publish a series of articles or a short book, in conversation with current secular positions.

Interdisciplinary Seminars typically work at one general topic for two or three years in a row. Students and faculty work together in small groups to research certain subtopics, which are presented and then discussed in three-hour seminars for all participants. All second-year Institute students are required to participate in an Interdisciplinary Seminar as one of their courses, and they are urged to work in a small group led by someone other than their mentor. The fruits of this mutual study show up in public conference presentations and in books on a single theme written by several people who have studied together.

The first Interdisciplinary Seminars were set up for the year 1976–1977. One was titled *Knowledge and Anthropology* and was led by faculty members Hart, De Graaff and Olthuis. The other was called *Philosophy of History* and was led by McIntire, Wolters and Hart. In 1977, the entire faculty, led by Hart and Sander Griffioen, organized a two-year Interdisciplinary Seminar named *NeoMarxism and Liberation Theology.* One aim of the seminar was to deepen the insight of the faculty and graduate students into the nature of responsibility in a contemporary context. The means was to engage in systematic reflection and dialogue with a well-articulated spirit of a direction different from Institute thinking, but with similar concerns about our world. Students and faculty wanted to contribute to the creation of room for responsibility, freed from the oppression of both authoritarianism and libertarianism. They considered dialogue with Marx and neoMarxism important, because at the time the development of a concept of responsibility was best done in relation to the cultural power of the revolutionary attitude in its struggle with reactionary forces.

Sessions were held every Friday morning. At first, introductory lectures were given in turn by several faculty members. There were four permanent work groups that convened every week and worked on a common theme, broken down into subthemes. A steering committee oversaw and coordinated the entire project. Each participant had one specific theme to work on and wrote a paper on that theme. Some basic core books were used by participants, and each subgroup had a bibliography.

In 1980-1981, the theme of the Interdisciplinary Seminar was anthropology, examining the nature of humanity from a biblical point of view. Studies explored biblical givens, modern research contributions, philosophical models, and the Institute's own approach. One subgroup worked on philosophical anthropology in relation to the theme of play in aesthetics, another worked on developmental anthropology and on interpreting models of understanding humanity, and the third worked on anthropology as it affects our work in history. The aim of this seminar was to develop a biblically responsible model for our understanding of who the human person is. With the help of this model, the Institute then hoped to be more effective in understanding the role of the person in various areas of life.

In 1983, the seminar on the thought of Dooyeweerd led to the publication of the book *The Legacy of Herman Dooyeweerd* on the occasion of the fiftieth anniversary of the publication of Dooyeweerd's magnum opus, *A New Critique of Theoretical Thought*. The book was written by six Institute professors and presents Dooyeweerd's contribution to several fields, including philosophy, religious studies and theology, history, aesthetics, and theory of political science. It also gives an appraisal by the Institute faculty of the contribution of Dooyeweerd to Christian thinking.

Interdisciplinary Seminar on Pluralism. One of the more successful interdisciplinary programs took place in the early 1990s on the topic of pluralism, with $59,000 in funding over three years provided by a grant from the Social Sciences and Humanities Research Council of the Canadian government. Paul Marshall and his group worked on toleration and pluralism, Robert Sweetman worked on the political strategies for dealing with pluralism in the Roman Empire and in the early medieval period, Hendrik Hart and Carroll Guen Hart worked on worldview and attitudes to homosexuality, James Olthuis worked on pluralism and family violence, George Vandervelde worked on native spirituality and self-government, Ken Badley worked on indoctrination in education in a pluralistic context, and Calvin Seerveld worked on how other "minority" artistic movements and figures made peace with the cultural powers of the day and how "off-centre" groups today demand plurality on the common cultural scene.

Paul Marshall coordinated the whole project and reported that under the general theme of "A Framework for Applied Ethics within the Context of Plurality," the program involved all of the faculty and twenty-six graduate students. The specific objectives of the research were, first, to examine the "moral ontologies" current in the academic fields of expertise of the Institute's faculty members, and second, to use this to state specific principles for the individual disciplines and the conflicts taking place within them. The research project was ". . . centred on addressing matters of applied ethics within the context of a pluralist culture."

These objectives were well achieved, said Marshall in his report. The tangible results of the program were very impressive. The research suggested how different ontologies (fundamental ways of looking at the world) need not be a barrier to cooperation, and it suggested how the possibilities of cooperation need to inform our ontology, that is, that ontology itself needs to have an ethical dimension.

The output from this three-year research program was most impressive. In addition to Marshall's international program stated above, faculty members gave papers at eleven academic conferences, and students gave three such papers. Members wrote thirty scholarly articles, including chapters in three books that came directly from the research. There were seven media presentations, twenty-nine public lectures and general conference presentations and workshops, twelve popular articles, and Marshall's fifteen articles for News Network International, which were carried to thirty countries. Olthuis edited the book *Knowing Otherwise: Philosophy at the Edge of Spirituality,* which contained many of the ideas developed in the seminar. Students wrote six master's degree theses and one doctoral dissertation based on their grant research.

The success of this research can be seen in other ways. Catherine Crawford's work on family breakdown has been used by a variety of agencies working with street kids. Lisa Smith's work on female circumcision has been used by agencies working with immigrant women. Ken Badley used his work as a springboard to write a major textbook dealing with different religions for Newfoundland high school students. Hendrik Hart won two awards for his writing on homosexuality. Paul Marshall developed an international audience for his work on pluralism, human rights, and religion, lecturing and meeting with government officials in eight different countries.

The huge majority of the grant money was used for research assistantships for the twenty-six graduate students who participated, seven at the doctoral level and nineteen at the master's degree level. Almost half of these students wrote theses, scholarly or popular articles or gave papers at conferences based on their research.

Cross-fertilization was a major benefit of the research. Participants were able to see common issues arising across the boundaries of different academic areas. This research, rarely done at the scholarly university level, enabled participants to develop a wide variety of interdisciplinary materials. It was very hard to communicate across academic boundaries, but a great advantage was that all Institute researchers shared common religious views.

The Institute Library

A good academic institution needs a good library, and a good library is very costly, requiring more money than the Institute could provide. Donations of good books were sought from professors, pastors, and publishing houses, and students could read books in carrels in the University of Toronto library. At the 141 Lyndhurst Avenue location, however, there was room only for a shelf or two of books. When the Institute moved to 229 College Street in 1972, Kerry Hollingsworth spent the summer setting up the library. He was the Institute's librarian until mid-1974.

Tom Henshell succeeded Hollingsworth as librarian. During his tenure, the head librarian of the Free University, Johan Stellingwerff, visited the Institute and met with his friend Robert Blackburn, the head librarian of the University of Toronto. As a result, the Institute was able to arrange for Institute students and faculty members to have complete access to the University of Toronto library for an annual per-person fee of $50. That gave them access to the library's stacks and enabled them to withdraw books. The university library, the largest academic library in Canada, was located only two blocks away from the Institute building. In many ways, it became the Institute's library. This meant that pressure was off the Institute to provide the wide range of books needed for the research of graduate students.

Later, the Board of Curators approved adding the following kinds of materials to the Institute's library collection: books that supported ICS courses, the collected works of leading reformational/Reformed scholars, books from various perspectives on the relationship between Christianity and scholarship, journals relevant to each field of study at the Institute, basic and relevant reference works, and materials that help preserve and record the history of the Association and the Institute and related organizations.

The library befitted greatly from generous bequests of books from the personal libraries of Dutch scholars Herman Dooyeweerd, M. C. Smit, and Hans Rookmaaker. Dooyeweerd specified in his will that the Free University could take any of his books it wished, but that the Institute could have any of the remaining books. After Dooyeweerd's death, Bernard Zylstra went to Amsterdam to select the books, and he arranged for them to be packed in one hundred wooden egg crates for shipment to Toronto, with shipment provided by Anne de Boer, a Toronto furniture dealer. Among the valuable books received was the complete Weimar Edition of Martin Luther's works.

In 1982, the Institute received the complete library of 15,000 to 20,000 volumes of Dutch historian and Free University professor M. C. Smit, which more than doubled the Institute's collection. Smit's research associate Harry Van Dyke, professor emeritus of history at Redeemer University College, was instrumental in arranging the gift. Cataloguing the library was an awesome task, but the Institute was able to get a government grant of $62,000, matched by $10,000 from the Institute, to get it catalogued. It was a ten-month project headed by Richard Reitsma, who worked with four other librarians and nearly competed the project. The Institute also received Smit's filing card reference system, which was beyond imagining.

The library also received a virtually complete set of materials by and about Hans Rookmaaker, professor of aesthetics at the Free University who died suddenly in 1977. The collection was assembled by Wendy Morrison Sereda, a former student of Rookmaaker and of the Institute. Included were six books by Rookmaaker, twenty-five cassette tapes of his lectures, and a set of about two hundred articles or reviews written by or about Rookmaaker. Rookmaaker was a strong encourager of Christian artists and a lover of jazz music. He was a warm friend of Calvin Seerveld, and on one occasion they met in Chicago at the home of Mahalia Jackson, who had received an honorary doctor's degree from the Free University.

In 1998, librarian Marcille Frederick Cook prepared a short bibliography of materials dealing with the Christian faith and learning in various academic disciplines, which she expanded in 2000. This was greatly expanded in 2005 when the International Association for the Promotion of Christian Higher Education designated the Institute's library to be the heart of its international Faith and Learning Network Bibliographic Database. This activity is described in Chapter 15.

In 2006, the Institute's complete library holdings were added to the library catalogue of the University of Toronto so that university students, as well as ICS students, could have access to the books in the ICS library.

Faculty Evaluation and Sabbatical Leaves

From the start, the faculty and the Board of Curators agreed that the Institute would not adopt the policy of tenure for the faculty. The feeling was that no one had the right to hold an academic position without periodic formal evaluation of the service given. Instead, the work of each faculty member would be reviewed periodically, even if after some years one would no longer receive periodic terms of reappointment.

The work of each new faculty member was to be thoroughly evaluated near the end of the second year of service, and again two years later and two years after that. At that point, the faculty member would receive a "continuing appointment," meaning that the appointment was permanent but that every five years the person's service would be re-evaluated. If the service was not found to be acceptable, the person would continue on the faculty one more year, at which point his or her service would end.

The Institute's periodic evaluations are very rigorous. At the time of evaluation, the professor prepares a complete curriculum vita, identifies what has been achieved during the period since the last evaluation, and projects a program of research and teaching for the next few years.

There are two steps to the evaluation. The first step is an evaluation by the faculty and the students who have been served by the professor. Student evaluation is done in a half-day session of very open discussion in which the strengths and limitations of the person are addressed. It is not a hostile meeting, but it is very frank. Strengths and areas for improvement are forthrightly addressed. Most often, the professor is highly appreciated and words of thanks are generous.

The second step is that a full written report is given to the Senate. That body then meets with the professor, all the issues are discussed, and the academic board reaches its conclusion. The academic board's decision nearly always includes appreciation and best wishes for the coming years, but occasionally leads to the termination of an appointment.

Summer Conferences, Seminars and Courses

In the 1970s, the Institute wanted to present a nonacademic course in addition to the academic course each summer. This program of two-week nonacademic courses, called "Basic Issues," continued for a few years. It included the following courses:

1974 Basic Issues in Philosophy, by Hendrik Hart
1975 Basic Issues in Education, by Arnold De Graaff
1976 Understanding the Scriptures, by James Olthuis
1977 Biblical Basics for a Christian Philosophy, by Albert Wolters
1978 "Art, Literature and Music in God's World," by Calvin Seerveld

For many years, the Institute also offered Interim courses in January that corresponded to the academic calendar of Calvin College and other undergraduate colleges that used the 4–1–4 calendar, giving room for special educational experiences. Generally, these Interim courses at the Institute were team taught by an Institute professor and one or two others, usually from Calvin College.

In 1982, the Institute organized and hosted a one-day conference on fund-raising to which other parachurch organizations started by Dutch immigrants as well as some other Christian ministries were invited. The aim was to share information on fund-raising in an open way by groups asking for money from the same religious community, so competitiveness and ill will would not develop among the organizations. The meeting was so successful that a second conference was held in 1984.

Starting in 1993, the Institute shared a summer school course program with Wycliffe College of the University of Toronto, a program that was very successful and ran for several years. A series of monthly public seminars during the academic year was begun around the year 2000 at which a graduate student or professor at the Institute gives a talk and leads discussion on research work in progress.

The Institute faculty knew that many Christian scholars were active in studies of Christian understanding of academic issues, so starting in 1970 the faculty set up summer academic conferences inviting Christian scholars to join them in discussing current thinking in various fields. From many of these conferences came books presenting current Christian scholarship. Many of these conferences are identified in Appendix 3.

Art Talks

In 1997, Calvin and Inès Seerveld made provision for an annual arts event called the Ruth Memorial Series on the Arts and Culture. Each year, for one or two days, a person or small group highly skilled in visual, dramatic, or musical arts presents a workshop that has considerable appeal. Presenters have been Marnie Giesbrecht and Joachim Segger, Rudy Wiebe, Adrienne Dengerink Chaplin, Nigel Goodwin, Jeremy Begbie, William Romanowski, Erica Grimm-Vance, Ron Reed, and John Franklin.

Distinguished Associates and Adjunct Faculty

In 1974, the Institute set up the position of Fellow to draw into the academic program people throughout the world who were willing and able to make academic contributions to the work of the Institute. A Fellow was identified as a person who is "a spiritually kindred competent scholar who is willing to make a tangible contribution to the work of the Institute." The appointment of a Fellow is for a five-year period and the services provided are normally given without compensation. The first people appointed as Institute Fellows in 1974 were Bob Goudzwaard from the Netherlands and Peter Schouls from Canada. In 1975, A. B. Cramp in England, H. Evan Runner in the United States, and M. Dirk Stafleu and Johan van der Hoeven in the Netherlands became Fellows. In 1992, the designation was changed to Distinguished Associates, a non-sexist term.

By the 1980s, the Institute was drawing on certain Christian scholars living in the Toronto area for short-term and usually part-time teaching appointments. In October 1985, the Senate and Board of Trustees established the designation of Adjunct Faculty to identify people who have the same confessional beliefs as are required of regular faculty, have the ability to integrate faith and learning, have a doctorate or professional equivalent of the faculty, and are able to give intellectual leadership. These people were asked to make a three-year commitment for service at the Institute that would, at minimum, include serving on Institute master's and doctoral thesis committees.

Lectures by Guest Professors

The Institute has always been open to hearing lectures from visiting Christian scholars who pass through Toronto, though there is little or no financial remuneration for this service. Among the more notable guest lecturers have been Hans-Georg Gadamer, Mikel Dufrenne, Paul Oskar Kristeller, Gustav Wingren, Herman Dooyeweerd, George Grant, Nicholas Wolterstorff, Richard Mouw, Alvin Plantinga, Hans Rookmaaker, Samuel Escobar, René Padilla, H. G. Stoker, Peter Schouls, James Houston, Herman Ridderbos, Stanford Reid, Clark Pinnock, Abraham Rotstein, Gregory Baum, Jim Wallis, Egbert Schuurman, Arthur Holmes, David Lyon, Alan and Elaine Storkey, Roy Clouser, Bruce Cockburn, and N. Thomas Wright. Distinguished scholars who have given short courses at the Institute include Bob Goudzwaard, Sander Griffioen, A. B. Cramp, Johan van der Hoeven, and M. Dirk Stafleu.

The Institute set up the Christianity and Learning Lecture Series to bring three lectures each year in February by Christian scholars who are not in the Dutch reformational line of thinking, people of proven academic competence who could enhance the interdisciplinary character of the Institute and be able to foster relations between the Institute and the wider academic community. Invitations to the lectures were given to professors and students at nearby universities and seminaries. Among those who have spoken in the series are: Martin Marty, Gustav Wingren, Stanley Jaki, Langdon Gilkey, Rosemary Radford Ruether, Merold Westphal, N. Thomas Wright, Adriaan Peperzak, Heike Oberman, John Caputo, Thomas Groome, Jean Bethke Elshtain, Walter Brueggemann, Ursula Franklin, George Tavard, Timothy Noone, Richard Kearney, and Miroslav Wolf.

Calvin Center for Christian Scholarship

Each year during the 1980s, the Calvin College Center for Christian Scholarship brought a team of scholars to Calvin College for a year of intensive study of a Christian approach to some area of public concern. It became a custom each June for the Institute to host the team for a two-day conference at which these scholars gave a public presentation of the conclusions they were reaching. The Institute provided a qualified respondent to each presentation. These were exciting conferences that brought forward valuable insights, and the critics provided by the Institute helped the Calvin scholars in the formal articulation of their reports. The conferences were:

1981	Alternatives to our present economic theory
1982	A Christian approach to behavioural science
1983	Forum on hermeneutics
1984	Toward a responsible technology
1985	The creation as cosmos
1986	Christian faith, health, and medical practice
1987	The crisis in Central America: A Reformed Christian approach
1989	Youth, electronic media, and popular art
1990	Gender roles
1992	The schools we don't deserve

International Study Centres

The Institute's publications as well as its vision for Christian academic study stimulated the formation of study centres in the United States and overseas. These were places where public lectures were held and where people could use and purchase books and papers produced by the Institute and from other sources. Such centres the Institute knew about were located in North Carolina, Minnesota, Kansas, Oregon, Australia, New Zealand, Ireland, and England.

Student Recruitment and Enrolment

The first students at the Institute came because of the general excitement about its opening and its lecture programs throughout Canada. In 1969, the first year the school was established in Toronto, the Institute counted thirteen full-time and ninety part-time students.

As the academic program and courses became better defined, the number of part-time students dropped sharply from the first years. In 1974, there were twenty-six full-time students in regular programs, with twelve others attending full-time but not in a certificate program, but only eleven part-time students. This lower enrolment was also caused by the Institute's becoming better known as a place for serious academic study, lack of degrees for the academic programs, and lack of student financial aid. The tuition fee for full-time students in 1974 was $750 for the year, and food and lodging costs were estimated at about $120 a month.

People were surprised that from the start the Institute drew students from overseas. Very early students came from Australia, Lebanon, Cyprus, and Japan, for instance, and in the mid-1970s, they came also from Australia, England, India and Malaysia. There seemed to be an international web of people interested in the kind of Christian higher education the Institute offered. The proportion of students from overseas has always been strikingly high.

After a time, the number of students from Dutch Reformed churches in Canada and the United States became quite low, though later the number increased again. As the counterculture faded, Christian students became less idealistic and more concerned with career aspirations and with getting a widely recognized degree and a solid job. Many students who had moved through elementary and secondary Christian schools and a Christian college felt that part of their education should take place in a secular university. The result was that the Institute was serving only a small number of the students whose families and Christian communities were providing most of the Institute's financial and prayer support. The Institute seemed to be serving as a sort of academic evangelistic outreach to nonsupporting Christian communities in North America and overseas. Over the years, a constant problem was getting a large enough student body to justify a larger faculty.

Already in 1975, the new students were all non-Dutch, and most were American. A major source of new students was from the work of Peter Steen in Pennsylvania and to some extent Trace James and the Young Life ministry in Minneapolis. The best way to recruit Institute students seemed to be through professors, campus chaplains, and other mentors who worked with undergraduate students over an extended period of time. Institute recruitment trips to undergraduate Christian colleges did not directly bring in many students, but they did bring personal contact with professors in those colleges who could encourage their students to study at the Institute after their graduation.

Student recruitment often proceeded by mail. A student would send a letter of inquiry with indication of an academic field of interest, and the Institute would reply with some helpful materials and suggestions for reading certain books. Often the Institute professor in the field in which the inquirer expressed interest would send a personal letter to the potential student. For most inquirers, learning of the Institute's reformational Christian approach was itself an education. Often this correspondence would progress over two or three years as a Christian educational outreach service before the student enrolled in the Institute.

In the early decades, the Institute professors did not have the time for extensive correspondence, nor did the Institute as a graduate school have the infrastructure to conduct this service, so in 1974 student recruitment became a service of the Association handled by its Educational Services Department. Recruiters were usually people who had recently graduated from the Institute and who were therefore well informed about the program from the inside out.

A problem with student recruitment was that new faculty members were appointed to the Institute with no thought as to whether the person appointed or the academic subject would interest prospective students. Appointments were made solely on the basis of whether the appointee had a good knowledge of the academic field with a reformational philosophical perspective and whether the field itself was considered a priority by the faculty and the Board of Curators. There was no initial contact with people at undergraduate colleges about fields of interest to students nor whether a particular person was well thought of by the faculty members. After a person was appointed, the Institute made little attempt to inform Christian college professors about the strengths of the faculty appointee. The Institute assumed that if it did the "right" things, students would automatically come.

Student Financial Aid

In the earliest years, there was no provision for financial aid from the Institute to full-time students who could hardly afford to study in Toronto. This alone greatly discouraged overseas students from attending. As that became apparent, appeals were made to Institute supporters to make special donations designated to help specific needy students. But the amount of money supplied for this, and the uncertainty of getting enough money for needy students, showed the need for a budgeted financial aid program.

A student financial aid program was set up in 1975 as a line item in the budget set by the Board. It was administered by a standing committee that included the Executive Director of the Association and another administrator, plus a student and a faculty member. Each student applicant needed to fill out a confidential form showing what financial resources the student could commit for Institute study each year, which was matched against the estimated costs for the year, including tuition fees. Where possible, the student was interviewed by the committee, and from all indications the student applicants were open and honest about their resources. Financial aid was usually given as a combination of grants, loans, and work at the Institute in the library, office, or sometimes in regular cleaning of the premises. Students were expected vigorously to pursue receiving grants and loans from government or other outside sources, which were all part of the calculation. Because all applicants were mature graduate students, parents were often reluctant to provide money, feeling that at this age a person should be financially independent.

The aim of the Financial Aid program was to permit all qualified people who wished to study at the Institute to do so even if they themselves did not have the money they needed for Institute study. Student aid was given only for full-time study toward an Institute degree, with priority given to doctoral students. Students needed to be making good progress toward a degree, and students receiving aid for more than one year would need to agree that the committee could check with the faculty about their progress toward the degree. Aid money would not be given for more than two years for a candidate for the master's degree, and not more than four years for the Ph.D. Since Institute tuition fees were quite low, partly because tuition fees at Canadian universities were low compared to American tuition fees, the difference between overall tuition income received by the Institute and student financial aid paid out was generally quite low.

Special provision was made for aid to two new international students each year. To receive aid, international students needed to show the desire for a clearly Christian vocation, to be realized in the students' home country, for which study at the Institute could clearly be significant. Priority was given to especially gifted applicants who could show that the environment in their home country was sufficiently congenial to the service the students wished to prepare for and that there was a church or school in the home country eager to have their services after graduation.

Special aid funds were also available, but the amounts were usually small. The Bernard Zylstra Scholarship Fund, set up in the year 1985–1986, was awarded based on donations to the Institute specifically earmarked for this. The Peter J. Steen Scholarship Fund, set up in 1984–1985 in tribute to Steen, who died of cancer at an early age in 1984, was granted to one student each year, with preference given to students from Pittsburgh and its tristate area. The recipient was selected from students who showed the Christian academic motivation that Dr. Steen encouraged in students but who did not necessarily have a demonstrated financial need for this grant.

Herman Dooyeweerd

Early Board of Trustees (from left top): Mr. M. Koole, Rev. L. Tamminga, Mr. G. Vanderzande, Mr. J. de Koning, Rev. P. Jonker, Dr. C. Seerveld, Mr. M. Vander Meulen, (seated), Rev. J. Joosse, Rev. A. Venema, Rev. M. deVries.

141 Lyndhurst Avenue

An early photograph of the founding fathers of the AACS,
rom left to right: Henry Venema, Casper VandeRiet,
Peter Speelman and Francois Guillaume.

A group of participants in the first AACS conference,
held in Unionville, September 1-3, 1959.

Current ICS building

7

Books as a Vehicle for Leadership

As a graduate school, the Institute has two strong mandates, teaching and research. Having taken a brief look at the teaching program, we now look at the research aspect. There are several ways that the research conducted by the faculty reaches out to other Christians. One way is by means of books written by faculty members for reading by academics and nonacademics. Another is through the many talks they give, both scholarly and popular. However, talks often do not leave tangible records, so a close look at what has been spoken is not possible.

Many books that have been generated by the Institute have come from papers given at conferences. Examining most of these books is more fitting to an academic volume and would provide too much material for this discussion. Instead, we will focus on books written by one or perhaps two Institute people, from which we can get a good idea of special contributions arising from Institute research. Following, in chronological order, are some of the books that have arisen from the Institute's research activity.

The Challenge of Our Age, Hendrik Hart (1968)

This book includes lectures given by Hendrik Hart in 1966 and 1967 when he began his work for the Institute. These lectures served as a sort of manifesto for the Institute's founding and development in the years that followed. It is a basic analysis of the spirit of the age at that time, and it gives direction for Christians in the years to come.

The book is a countercultural statement in the best sense of that term. It closely analyses commonly held Western views, such as secularism, humanism, scientism, human self-sufficiency, pragmatism, and rationalism. The views of Ralph Waldo Emerson, John Dewey, and Harvey Cox are identified as pivotal statements articulating what is wrong with Western culture. The book is a precursor to the Institute's pioneering studies of Christian worldview that started a few years later.

This age with its scientism and pragmatism, says Hart, challenges us to look for perspective above ourselves and our own culture, to work with deep Christian spirituality, and to develop a rich knowledge of our Creator. He writes, "Life in the Kingdom of God is the fullness of life in subjection to God's Word in *communion* with the Holy Spirit." The challenge and responsibility are to understand our world and to recognize that religion is all-encompassing. To be spiritually prophetic, he says, we need thorough grounding in the Bible, which is the canon of the new creation. Christians need to be awakened and become alarmed. This is a direction-giving book.

A Christian Critique of Art and Literature, by Calvin Seerveld (1968 and 1995)

This book contains early lectures by Seerveld on artistic and literary criticism delivered in 1962 and 1963 at ICS summer study conferences in Unionville, Ontario, and in Banff, Alberta. They contain Calvin Seerveld's early pleas to fully entrust our aesthetic lives to Christ.

Seerveld's creative intellect expresses itself in an exuberant flair not out of place in the counterculture of the 1960s. The book is written with the reformational Christian approach that insists that all of culture necessarily reflects certain prior core commitments. This permits him to present a deeply Christian critique of the arts, yet one that respects their dignity and integrity. He approaches art and literature from his experience in philosophy. This material is written not only for artists and philosophers but also for the general public.

Insight, Authority and Power: A Biblical Appraisal, by Peter Schouls (1972)

The biblical example of the ministry of Jesus in the face of leaders who lacked insight about God's rule in the world is the central thrust of this small countercultural book. Peter Schouls writes, "Those among the people of God who claim authority but have no knowledge are called hypocrites by Christ." He argues that "Authority is *never* gained except through gaining insight or knowledge" and "Power is exercised legitimately *only* by people possessing authority because of insight."

This view was attractive to leaders at the new Institute who were sure they had good insight but wondered about people they found in decision-making positions. Implicit was the view that leadership structures should never be hierarchical, a view that was practiced in the early years of the Institute, during which time Schouls was chair of the Institute's Board of Curators. The concrete meaning of this biblical teaching was controversial in the turbulent times in which it was expressed. This material originated in AACS lectures that Schouls presented in three western locations.

I Pledge You My Troth: A Christian View of Marriage, Family and Friendship, by James Olthuis (1975)

When God created Adam, he said that humans should not be alone. But loneliness and broken personal relations are all around us. Many people have difficulty relating with other people. This book deals with interpersonal relations in marriage, family, and friendships, which Olthuis presents as God's gifts for humans.

To be human, says James Olthuis, requires us to be in relation with other people. Humanity is a biunity, created for partnership. Discussing gender differences, he says God called the marriage of husband and wife to be an exclusive, lifelong partnership of love, that is, of troth and fidelity. The key concept in marriage, and also in family relationships and friendship, is troth, which means trust, reliability, stability, scrupulousness, authenticity, integrity, and fidelity. God's call to love him and our neighbours is a unique dimension of our creation as humans.

Olthuis discusses in clear and open ways what a family is and how it should function and also the meaning and importance of friendship. The book was widely accepted and became a best seller, the first book from the Institute published by a major publisher.

God, History, and Historians, edited by C. T. McIntire (1977)

From the time of Augustine to the nineteenth century, it was accepted that history has meaning and a role in the divine plan. Under pressure from rationalism, positivism, and Marxism, this view was replaced by a secular one. At the start of Hitler's conquests, however, Reinhold Niebuhr turned that secular view around with his seminal writing on *The Nature and Destiny of Man*. "The renewal of interest in a Christian view of history emerges from two sources," writes C. T. McIntire in his Introduction. "The primary one is a response to the catastrophes of our secular age," and "the secondary one is the 'problem of history' in Old and New Testament studies and theology."

The selections in this book, written by twenty-one leading thinkers of the twentieth century, "reveal the range of issues included in a Christian view of history, as well as some of the diversity and disagreement which exists," writes McIntire.

Part I is devoted to the questions of the meaning of history. Part II on the nature of history and culture deals with what is often called the philosophy of history. Part III is on the study and writing of history. The book contributes to the theology of history, which most non-Christian viewpoints neglect. The book is engaging for anyone who has been led by recent crises and catastrophes to question the assumptions that underlie our secular civilization. Oxford University Press published the book.

Herbert Butterfield: Essays on Christianity and History, compiled by C. T. McIntire (1979)

The essays in this book were written by Herbert Butterfield, a leading British historian who wrote widely on Christianity and history and who spearheaded the general revival of a Christian view of history. C. T. McIntire had worked with Butterfield in Cambridge, England, and Butterfield provided for this book copies of some of his material that was not otherwise accessible.

Rainbows for the Fallen World: Aesthetic Life and Artistic Task, by Calvin Seerveld (1980)

The six essays in this book present Calvin Seerveld's Christian perspective on art and aesthetics. He asks whether visual art is just something constructed in the mind, which, like fiction and parables, sets up something that never really happened. His answer is that God made rainbows for the fallen world.

Following a printing of his own translation of Psalm 19, he directs attention to creaturely reality and how aesthetic theory relates with reading the Bible. God's people are called, says Seerveld, to find out what art is like and why God has put artistic talent among us, as well as to affirm that art can be a legitimate full-time service. His thesis is that God requires aesthetic obedience of everyone. Following his insistence that art is not esoteric, he says that art shows its redemptive service if it reveals the way of the Lord for the aesthetic dimension of our daily lives.

After directing attention to the nature of created reality, Seerveld shows how aesthetic reality relates to the reading of the Bible. Then comes the philosophical rationale for his analyses of concrete affairs as well as an essay on art in schooling. Finally, he points out how God's people are called to proceed faithfully. The book contains many reproductions of artworks.

Understanding Our World: An Integral Ontology, by Hendrik Hart (1984)

With this book, Hendrik Hart contributes to the renewal of

systematic philosophical thinking by constructing an integral ontology dependent on a Christian worldview. He makes explicit a categorical framework that includes the most general structures of our world, aiming to help integrate scholarship and relate it integrally to the rest of human culture. This is an ontology, an understanding of the nature of existence in the world, that is a unifying view of the world in philosophical terms, using concepts implied in and at the same time guided by a Christian worldview.

Hart's ideas are oriented to Calvinian Christianity and its tradition, best known for its rejection of the ultimate authority of reason. He concludes the book with a statement of his core Christian beliefs as the commitment on which his thinking and this book are based.

Thine Is the Kingdom: A Biblical Perspective on the Nature of Government and Politics Today, by Paul Marshall (1984)

Paul Marshall gives us a foundational statement of the nature of politics from a Christian point of view. His focus is on *understanding* politics, since we need to *think* to become politically involved. He argues against the view that a Christian approach to political action focuses on individual morality, calling instead for concrete political morality. He also deals with how governments should approach questions of public morality.

The book outlines how the Bible develops political order as the authority that God has set up to establish just relations between persons and groups. It considers the purpose of government and the meaning of justice. Guidelines are given for Christian political action today. The book introduces biblical teaching on the nature of economics and on the place of the poor in society.

Marshall complains that Christian politics today tends to embrace a secular ideology with only a veneer of faith. He provides a thorough biblical understanding of politics as an institution and offers a Christian analysis of policies related to the welfare state, international relations, and, especially, the nuclear arms race. The discussion is set in the context of our age in which the Kingdom of God has come but in which sin remains until the return of Christ.

The Transforming Vision: Shaping a Christian Worldview, by Brian J. Walsh and J. Richard Middleton (1984)

Brian Walsh and J. Richard Middleton wrote this book while graduate students at the Institute, both having been students in the worldview course taught by Albert Wolters. The book arose out of some twenty courses the two taught through the Institute on university campuses in southern Ontario between 1977 and 1983. The aim of the courses was "to help university students develop an integrated Christian worldview, both faithful to the Scriptures and motivating for Christian obedience in a secular age."

The authors want Christianity to receive social and cultural embodiment. Our world, they say, needs a Christian worldview to shape our understanding of what the world really is.

The book starts with stories showing worldviews of cultures different from those common in North America. Worldviews, the authors say, "are best understood as we see them incarnated, fleshed out in actual ways of life." They are not systems of thought but perceptual frameworks, ways of seeing. Everyone, they say, has a worldview. By their nature, worldviews are shared, communal, and only with shared worldviews can people have community. Worldviews are intensely spiritual, and they underlie all scholarly work. There are many different Christian worldviews, but the basic biblical worldview deals with the biblical givens of creation, fall, and redemption.

Modern worldviews, according to the authors, suffer the problem of dualism, giving a split-vision worldview that "separates reality into two fundamentally distinct categories: holy and profane, secular and sacred." The modern secular worldview started when people lost interest in religion, in part through the rise of science, and abandoned the sacred for the secular worldview.

Walsh and Middleton sketch a Christian worldview based on God's covenant with the world and with humanity. This requires that we give up the idols of our time. The conclusion of the book calls for a view of scholarship that is not religiously neutral but is built on a Christian worldview.

Creation Regained: Biblical Basics for a Reformational Worldview, by Albert Wolters (1985)

A worldview, says Wolters is ". . . the comprehensive framework of one's basic beliefs about things." The Protestant Reformation discovered afresh the biblical teaching and scope of sin and redemption. This scope allows us to reflect on biblical worldviews, a category of things that is distinctly different from theology and philosophy. A person's worldview is a guide to one's life in a way that is intuitive, not academic.

Everyone has a worldview, whether or not it is examined. A worldview is a matter of wisdom and common sense. A Christian's worldview should be shaped and tested by the Bible.

Wolters opens up the meaning of worldview in terms of the basic biblical categories of creation, fall, and redemption. He shows how our understanding of these categories shapes the structure and direction of life. He writes that "*structure* denotes the 'essence' of a creaturely thing, the kind of creature it is by virtue of God's created law. *Direction*, by contrast, refers to a sinful deviation from that structural ordinance and renewed conformity to it in Christ."

This book is one of the earliest Christian statements about worldviews. It arises from Wolters's teaching of a course on worldview at the Institute.

History and Historical Understanding, edited by C. T. McIntire and Ronald Wells (1985)

The eight essays in this book are contributed by various writers. The essays all deal with the common theme of the insights that the Christian faith may bring to our understanding of historical process and historical knowledge and study, and they are followed by an explanation of how these insights can be used. The aim is to bring the Christian faith into an area of study that is widely taken to be secular.

Keeping Our Troth, by James Olthuis (1986)

James Olthuis presents a biblical view of home and marriage, of family and friendship. In an era of anxiety and broken illusions, happiness is not a gift that comes pre-packaged with marriage. The book provides a compass and chart for marriage, dispelling some of the illusions and myths that befuddle many couples. Olthuis says that "With proper preparations and a good map, marriage can be a fulfilling and rewarding adventure even in these tempestuous times."

The book offers a refreshing and thoughtful view of the home and marriage that is informed by the best in both modern psychotherapy and the Christian tradition. It shows how the age-old concept of *troth*, implying not only trust in one another but in God and oneself, provides a strong foundation for marriage and frees couples for genuine intimacy.

Useful for preparing couples for marriage, the book identifies five stages of marriage. Each stage is illustrated with case studies and presented with warmth and understanding. The book offers practical helps, suggestions, and spiritual insight on the development and nurturing of intimacy. This book is a follow-up to Olthuis's earlier book *I Pledge You My Troth*.

***On Being Human: Imaging God in the Modern World*, by Calvin Seerveld (1988)**

To get straight the meaning of being human, says Calvin Seerveld, we need to listen to Scripture. This book consists of seven brief meditations, originally given at a conference in Zeist, the Netherlands, for professors, students, and nonacademicians who are interested in Christian philosophy. Included are Seerveld's own translations of the Bible texts chosen, as well as eleven psalms he translated and the versification of those psalms for singing.

The book engages all our senses while vividly illustrating what it really means to be human. Through the use of Scripture, stunning artworks, original songs, and prayers, Seerveld explores the miracle of being human in the image of God.

***The Holy Spirit: Renewing and Empowering Presence*, edited by George Vandervelde (1989)**

This book contains material presented at a conference that was organized by Vandervelde. James Dunn provides "two profound New Testament studies which explore the relation of the Spirit to Jesus himself and to the church which is his body." Richard Gaffin writes of the Spirit in Paul's theology. Garth Wilson makes clear what the Holy Spirit means in the Reformed tradition, Jan Veenhof exposes a false dichotomy between the natural and the supernatural, and Richard Mouw argues against a merely individualistic and religious reading of the work of the Spirit. In the longest chapter, Vandervelde asks why the church today does not value more highly the gift of prophecy, and he urges a revival of this spiritual gift.

***Setting Our Sights by the Morning Star: Reflections on the Role of the Bible in Post-Modern Times*, by Hendrik Hart (1989)**

In dealing with the question of what the Bible really is, Hendrik Hart uses the metaphor that the Bible is light. The Bible presents Jesus Christ through the light of the Holy Spirit. The Bible speaks of Jesus as the Morning Star, which appears just before dawn when the sky is darkest. God's Spirit is the spirit of troth whose way of life we must follow, giving him control of our hearts and minds. Our openness to the light of the Spirit, says Hart, relativizes our convictions about the truth of tradition and doctrinal statements.

***Search for Community in a Withering Tradition*, by Kai Nielsen and**

Hendrik Hart (1990)

When Kai Nielsen was one of Canada's most prominent philosophers and a person who identified himself as an atheist and a Marxist, he often presented his views on the nature of reality at the annual meetings of the Canadian Philosophical Society. In 1984, Hart gave a paper at the meeting a year after Nielsen's address as president of the Society, in which he argued that Nielsen's atheism was covertly supported by a religious appeal to reason and rationality. Following that, a friendly if spirited annual dialogue was underway. After a few years of this public discussion, the two decided to publish their divergent views in a book.

The two agreed to disagree on almost every detail of philosophical thinking. They did agree that in both the Marxian and the Calvinian heritages, the tradition of reason is withering. The views of each embodied strongly held religious beliefs, but they agreed that conversation even with such great differences was not fruitless. There was the common conviction that conversations of this sort were important to the continued flourishing of humanity in community.

Nielsen claimed that belief in God is irrational. A key issue in the debates was the question of what reason and rationality really are, and in what is rationality rooted.

The book consists of alternating chapters by each author, with each trying to show the unacceptability of the views of the other. Nielsen graciously invited Hart to write the concluding chapter, in which Hart presents a powerful argument for a Christian view of knowledge in God's world.

Subversive Christianity: Imaging God in a Dangerous Time, by Brian Walsh (1992, 1994)

This critique of modern liberal democracy is about worldview formation. Its context is the cultural captivity and cultural collapse of a Christian mind in our age, which denies in practice a Christian worldview. How should we understand, for example, the ways that corporation leaders and labour unions are at each other's throats, both denying any Christian responsibility?

We live in the midst of cultural idolatry, says Brian Walsh, but our Christian vision of life is much like that of our secular culture. Christians seem concerned only with souls, living with a dualist mind-set that denies the Lordship of Christ. We should mourn that we are captured by our culture. Paul and Silas were subverting the culture in which they lived, as was the prophet Jeremiah. We need to set up with good hope alternative structures with Christian vision.

Political Theory and Christian Vision: Essays in Memory of Bernard Zylstra, **edited by Jonathan Chaplin and Paul Marshall (1994)**

Ten students and four academic colleagues contributed to this memorial book in tribute to Bernard Zylstra, who died of cancer in the strength of his years. The book's four sections identify Zylstra's strong interests: Normative Foundations, The Nature of the State, the State in Plural Society, and Political Economy.

Zylstra was strongly influenced as an undergraduate student by H. Evan Runner and, as phrased by Chaplin, absorbed Runner's maxim ". . . that all knowledge, including academic knowledge, is rooted in faith and, hence, that every dimension of the academy, indeed every dimension of life itself, needs to be reformed in a Christian way."

The authors creatively develop ideas brought forward by Zylstra, whose work Chaplin articulates as a "multifaceted enterprise with large and somewhat audacious horizons. Its aim is to investigate systematically, and on the basis of a clearly articulated religious and philosophical vision, the full range of dimensions of political reality, and to do so in close correspondence with related disciplines such as sociology, economics and law. . . . His particular interests lay, for good strategic reasons, in the philosophical and methodological questions that underlie the study of empirical political systems."

The Woman Will Overcome the Warrior: A Dialogue with the Christian/Feminist Theology of Rosemary Radford Ruether, **by Nicholas Ansell (1994)**

Written from within contemporary evangelical Christianity, this sympathetic critique of Rosemary Radford Ruether's thought is directed to those who are open to her position. Nicholas Ansell finds a number of significant points of contact with Ruether's Christian feminist theology, though he has major disagreements with her on topics like eschatology.

Truth Is Stranger Than It Used to Be: Biblical Faith in a Postmodern Age, **by J. Richard Middleton and Brian J. Walsh (1995)**

In Part I, J. Richard Middleton and Brian Walsh identify their understanding of postmodernism by means of four worldview questions. They give a historical overview of the shift from modernism to postmodernism, followed by the main answers current in our postmodern culture for our place in the world, human identity or selfhood, and the problem of good and evil. They emphasize that all postmodern views are human inventions conditioned by the social context in which they occur.

In Part II, the authors bring forward the resources of Scripture and a biblical worldview to bear on postmodernity. They affirm that "The Scriptures have the resources to address the postmodern condition, speaking a redemptive word of healing for our times." They argue that postmodernism can open the way for a faithful reading of Scripture, showing new and exciting dimensions of the biblical text.

The authors conclude that "Modernity is coming to a grinding halt, its ideals unravelling, its accomplishments incomplete." At the end, Middleton and Walsh ask, "How then shall we live? We need a renewed rooting in the Scripture with an understanding of what it means to live out of the Christian faith with authenticity in our contemporary culture." But, they note, a simple reading of parts of the Bible will not help us confront postmodernism. It is the hard parts that we turn away from that challenge our fixed categories and give us insight into the postmodern world.

The biblical story is not always safe, the authors insist. Our times are dangerous, but by holding a faithful and risky discipleship in a postmodern world, we are promised the blessing of the Holy Spirit who guides us into all truth.

An Ethos of Compassion and the Integrity of Creation, edited by Brian J. Walsh, Hendrik Hart, and Robert E. VanderVennen (1995)

This book contains the major papers and responses given at the international 25th Anniversary Conference of the Institute. The goal of the conference, wrote Henry Fernhout in the Introduction, was to consider anew the strength and weaknesses of an orientation to creation order in reformational philosophy and at the roots of the Institute. Is creation order the right normative ground amid rising changes in our world in which postmodernism is so important? Does creation order provide us with a healing orientation today?

The conference and the book deal with ethical issues, gender relations and sexuality, international political order, artistic freedom, and challenges in higher education. Contributors all affirm that order in our life experience is real. Orderedness is a gift and also a call.

This is an extremely rich volume, bristling with new ideas and responses to the use of creation order as a norm. The book gives no place to smugness. All contributors affirm creation order. They often disagree on how others respond and use order, yet agree that living and thinking in ordered ways may not become stagnant.

Hendrik Hart writes that compassion must be a key part of our thinking and acting in an ordered world. The book contains three responses to Hart's presentation, which take some issue with his suggestions, and includes Hart's response to his critics. Allen Verhey insists that biblical hermeneutics must be as prominent as science in medical ethics. Calvin DeWitt asks "When is 'Against Nature' against Nature?"; James Olthuis provocatively asks "When is Sex Against Nature?"; and Elaine Storkey considers "Is Male Dominance Against Nature?" Langdon Gilkey considers the ambiguity of order.

In their summing up of the contents of the book, Jonathan and Adrienne Dengerink Chaplin add that creation order should not be conceived primarily in terms of an order of law and lawgiver. They conclude, "Biblical hermeneutics remains central to the task of creational hermeneutics."

Pledges of Jubilee: Essays on the Arts and Culture, in Honour of Calvin G. Seerveld, **edited by Lambert Zuidervaart and Henry Luttikhuizen (1995)**

This book breaks new ground in the fields of cultural theory and aesthetics, highlighting Calvin Seerveld's legacy as a scholar, teacher, and leader. Contributors are seventeen of Seerveld's former students and others who have been in dialogue with him about issues in the arts and culture. The book reflects the community of scholars that has developed of those who have learned from Seerveld's work and who pursue transformational aesthetics in the Reformed Christian tradition.

These essays test the fruitfulness of Seerveld's aesthetic theory for various fields of study that have opened up in recent years. Some contributions examine the cultural theories of Derrida, Dewey, and Heidegger with the kind of close and engaged reading of philosophical texts that characterize Seerveld's teaching and scholarship. Other lively, focused, and reflective essays deal with areas in which Seerveld has given cultural leadership. A listing of Seerveld's written materials and speeches fills twenty-two pages.

A Kind of Life Imposed on Man: Vocation and Social Order from Tyndale to Locke, **by Paul Marshall (1996)**

This book is an academic study of the Christian idea of calling to the kind of work one does. The theological notion of calling, the idea that everyday work is the locus of Christian obedience, formed the core of much of the economic and social theory of Protestantism in its earlier years, and Paul Marshall studies its development in England from 1500 to

1700. The doctrine of calling was a key element in various English social theories. It emphasized personal responsibility, yet it still treated the social order as divinely sanctioned, and it produced a distinct "Protestant" work ethic.

Worldviews: The Challenge of Choice, by Ken Badley (1996)

This attractive book was written by Ken Badley while he was Professor of Educational Philosophy at the Institute. The book was commissioned by the Integrated Educational Council of Newfoundland and Labrador for use as a textbook by students in grades 11 and 12 in the high schools of the province. It introduces high school students to issues of morality and ethical decision making, as well as to religious and spiritual belief.

The raising of questions rather than a dogmatic statement of answers is a prominent feature of the book. Speaking of our view of the world as our worldview, questions arise like "How is our worldview connected with religion? How might we respond to some of the challenges facing our worldview? Why do we make the decisions we do?"

The book deals sensitively with social issues that teenagers face, such as sexuality, the environment, family and peer relations, religious differences, peace and security, high-tech medicine, poverty and social justice, the meaning of life, life and death issues, discrimination, and tolerance and understanding.

Presented are various religious views like Buddhism, Islam, Christianity, Hinduism, Judaism, Sikhism, Bahá'i Faith, Jainism, and the traditional spiritual beliefs of Canadian Aboriginal Peoples. The book draws the eye with its many coloured illustrations and cartoons throughout.

Knowing Other-wise: Philosophy at the Edge of Spirituality, edited by James Olthuis (1997)

Arising out of the Institute's Interdisciplinary Course, which studied pluralism, this book calls into question the Western philosophical tradition of giving pride of place to reason in the acquisition of knowledge. Reasoning, the book affirms, is only one of the many ways in which we know the world, not the only way. We know by touch, by feel, by taste, by sight, by sounds, by smell, by symbols, by sex, by trust.

Recent discussions on feminism, postmodernism, and environmentalism make clear that what it means to exist and to have knowledge must be infused with ethics. This book suggests the importance of nonrational ways of knowing, a spiritual knowing of the heart with the passionate eye of love. We know more than we think.

Tracing the connections between epistemology, ethics, and spirituality—between "knowing" and the "other," between an other and the Other—these essays by Olthuis and other Institute professors and graduate students serve as points of convergence between postmodern discussions and the Calvinist spirituality that is the home for the writers of this collection of essays.

***Solidarity and the Stranger: Themes in the Social Philosophy of Richard Rorty,* by Ronald A. Kuipers (1997)**

This book is a sympathetic and incisive study of Richard Rorty's efforts to put human thought in the service of the many problems we face at the close of the twentieth century. Ronald Kuipers uses the figure of the stranger to explore the ethical tension between an individualistic ethos and Rorty's evaluation of the liberal private-public dichotomy. He urges us to work through Rorty's worldview so we can listen to the story told by one of the most culturally important thinkers of our time.

***Their Blood Cries Out: The Growing Worldwide Persecution of Christians,* by Paul Marshall (1997)**

Paul Marshall points out that more than 200 million Christians around the world suffer imprisonment, abuse, and even death because of their faith. The book documents stories of their suffering. The book arises from Marshall's long-term ICS research on human rights.

***Heaven Is Not My Home: Learning to Live in God's Creation,* by Paul Marshall with Hilary Brand (1998)**

Many Christians sing with conviction, "This world is not my home, I'm just a' passing through," as though this world is merely incidental. Paul Marshall argues that the Bible portrays this world as good; it is distorted by sin, but destined for reunion with God in Jesus Christ. God loves and cares for this world. Thus, he says, Christians should not be "shirking their divinely given responsibility to sustain, nurture, renew and really *live* in God's world." In this book, he gives "a brief overview of our *spiritual orientation* as we live as God's people in God's world." He also issues a deep and heartfelt challenge to what we think and believe about the world.

***Walking the Tightrope of Faith: Philosophical Conversations about Reason and Religion,* edited by Hendrik Hart, Ronald A. Kuipers,**

and Kai Nielsen (1999)

This book was written in response to the earlier book by Hendrik Hart and Kai Nielsen, which dealt with Nielsen's views on philosophy and religion and Hart's earlier criticisms of those views. It consists of eleven essays on the relation of reason and religion. The book is of special interest to students of the philosophy of religion who wish to examine the encounter between religious faith and secular humanism in an increasingly postmodern time. The book includes such difficult topics as the limits of the rational justification of human knowledge, the role of prereflective commitments in intellectual life, the nature of truth, and the possibility for peace in a world consisting of often violent, varied religions.

Art and Soul: Signposts for Christians in the Arts, by Hilary Brand and Adrienne Dengerink Chaplin (1999)

This book arose out of courses Adrienne Dengerink Chaplin taught to university and art college students while a graduate student at the Institute. The book is a guide for artists as society makes a transition from a modern to a postmodern era. In modernity, a naturalistic view of science seemed to swallow up everything around it, marginalizing the arts. In postmodernity, aesthetics and literary theory threaten to swallow up everything else.

The book starts with a section on some of the conflicting influences that Christians entering the arts might encounter. It presents three competing worldviews, followed by basic biblical themes on the activity of art and the application of these worldviews to art. The section ends with identifying some practical ways of serving God as artists in the twenty-first century. Because art expresses the times in which we live, the authors argue, artists need to develop a clear worldview of their own from which to approach their artistic work.

The book has a wide range of illustrations that show the conflicting influences artists experience as they produce artworks. The authors correlate the biblical themes of creation, fall, and redemption with making art. They examine the nature and purpose of the arts and the ways we experience and interpret them. Practical guidelines are also given for producing art.

Shades of Darkness, Points of Light: Calling, Professionalism and Shalom, by Carroll Guen Hart (1999)

There are many signs that professional services are in a crisis, with professional people disillusioned by the unethical demands often placed upon them. The question arises as to how the Christian community can serve professional people with more than pastoral care. Christians together should do some hard reflection that honours the complexity of this human and cultural situation.

Carroll Guen Hart gives historical reflection on this from ancient to medieval to modern times. First, the professional man came to be treated as a "gentleman." Then the gentleman professional came to take a place as a leader of society. Later, the "expert professional" became important. The Industrial Revolution made personal achievement more important than gentlemanly class. The democratization of education offered education for everyone. Moreover, professionals came to be replaced as cultural authorities by specialists who became quite narrowly focused and resented any actions in their field by nonspecialists. The "expert professional" became almost completely differentiated from the traditional aristocratic forms of power.

The author writes that communal discussion is needed on the biblical idea of calling and shalom, with awareness of God's good creation but also of sin. Self-regulation of professions has become a socially important issue in our time, with professionals needing to ask how their service relates to our being human.

Towards an Ethics of Community: Negotiations of Difference in a Pluralist Society, edited by James Olthuis (2000)

The writers of the ten essays in this book on social and comparative ethics are all faculty members or graduate students of the Institute. The book is one fruit of the Institute's three-year interdisciplinary study of pluralism. It introduces readers to some of the most challenging and divisive dilemmas of our increasingly pluralistic and postmodern world.

We live among neighbours, friends, and acquaintances. But the people we live among turn out to be "strangers" of different races and religions. People insist that their cherished distinctiveness be publicly recognized and accepted, and our boundary lines are no longer neat. We need to shape a civic ethos that celebrates differences and embraces strangers to affirm the special giftedness of others. The liberal-modernist response of expanding our definition of who is the "same" will not do.

The authors of these essays suggest an ethics of connection in which difference is not the enemy to withstand but the friend to stand with. Difference is not deficiency or personal deviance. Community is not the promotion of sameness but of being together in difference and diversity.

The book suggests some ways to negotiate healing in today's wilderness of postmodern pluralism. This is worked out in many different ways in chapters written by scholars in various areas of study. We are urged to dismantle our sacred/secular and public/private splits.

Bearing Fresh Olive Leaves: Alternative Steps in Understanding Art, by Calvin Seerveld (2000)

The six chapters in this book are edited versions of previously unpublished lectures given by Calvin Seerveld. Each chapter addresses the task of art in society and in God's world today, as well as the false dichotomy between theoretical thought and the producing of art. This book, a companion volume to *Rainbows for the Fallen World*, includes sixteen colour and 71 black-and-white illustrations.

In the Fields of the Lord: A Calvin Seerveld Reader, edited by Craig Bartholomew (2000)

This extensive book contains creative writings and lectures by Seerveld that are not available elsewhere. They cover using the Bible to gain an understanding of philosophy, education, work and daily life, arts and the aesthetic, Bible songs and dance. The fifty-one chapters range from popular to academic. They show Seerveld's comprehensive vision of neo-Calvinism and his wide-ranging abilities. Included are twenty-seven black-and-white illustrations.

The Beautiful Risk: A New Psychology of Loving and Being Loved, by James Olthuis (2001)

In this book, James Olthuis proposes a new model for psychotherapy, a relational approach of being-with that emphasizes connecting with, caring for, and suffering with clients. He sees this as a contrast to the standard model rooted in the spirit of modernism that emphasizes expertise, testing, control, method, rationality, independence, conformity, and cure and that sees clients as people with defects that need to be diagnosed, fixed, and cured. Olthuis wants to join clients on their journeys to richer and more faithful lives. This is a new relational therapy and calls not so much for solutions to problems but for connections. The book arises out of Olthuis's long-term practice of psychotherapy and reflection on its foundations.

Philosophy as Responsibility: A Celebration of Hendrik Hart's Contribution to the Discipline, edited by Ronald A. Kuipers and

Janet C. Wesselius (2002)

This book consists of thirteen chapters written by former students and colleagues of Hendrik Hart upon his retirement. It celebrates his contribution to developing a radical Christian approach to philosophy. As Hart's colleague and close friend James Olthuis writes, "Hart's philosophy finds its grounding not in the so-called certainties of reason, but in the experienced confidence and hope of faith. . . . For Hart philosophy begins and ends with the pre-philosophic in the exigencies of faith and the actualities of daily life."

Running through the wide range of topics covered is the general theme that in Hart's work, philosophy must be responsible and be pursued in the service of human flourishing.

***Voicing God's Psalms,* by Calvin Seerveld (2005)**

For most of his adult life, Calvin Seerveld has had a passionate, nonprofessional interest in translating passages from the Bible, especially the Psalms. He insists that psalms are oral writing meant to be read aloud or sung, so this book includes his translation of thirty-nine psalms and his versification of twenty-two of them, set to tunes from the Genevan psalter. The book also includes a CD with his reading of many of these psalms, plus solo performances of psalm melodies skilfully played by musicians on recorder or saxophone.

These carefully crafted psalm translations and versifications highlight the rough and tender voice of the Psalms, and the book offers suggestions for helping the Psalms come alive in our private and public worship.

8

Wedge and Book Publishing

The first book to come from the Institute and its Association was published in 1960 by Glenn Andreas in his hometown of Pella, Iowa. He published the speeches given at the student conference in the summer of 1959, and again for the next two or three years as well.

As early as the mid-1960s, the Association wanted to publish other speeches given at meetings it sponsored, and so it decided to publish and market them itself. Willem Hart designed the books and gave them attractive, colourful covers. Guardian Publishing Company of Hamilton, Ontario, published and sold the first books produced by the Association. About 1965, the Association began publishing books itself, with printing and distribution handled by Guardian. A considerable number of paperback books were published this way and sold to people interested in the work of the Institute. The people who worked at this were not professionally trained in book publishing but used their common sense and learned on the job. By 1968, fifteen books had been published, and, to the amazement of Association members, 30,000 copies had been sold. These books were well received all over the world. By 1972, over thirty titles were available in the Association's "Christian Perspective Series."

In 1967, the Institute was begun, and the Association was engaged in too many activities to do a good job at book publishing. It decided to have its friends set up a separate publishing company, with the hope

> **Willem Hart** is a graphic artist who always generously made his artistic gifts, abilities, and talents available to the Institute. He is characterized by integrity and a great sense of humour. He was irenic and not adequately appreciated for what he put into artistic design for the Institute. He always put in extra time for the Institute and for *Vanguard,* and he often did not charge enough for his services. He was deeply in tune with the Institute as a reforming agency and had a heart for what it was doing.
> —Gerald Vandezande

that it could be run by people knowledgeable about the business. Wedge Publishing Foundation was set up and incorporated in March 1970 to serve unofficially as the university press of the Institute. Wedge was to have two missions, to publish books and to publish the bimonthly magazine called *Vanguard*, a revised form of a magazine published earlier in Edmonton.

The Association agreed to let its Development Director, John Hultink, leave its employ to become Wedge's International Director of Development. At the same time, it noted that Robert Carvill, who worked half-time for the Association as its Director of Communications, would also be working half-time as Editor of Wedge. Adrian Peetoom served part-time as Executive Secretary of Wedge.

The bylaws of Wedge identified its purpose as follows:

> To foster and promote interest in the study of and commitment to Christian living in contemporary society, and in the furtherance of the aforesaid purpose (1) to carry on editing, printing, publishing, selling and distribution of: books, papers, journals, reports, research works, pamphlets, circulars and similar commodities; (2) to establish, create, administer, maintain and disperse a fund or funds, either of money in the Corporation or its earnings and from donations, gifts, legacies, devises and contributions from the public; and (3) to do all such things as are necessary to the attainment of such objects.

A Basis Statement was adopted that was very similar to that of the Institute, with the addition of this section: "Publishing is to be undertaken in the God-given freedom of voluntary submission to the Revelation of God. The responsible freedom of the publisher must be protected against any constraint or domination of church, state, industry or other societal structure."

The stated aim of Wedge was ". . . to bring a vision for cultural-formative action to all who will hear. The strength of our reformational vision lies in the integrating perspective it brings to a disparate and fragmented way of life. Communication should be a united effort, bringing an awareness of the basic issues of life from as many sides as possible."

Wedge existed in Toronto for only ten years. It had an amazing publishing record, but internally it was a frustrating mess. One problem was that it tried to do too much with too little. Committed people with a vision that knew no bounds thought they could do as much as they wanted. The story of Wedge Publishing Foundation follows.

Vanguard

When Wedge started in 1970, it accepted the offer of the Christian Action Foundation in Edmonton to take over its new, small bimonthly magazine called *The Christian Vanguard*. The publication, with its name changed to *Vanguard*, aimed to set forth the biblical reformation of life. The December 1970 issue stated: "*Vanguard*, Christian vision for the seventies, seeks to proclaim Christ as the Redeemer and Renewer of all things. By faith in Christ, man may dedicate the fullness of life to God in loving and obedient service. We confess that all human activities, relationships and institutions must be directed by the authoritative Word of God." *Vanguard* wanted to articulate a vision, to identify constructive and unconstructive attitudes, and to show people how to live out in their lives the vision of life in God's Kingdom. It was addressed to whoever would like to develop a Christian life perspective—people in leadership positions, educated people—and also to non-Christians.

Robert Carvill and Bert Witvoet were co-editors of *Vanguard* from the time of its move from Edmonton to Toronto in November 1970 until December 1972. Carvill alone was editor from then to February 1974. Bonnie Greene was editor from May 1975 until October 1977, and Witvoet was editor from June 1978 until December 1981. The early Editorial Committee consisted of John Olthuis, Gerald Vandezande, James Olthuis, James Visser, and Louis Tamminga.

In its early years, the voice of *Vanguard* was that of the counterculture. The cultural critique was that of reformational Christianity, to be sure, but it was vigorously critical. Initially, many of its targets were within the church and were viewpoints held by Christians. But there was bite to it. *Vanguard* established an early, very public presence at the Urbana Conference of InterVarsity already in January 1970. Forty students from the Institute, Trinity Christian College, and Dordt College came to the Urbana conference to bear witness to the need of radical reformation. They wanted an alternative direction for the conference, so they put out a daily newspaper, called *Vanguard*, edited by Carvill. About four issues were published and printed, with copies in the thousands handed out each morning. *Vanguard* co-opted the conference, stealing its cultural thunder. It stood in opposition to the radical individualism of evangelization, which did not oppose racism and corrupt politics. Their complaint was that Urbana was not into *communal* social action. *Vanguard* said that InterVarsity reduced the all-embracing, world-saving news of Jesus Christ to individuals and their salvation. Instead, they said, Christ must have pre-eminence in labour halls, factories, TV studios, college classrooms, and parliament as well as in church. The gospel must be lived wholly by the people of God before his face.

Many people responded to this perspective with great enthusiasm, both students and older people who were open to the radical demands of faith. Main speakers who showed sympathy with *Vanguard* included Samuel Escobar and Tom Skinner. The leadership of InterVarsity was aghast at *Vanguard* and was very angry, with some animosity for the Institute, which lasted for a few years.

In later years *Vanguard* still contained social criticism, but the articles did not have the same sting and bite of earlier issues, when it was hitting targets close to home. Targets became more national, public, and sociopolitical, with topics like food, African racism, politics, and children's books. More writers were included who were not from the reformational "movement." There was less blood spilled and less critique in *Vanguard* of the Christian Reformed Church and of Christian day schools.

In May 1977, *Vanguard* editor Bonnie Greene wrote a memo saying that *Vanguard* had gone through a classic metamorphosis from an ethnic paper intended to maintain a vision to a paper that attempted to translate that vision in concrete terms to a heterogeneous audience. Most ethnic papers, she said, don't survive that transition, and we don't know yet whether *Vanguard* will. *Vanguard* worked at approaching the world of books, politics, economics, business, education, arts, and the like from a Christian vantage point. "We've been using the concept of a magazine that offers critical commentary on public issues from a Christian perspective," she wrote. "*Vanguard* is a good format for showing that journalism, too, must be brought under the rule of Christ."

There was significant unease at Wedge's Board with such a broad editorial policy for *Vanguard,* so a committee was appointed to study the matter. Its report showed a difference of opinion among the Board members. Some wanted Wedge to keep its position of communicating the meaning of living a life with a reformational focus. They stated in a written statement that "We seek a distinctive form of Christian cultural action by means of confessionally based voluntary organizations and institutions, notably in education, scholarship, politics, economics, labour relations, and the arts. . . . *Vanguard,* in accepting the principle of sphere sovereignty, will attempt to explicate the meaning of this principle for the restoration of human responsibility in the political and economic sectors of society but also in structures such as the church, marriage, family, school, university, labour unions, and the media, as the alternative to the depersonalizing, impoverishing and alienating capitalism at home and abroad."

The others advocated a policy that replaced emphasis on "distinctively Reformed" with "biblically obedient." They, too, wished to reform the attitudes and actions of readers with writing rooted in the meaning of creation as God has revealed it to us as covenantal communion of people with God in Christ. But how closely should *Vanguard* work with the reformational view that came from Dutch culture?

The "reformationals" won out, and Gerald Vandezande, Tom Malcolm, and Paul Marshall left the Board. Bonnie Greene was also unhappy and soon resigned her position. She felt that the newly articulated position was somewhat inward-turning. In its earlier years, *Vanguard* had spelled out a religious vision for life focused on Reformed Christians, but she said that it should not always direct itself to an audience that limited. People from many Christian perspectives needed help in living out the vision. There was the danger that *Vanguard* could appear to be too Christian Reformed.

In June 1979, the Wedge Board decided to send a special appeal to subscribers to *Vanguard* in the hope that there would be enough financial support to continue publishing. But that last-ditch support did not come. So in September 1979, on the recommendation of Zylstra, control of *Vanguard* was passed to an independent non-profit organization, thus removing it from the control of Wedge. Glenn Andreas objected to this move, and he was not appointed to the initial membership of the group publishing *Vanguard*. Not long after that, *Vanguard* ceased publication.

Wedge Book Publishing

Wedge, in effect, served as the university press of the Association, though it could publish books independently of the Association and the Association was not limited to publishing its books through Wedge. Wedge also provided an important service by selling books published by other firms as well as books it published itself. It sold books chiefly by mail, and its lists of titles available always placed in front of people good books they might not otherwise have known about. Wedge also sold some books that were not readily available to Canadian buyers. From 1974 through 1980, Wedge sold 46,597 copies of books.

During the 1970s, Wedge published a large number of books that brought fresh insight to Christian living and Christian thinking. Nearly all the books Wedge published were academic. One of the most notable ones was Bob Goudzwaard's *Capitalism and Progress: A Diagnosis of Western*

Society, translated from the Dutch by Josina Zylstra and copublished with Eerdmans Publishing Company. The book contained the heart of lectures Goudzwaard had given at the Institute.

An overwhelming problem that Wedge faced was lack of money. The market was very good for Wedge's academic books, but proceeds were never high enough to pay the costs of the books. It also lacked a capital fund to pay upfront the costs of producing books. The Institute often provided loans for the production costs of books it wanted published and even made outright grants to Wedge for books, but the Institute itself could barely stay afloat financially. Wedge's income was so low that the company was always seriously understaffed and Board members often did staff work, which caused its own problems.

In 1969, John Hultink, while still working for the Association, started Tomorrow's Book Club (TBC) as a way of marketing Association books. He moved this to Wedge when he moved there. Members of TBC paid $2.50 a year and then received the books that it sold at twenty to thirty percent off the advertised selling price of the book. TBC would send out a list of book manuscripts it received and would publish a book only if enough members placed prepublication orders. Generally, five hundred to a thousand such orders were needed for a book to be published.

In March 1970, Hultink reported that $40,000 worth of books had already been sold through TBC. But, in fact, the program did not work. By 1973, Wedge and TBC were so deeply in debt that TBC was closed and Hultink left the employ of Wedge.

Glenn Andreas contributed major sums from the United States through the AACS Foundation. In 1976, Wedge also received a grant of $50,000 from Dwayne Andreas, a brother of Glenn Andreas, who lived in Florida. In 1980, Bernard Zylstra reported that the Association had subsidized Wedge over the years to the extent of $134,000, most of which came from donations by Glenn Andreas.

At one point, the Institute set up a special fund to which it asked its supporters to contribute money so that a revolving fund could be built to pay the production costs of books, money that would be repaid from the sales of books. But the fund never grew to the point where it could be very helpful. Wedge also wanted to augment its academic books with more popular books like biography and fiction, but nothing came of that, either.

Wedge also tried to interest trade publishers in publishing some of its better academic books, but met with little success. Trade publishers generally want to anticipate sales of 5,000 copies of books they publish, but academic books generally sell, at most, only 1,000 to 1,500 copies.

A further problem was that Wedge was publishing books without a budget, that is, without an estimate of costs or income from sales. The decision to publish a book was often made because one Board member or another wanted it published. Board meetings were often combination Board and staff meetings, with impossibly long agendas and the Board deciding details that should have been left to the staff.

A related problem was that the Board included very able members who acted individualistically and worked poorly together in book publishing. Bernard Zylstra, Gerald Vandezande, and Glenn Andreas often had problems working together. At times, the relations of one or more of them with the gifted but strong-willed editor, Bonnie Greene, were stormy. It was hard to imagine how such poor leadership could come from people who liked and respected each other and who wanted to see the same outcomes from the work.

In January 1978, Bonnie Greene resigned as editor because of the difficulties of working with the members of the Board. Tom Malcolm resigned from the Board three months later. Harry Westerhof had resigned from the staff in the summer of 1977.

Josina Zylstra became Executive Director at Wedge in April 1978. The same month, Bert Witvoet was appointed Managing Editor of *Vanguard* and Assistant Book Editor. The Editorial Committee of *Vanguard* at that point consisted of Ed Vanderkloet, Bert Witvoet, Albert Wolters, and Bernard Zylstra.

In May 1979, Glenn Andreas, on his own initiative, deputized Josina Zylstra to serve on the Wedge Executive Committee. Board chair Ed Vanderkloet took serious exception to this, and he resigned from the Board in January 1980. In February, the Board learned that Andreas would continue to contribute to the publishing of Wedge books only if the membership of the Board were significantly changed. In March 1980, the Wedge Board voted not to re-elect Andreas to another five-year term on the Board. With that, funding from Andreas came to an end.

In September 1980, Wedge asked the Association to pledge its support to Wedge of $25,000 to $30,000 a year for the next five years so that Wedge could publish some excellent books arising out of the Kuyper/Dooyeweerd tradition to which the Association was committed. But the Association turned down the request, largely because it could not afford to pledge the money. Consequently, Wedge was no longer able to publish books.

In 1981, Wedge negotiated the transfer of its name and assets to John

Hultink, now owner of Paideia Press. Most of its books were transferred to his location in Jordan Station, Ontario, and Wedge moved out of the Institute Building in May 1981.

Book publishing is an enormously satisfying activity, especially when the books advance exciting new ideas and can enrich the individual and communal lives of persons who wish to benefit from them. But the personal satisfactions of different persons differ somewhat, and the people with leading responsibilities in Wedge were too individualistic to be able bring their desires together. Wedge had a remarkable and rich decade of publishing both a magazine and books, and it is a tragedy that the ministry could not continue.

The Institute and Book Publishing

When Wedge moved out of the Institute Building, with it went the service of selling books and papers that was an important ministry of the Institute. Thus, the Institute decided in 1980 that it would take up the task of selling books and academic papers to interested persons. It continues to keep an inventory of about fifty different books and about one hundred academic papers that it sells from the Institute bookstore to those who request them. Nearly all these sales are by mail order. The Institute buys the books from publishers at their standard discount and charges the publisher's list price for the books plus a fee for postage and handling. Newer books are publicized and listed in each issue of the Institute's newsletter *Perspective*.

A more difficult problem posed by the removal of Wedge was how to get the academic books generated by the Institute published. At times, the Institute would try to get a trade publisher to publish a certain academic book, and a few books from the Institute were published that way. But there were also books that would appeal only to academic readers that were harder to sell.

To give a bit of background, in 1989, Harold Bohne, Director of the University of Toronto Press, wrote in a book titled *Scholarly Publishing in Canada* about the marketing and distribution of scholarly books. Academic books are advertised and marketed chiefly by direct mail, he said. Scholarly books generally will sell 500–1,500 copies worldwide, whether they are published by university presses or by trade publishers. Even highly regarded, best-selling academic books hardly top 2,000 copies. Bohne wrote: "The process of scholarly publishing, including the marketing of scholarly titles, must therefore be viewed as an extension of the research itself, the results of which, to be useful to other scholars and society, must be disseminated as widely as possible. The process of scholarly publishing therefore should not be viewed as a business, even though to succeed it must be carried out in the most business-like and professional way money can buy."

In early 1982, Lee Hardy, a professor at Calvin College, told me of the rather new non-profit publishing program of University Press of America (UPA), with which he had some experience while at Duquesne University. UPA had a copublishing program that required some of the work of preparing the book for publication to be done by the non-profit group or individual that presented the book. This meant that the work and financial cost of publishing were shared between UPA and the author or organization that wanted the book published. This arrangement made it possible for a small number of copies of each book to be published at a reasonable selling price.

The Institute made an agreement with UPA later in 1982 for the publishing over a period of years of a series of books called "Christian Studies Today." The Institute appointed a Book Committee, chaired by Hendrik Hart, that would decide whether it would be good for the Institute to publish a certain book. Then it would send the text out to two reviewers professionally competent in the subject of the book to advise on whether to have the book published. If the reviewers' reactions were affirmative, they would be asked to recommend improvements to the text. The author or editor of each book never knew who the evaluators were. Upon positive recommendation, the committee would proceed to have the book published.

When a text was ready to be prepared for publishing, a person or organization outside the Institute would typeset and lay out the pages. After a few years, computer software allowed the Institute to complete the book layout itself, and laser printers gave the text a professional look. Graphic artist Willem Hart designed attractive book covers.

The pages ready for printing and the artwork for the cover were sent to UPA, which would produce the book. UPA typically would print about 500 copies of each book, half in paperback and half in hardcover format. The Institute was required to buy 100 copies of the book at a twenty-two percent discount off the publicized selling price. It would then sell the books at list price. Generally, the Institute and UPA sold equal numbers of copies of each book. Usually, after a few years, the book would be sold out, and sometimes a second printing was made. UPA submitted annual reports on how many copies of our books were sold, including copies sold by the Institute.

The program worked well for the Institute. In 1998, for instance, UPA reported that since 1983 they had sold a total of 9,208 copies of the books they published for us, for a wholesale income of $168,600. Most importantly, however, major new ideas on Christian scholarship arising from the Institute were getting into the hands of scholarly readers who were in leadership positions.

Most of the books copublished with UPA consisted of papers presented at academic conferences held at the Institute. It was gratifying to the Institute that a few books it published with UPA came from work done at the Free University in Amsterdam or Calvin College. This cooperative book publishing program continued to the late 1990s. A list of the books copublished with UPA through 1997 is shown in Appendix 4.

9

Educational Services

The Institute's Charter says that one of the aims of the Institute is "to exhibit the coherence of all reality in Christ and in this way to equip people to direct their lives by the Gospel." That is a large order, and it indicates that academic research and teaching are only part of what the Institute intended to be working at. The Institute wanted to educate *everyone*.

An important task of the Institute's Educational Services was to reach people with the new insights that were being developed by Institute professors and other people they were working with. A wide range of people are the targets of this outreach: academicians, undergraduate and graduate students, professionals, and the general public, including people who do not have the educational background to understand academic and theoretical issues. People everywhere can be helped to gain insight into the spirits at work in the world and to find principles that they can put into practice to bring healing to the world and show Christ's reign over all of life. Drawing in people who can contribute to the biblical reformation of scholarship and to the development of a Christian worldview is of great importance to the Institute.

Educational Services was also seen as a way of closing the loop; donations by supporters become benefits coming back to the supporters as insights on Christian worldview and how to put those insights into practice.

The earliest form of Educational Services, in this case provided to university students, was the annual summer conference that started in 1959 at Unionville, Ontario. This was followed by having some of the speakers lecture in western Canada. Academic and nonacademic education outside of Toronto was a service provided by Institute professors when Hendrik Hart lectured in many parts of Canada in 1967–1968, joined in 1968–1969 by James Olthuis and Bernard Zylstra.

A University for the People

Discovery Conferences

When instruction began in Toronto in 1969, the Board was concerned that the Association would lose contact with its members throughout Canada and northern United States. So a series of travelling lectures was set up for Institute-related people to speak and lead discussions. The program was called Discovery Lectures, with the overarching theme of "explorations in contemporary living." The series ran for six years, with the following content.

> The 1969 topic was "The Family," with two teams of five speakers, with attendance of about 3,500 people at lectures given in eleven places in Canada and in Illinois, Iowa, Washington, and Michigan.
> The 1970 topic was "The Institutional Church," with five teams of three speakers in nineteen Canadian locations plus New York, Iowa, and Washington.
> The 1971 topic was "Christian Education in the 1970s," with three teams of five speakers in sixteen Canadian locations plus New Jersey, Pennsylvania, Tennessee, Illinois, Michigan, Washington, and Iowa.
> The 1972 topic was "The Word of God Shall Stand Forever," with one team of five speakers in five locations.
> The 1973 topic was "Toward Maturity in Christ," with one team of five speakers in five locations.
> The 1974 topic was "Seeking the Abundant Life," with one team of five speakers at five locations.
> The 1975 topic was "Aesthetic Obedience and Art for God's Sake," with six speakers at six locations.

The Discovery program was large, and it was difficult to arrange and pay for. As the program continued, it became increasingly difficult to get good speakers to make the commitment needed of them. Promotion itself was a major task. In 1969, for example, 75,000 copies of promotional literature were printed, including brochures inviting people to each local lecture.

In 1972, arrangements were made to videotape the lectures so that a large number of locations could have the video played instead of having the lecturer physically present. Even some cable television channels showed some of the lecture programs. This was in the days when universities were experimenting with video lectures, hailed as a great instructional breakthrough. Before long, however, it was generally accepted that this system would not work. People looked for entertainment from their television, not talking heads giving lectures. So the Institute's Discovery Lecture series ended in 1976.

For a few years after 1976, the Association arranged instead for an

Institute professor to give a lecture in several locations. For example, in 1977, Thomas McIntire presented a lecture on "God's Word in a Secular Age" in nine locations.

The lecture series had a good effect in many ways, but it became clear that this was not a good medium for in-depth presentations of important issues. Basic overview lectures will serve for a while, but people will not be satisfied very long with presentations at an introductory level. Many of the lectures, however, were printed in booklet form or in books, to give them more lasting value and place them before more people.

In 1985, the need was once again felt for a series of talks by Institute people for its supporters, so a series called "Maps and Compasses" was presented by five speakers in nine locations in Canada and the northern United States.

Bibliographies and Cassette Tape Ministry

In the 1970s, Institute faculty members each produced bibliographies of materials that gave fundamental insights and Christian perspective in their academic fields. These were especially used in Institute correspondence with people inquiring about study at the Institute. The idea was that people reading materials cited in the bibliographies would learn about certain subject areas even though they were not studying at the Institute.

When Institute student and staff members Richard Middleton and Brian Walsh published their book *The Transforming Vision*, they also included a very substantial bibliography of materials both in academic fields and also in areas of cultural importance. And in 1998, Institute librarian Marcille Frederick prepared "A short bibliography of Christian faith and learning in various disciplines," which the Institute made available without charge to interested persons.

From the early 1970s to the late 1980s, the Institute ran a cassette tape service, offering at cost tape recordings of a number of speeches by Institute professors, guest lecturers at the Institute, Discovery lectures, and workshops given at the Institute summer conferences for the general public.

The Academic Papers Program

A graduate student may put lots of time and energy into writing a paper that turns out to be of excellent quality. It may even include some fresh insights that others would be glad to know about. Should such a paper simply die in the hands of the professor who reads and grades it?

The negative answer to that question has meant that there have always been some student papers in copied form lying about the Institute. In 1978, the Institute set up a "Paper of the Month" subscription program, committing itself to identify ten academic papers a year that it wished to have a broader readership than most unpublished papers receive. The papers would include student papers recommended by the professors who received them, unpublished provisional papers by faculty members, reproductions of published faculty papers with permission granted by the publisher, some papers given by guest lecturers at the Institute, and some other papers that were written by various people with the same distinctive perspective that the Institute promoted.

People were invited to subscribe to the program for $15; for this, they would be entitled to receive ten papers. Every three months, they received descriptions of three academic papers made available in the series, and they could inform the Institute if they wished to receive any of the three. They would receive only the papers they selected. When they got down to having one or two papers left on their account, the Institute notify them that they should send another $15 if they wished to continue to be active in the program. There was no time restriction for the program, so a person could use up the allotment of ten papers quickly or slowly, or, in a few cases, not at all. Libraries could subscribe for an annual fee of $12.50, for which they would automatically receive all the papers for each year they subscribed. This program helped interested people to "think along" with the Institute as it developed new ideas.

By October 1978, there were 253 subscribers to the program, including 22 who lived overseas, as well as twenty-eight library subscribers. Between January and October 1978, some 1,653 papers were sent out to subscribers. A year later, there were 284 subscribers, some of whom had resubscribed five or six times. The program continued until 1987, when the Educational Services program at the Institute was discontinued. Approximately eighty-five different papers were distributed through this program.

The Academic Papers program was an alternative to the Institute's setting up its own academic journal. This program placed good papers in the hands of interested reformational scholars but also encouraged Institute scholars to publish in existing journals so they could receive a wider reading than would be possible if much of their publishing was in an in-house journal.

Besides the subscription program, the Institute also regularly mailed without charge all its academic papers to campus chaplains of the Christian Reformed Church, to a number of college and university professors who requested getting them, to some people in particular educational positions overseas, and a few other people, about ninety in all. This gave them a resource of Institute materials for their counselling of students and kept the Institute before them as a graduate school to recommend to their students.

In addition to this program, the Institute reproduced some of its best master's degree theses and distributed them at a fee that covered its cost to people who were interested in the academic field of the papers or who wished to learn along with academic developments at the Institute.

Anakainosis

In 1978, Albert Wolters received the go-ahead to produce an informal quarterly journal that would be a way for reformational scholars worldwide to share fresh ideas they were working on with others. Kerry Hollingsworth served initially as managing editor. Named *Anakainosis*, meaning *renewal*, and with a subscription rate of $10 a year, the paper was produced at the Institute and carried a number of excellent articles that were not yet ready for publication in the scholarly literature. At times, writers would ask for response from others on ideas being tested.

Anakainosis also included some features of a newsletter, providing information on articles and books, academic conferences, study clubs, research projects, various lecture series, and the like. It aimed to acquaint its readers with the history of scripturally directed scholarship, especially that of the past one hundred years. It tried to be a vehicle of communication between all who reject the religious neutrality of reason, and it sought to elaborate alternatives to secular scholarship from an open allegiance to Scripture.

When Wolters left the Institute in 1984, various graduate students served serially as editors, including Chris Gousmett, Mark Roques, David Woods, and Nigel Douglas. The paper folded in 1987 when Educational Services activities ended.

Coalition for Christian Outreach

The Coalition for Christian Outreach was set in place around 1970 by people living in Pittsburgh, Pennsylvania, as a massive outreach ministry to college and university students in western Pennsylvania. The Coalition trains and supports young college and university graduates to serve as full-time consultants on campuses. Their mission is to bring students to Christ and especially to help Christian students develop a

Christian worldview and apply it to their chosen area of study. Bob Long was Director of the Coalition for many years.

The Coalition was started by Presbyterians, and their ministry and worldview are quite similar to that of the Institute, except that they do not have their own school. During the academic year, their staff members fan out to a large number of colleges and universities, many also serving part-time on the school staff. Each summer, the Coalition has a training session of a week or two for new staff members for which, initially, they drew significantly on Institute faculty for leadership, especially Albert Wolters, Calvin Seerveld, Bernard Zylstra, and Brian Walsh.

Each February, the Coalition holds a massive weekend conference for students called Jubilee, during which a thousand or more students gather in the large Hilton Hotel in downtown Pittsburgh. Many Institute faculty have been speakers at the annual conferences, and many Institute people have attended the Jubilee conferences. At each conference, attendees see a table of resources from the Institute and someone recruiting students for the Institute. Peter Steen was an early staff member of the Coalition.

University Christian Perspective Courses

It was Peter Steen who persuaded the Institute to start teaching Christian Perspective courses on nearby university campuses, as the Coalition for Christian Outreach was doing. From his position with the Coalition, and later from his own ministry called Christian Educational Services, Steen would get on university campuses and arrange to teach non-credit courses. He realized that the Institute was ideally placed to do this with its special Christian philosophy and its location right across the street from the University of Toronto.

In 1976, the Institute set up Tom Malcolm, a former Institute student who had been a protégé of Steen in Pennsylvania, to start teaching at the University of Toronto. Malcolm had earlier connected with InterVarsity leaders there, and they sponsored his course as part of their program. The Institute prepared an attractive brochure describing the program, which was called "Hearing and Doing." The brochure asked, "Interested in a Kingdom vision for the university? Wondering what redemption has to do with politics, psychology or education? Feeling a gap between Bible study and living in our culture? Finding answers to these questions is what Hearing and Doing is all about."

Malcolm's course was successful, and soon other Institute students joined the teaching program. Harry Anastasiou and Terry Tollefson were among the early Institute students who joined Malcolm. Later, Brian

Walsh wrote this about the program:

> The vision of the program was to provide a service to university students which would assist them in developing a Christian perspective in their studies. It was a Kingdom vision—to claim university education (and beyond that, all of culture) for Christ. Inter-Varsity provided access to the university and Christian credibility. Student teachers have had good influence in shaping policy and programs for Inter-Varsity.

The Institute's university teaching fit well with other campus ministries, which tended to look on Christian students as parishioners for Bible study or counselling or as potential for campus evangelism, for the Institute addressed them *as students*. The Hearing and Doing program addressed the tension Christian students feel in a secular university, where underlying spirits and worldviews compete for their allegiance. The Institute wished to bring these competing worldviews to light and examine them so that students could understand and cope with the tension they bring. Christian students should be challenged to *think* as students, as well as to worship and pray.

Needing direction in organizing the other Institute graduates who joined him in teaching, in 1977, Malcolm, assisted by Harry Anastasiou and Brian Walsh, developed a twenty-five-page syllabus of materials that could be used in the courses. Courses developed for the university teaching program included Christian Worldview in a Secular Culture; Christianity and Scholarship; Political Action; Being Human; Reflections on Art; and Christianity and Natural Science. Two study manuals arising out the campus teaching were Adrienne Dengerink's on art and Jonathan Chaplin's on politics, both of which were distributed widely to interested readers who could study them privately or in groups. The university campus teaching led to the writing of the highly regarded book *The Transforming Vision* by J. Richard Middleton and Brian Walsh.

Non-credit courses were taught at the University of Toronto and its Scarborough and Erindale campuses, York University, McMaster University, Ryerson Polytechnic University, the University of Guelph, and the Ontario College of Art. Courses were also taught at St. Andrew's (Islington) Presbyterian Church and the Anglican Church of the Redeemer. In addition, Nick Loenen and Ed Piers taught non-credit courses in the lower mainland of British Columbia.

More than thirty of the Institute's graduate students taught in this program during the eleven years it existed. Students taught each course once a week for the eight-month academic year, and they were usually paid $1,200 for teaching the course. For most of them, the money was counted toward the financial aid they needed to study at the Institute.

This teaching was an extremely valuable experience for Institute students. They found that the theoretical insights for which they worked hard at the Institute were very attractive to university students, and therefore what they were learning at the Institute had some market value. And it gave them teaching experience they would not otherwise get. In addition, the program brought university students into the orbit of the Institute, some of whom later enrolled as Institute students. The course was often a very moving, life-transforming experience for the university students.

Teachers were required to give their supervisor monthly oral reports and submit a written report at the end of each year. Their students were asked to turn in a written evaluation of the course and of the teacher's effectiveness. Typical was the written statement from Peter Schoenherr, a graduate engineering student, who said, "The biggest benefit I derived from the course was its emphasis on applying Scripture to all of life's activities, and that people engaged in any of the trades or professions have an active role in developing God's creation." Another student commented, "I realized that I should reflect God's image not only in the 'spiritual' part of my life, but in every aspect of my life."

Institute student supervisors for the program, following Tom Malcolm, were Terry Tollefson, Brian Walsh, Malcolm MacRury, Susan Bower, and Anne Burghgraef Roques. Each of them worked about half-time doing supervision while they were also teaching one or two courses themselves, as well as simultaneously being in charge of Institute student recruitment.

Weekend Conferences for Students at the Institute

In 1983, Malcolm MacRury, who was working in student recruitment, proposed that the Institute host an annual winter conference for students patterned after the Jubilee Conference in Pittsburgh. The hope was to draw fifty to a hundred students from the Institute's university campus courses, Canadian universities, and Christian colleges, as well as people from InterVarsity, the Christian Reformed Church, Pentecostal churches, St. Michael's College, and the like.

The aim was that the conferences would excite students about the Institute and would help draw students who wanted to discuss Christian academic perspectives. The conferences would focus on the theme of hope in the context of analyzing the present state of the world. The analysis would deal with the religious, artistic, philosophic, historical, and political situation, which might point to directions for renewal in church, state, the arts, schools, and so on.

These conferences were held for about four years and were very successful. The conference would close with a special event on Saturday night and a worship service Sunday morning. Institute students were leaders at workshops, and well-known speakers included Arthur Holmes of Wheaton College, Gillette Elvgren of Pittsburgh University, Thomas Langan of the University of Toronto, Janine Langan of St. Michael's College, and Toronto neurologist Harley Smyth.

Correspondence Courses

In 1986, the Institute began a Correspondence Course program after receiving encouraging responses to a sampling of opinion about such a program from part of the Institute's mailing list. By that time, the Institute and scholars with a similar Christian viewpoint had published a considerable amount of excellent material in the form of nonacademic books and articles that could be read with much profit by people who were given some incentive to do so.

Thus, a series of courses were set up. There were no academic standards a person needed to meet to register for a course, only the willingness to undertake the study. The courses carried no academic credit and were intended only for the reader's benefit. The program was an "adult education" activity. The aim of each course was to give the registrant the opportunity to read and think about insightful material in a certain field written from a Christian perspective.

The tuition for each course was $150, and for that the registrant received books and papers for 400 to 500 pages of assigned reading, a Reader's Guide with a suggested order in which to do the readings, and a number of thoughtful questions to explore. Extensive evaluation of the written work by the author of the course or a person similarly qualified was offered, and each registrant received a pass or fail grade. Written work to be evaluated required answers to ten questions selected by the student, who was to write not more than a page for each of the answers. If a person received a "fail" mark, which almost no one did, there was the option for the student to revise the writing based on suggestions and then have it re-examined for a $25 fee. If the student did not complete the course by sending in their written work, there was no penalty or stigma.

Courses were set up in nine areas, each prepared by a competent scholar in the field. The courses and those who prepared them were Christian Schools: Their Bases, Goals and Practices, by Harro Van Brummelen;

Christian Worldview, by Brian Walsh; Technology in a Christian Perspective, by Charles Adams; Science in a Christian Perspective, by Robert VanderVennen; God's Covenant Gift of Land, by Harry Fernhout and Donald Sinnema; Christian Views of History, by Thomas McIntire; Encounter with Sociology, by Robert MacLarkey; Introduction to the Economy, by Jasper Lesage, and Politics in a Christian Light, by Jonathan Chaplin.

Some courses were more popular than others, of course. The Christian Worldview course was very popular, but the course that was best received was the one on Christian schools. Groups of teachers and school board members in some areas were encouraged to get together regularly to discuss together material in a given part of the course, and often some or all members of the group would write out their own answers to the questions for evaluation. Some school boards of Canadian Christian schools would require new teachers who had not studied at a Christian college to take the course, and often the school would pay the cost of the course. For the last several years of the program, John Hull carefully evaluated the work of each student in the Christian schools course. By 1993, a total of 298 people had registered for the courses, and in later years, between ten and twenty teachers took the course on Christian schooling each year.

Staffing for Educational Services

In its early years, the Educational Services program of the Institute was served by gifted and creative young people. The first person specifically appointed to that service was Albert Wolters, who started in 1972. In 1974, he was followed by Tom Malcolm, who was succeeded at the end of 1976 by Roseanne Lopers Sweetman, who served also as part-time librarian. In those years, Marcia Hollingsworth also worked on many of the programs.

Until 1987, the task of the Educational Services Department included student recruitment, supervision of the university campus instructional program, and promotion of all the Institute's educational programs, including both the academic work of the Institute and the many educational outreach programs.

In 1983, Bernard Zylstra became president of the Institute, as the Association and Institute were folded into one structure. At that time, I became Director of Educational Services, working four days a week. At the end of 1987, the Board of Trustees decided it could no longer afford to maintain the program. I continued to work two days a week until 1999 on editing and producing Institute books.

10

Curriculum Development Centre and Patmos Art Gallery

Evidence that the Institute was not merely an ivory tower came in the companion organizations spun off from the academic work of Institute professors. Already in 1974, the Board of the Institute decided that the Institute would limit itself to teaching and research in theoretical matters, addressing itself to foundational and interdisciplinary studies. The specific issue that brought about this decision was a recommendation from some professors that the Institute offer clinical education for people who wanted to be educated for service as psychotherapists, drawing on the special expertise of Arnold De Graaff and James Olthuis.

Nevertheless, Institute professors joined with others in the book publishing of Wedge Publishing Foundation, in writing for and producing *Vanguard* magazine, in developing the Curriculum Development Centre, and giving encouragement to Patmos Workshop and Gallery. Each of these efforts became structurally independent of the Institute, following the Kuyperian pattern of separate organizations for disparate activities. The first two of these activities have already been described; this chapter will focus on the Curriculum Development Centre and the Patmos Art Gallery.

Curriculum Development Centre

In the late 1960s, when Arnold De Graaff was a professor at Trinity Christian College in Palos Heights, Illinois, he began to lead summer workshops in which Christian school teachers, mostly from Ontario, developed teaching units to use in their classrooms. He and the teachers would deal with issues of pedagogy but also with more foundational matters, such as anthropology and the nature of the child; what is knowledge (dealing with factual knowledge and also confessional knowing); and authority relationships, discipline, and order within the classroom. They worked together to develop an integrated program of studies for elementary and secondary schools.

When De Graaff moved to the Institute in Toronto, he continued these summer sessions, which then became part of the SPICE (Summer Program in Christian Education) in-service program sponsored by the Ontario Christian School Teachers Association. In the summer of 1970, for instance, twenty-four Christian school teachers worked with De Graaff to develop an integrally Christian curriculum for Bible studies and social studies. The Association supported the activity, among other ways, by giving $1,750 to teachers working during the summer on the project.

In 1973, De Graaff and his coworkers Jean Olthuis and Anne Tuininga published a 617-page loose-leaf guide called *Joy in Learning: An Integrated Curriculum for Elementary Schools*, designed especially for use in the early elementary school grades. The brochure promoting the teachers' guide said:

> This unique guide presents a Christian view of life in terms of the daily experiences of the children and the common subjects they study. Such everyday subjects as land, air, water, seasons, space, weather, heat, electricity, transportation, the city, stores, laws, butterflies, mushrooms, etc., are consistently placed and looked at in the light of Scriptures. The Bible, starting with Genesis 1, truly serves as an eye opener: to see (again) how God intended life to be from the very beginning, how He subjected the whole creation to His will, and how, in Jesus Christ and by the power of the Holy Spirit, we may again begin to experience God's peace if we obediently seek to follow His good order for life.
>
> In a natural way through their learning activities, the children are helped to develop a distinctly Christian view of life, leading them to praise and serve God and become His disciples and witnesses. As an integrated curriculum, the manual provides for the teaching of all the traditional subjects, allowing for the integration of social studies, science, reading, math, music, physical education and art. By providing a total, integrated program, the child's learning can progress in a natural way during the course of each day without being broken up artificially.

The curriculum that *Joy in Learning* developed, then, did away with thinking of different subjects as being separated and isolated from other subjects. It also advocated an open and more informal classroom in which children often worked on their own or in groups and discouraged having classroom desks in a row facing the front. It presented a Christian view of life in terms of the daily experiences of children and of the common subjects of study.

When the guide was published, 1,000 copies were printed, though each teacher needed only one copy. But to the delight of the authors, all 1,000 copies were sold in the first year and a half, and orders were received from twelve different countries. Copies were sold to Mennonite, Pentecostal, and Lutheran school systems and to schools in such countries as India, Australia, Bolivia, and Venezuela. The guide received highly favourable reviews written by respected educators in education periodicals.

With activity at this level, it became clear that some organizational structure was necessary to sustain and develop the program. The Institute's Association undertook to adopt the program as part of its mission to work toward "the advancement of Christian scholarship." Staff members were needed, and they required payment for their services. The Curriculum Development Centre (CDC), as it came to be called, became a part of the Association in 1974, parallel to the Institute. The Association gave CDC a room in its building in which to work and assistance with many of the things needed to run an office. Harry Houtman, Director of Finances for the Association, was permitted to spend part of his time raising funds for CDC. At first, Arnold De Graaff's time was considered part of his regular service to the Institute, but in 1975–1976, he worked one day a week for CDC and his salary for this time was paid by CDC. In 1974, Jean Olthuis and Anne Tuininga each worked four days a week, and Mary Gerritsma worked one-third time.

In 1974, CDC became incorporated as a non-profit agency and gained legal status to receive donations and issue official receipts that could be used for income tax deduction. The thinking was that people supportive of separate Christian schools should be willing to help with the costs of preparing Christian school teachers to do a better job. CDC became legally distinct from the Association, forming its own Board, but its services were considered to be part of the Association's ministry and CDC was accountable to the Association Board, especially for its finances. The by-laws of CDC contained a statement of its basis that was very similar to that of the Association, with the addition of sections on curriculum and on its perception of the nature of the child in the school.

The CDC Board appointed a group of fourteen educational consultants to advise it on its services, people knowledgeable about Christian school education who agreed with the educational philosophy of CDC. Early members of the CDC board were Deborah Steele Marshall, Helen Breems, and John Olthuis, with Marshall as chair.

In 1975, a seminar called Basic Issues in Education was organized by CDC and was attended by about fifty people of very different backgrounds, most of whom were teachers. There were two simultaneous seminars, Integrated Approach to the Teaching of Reading and Learning to Use *Joy in Learning*, directed by Jean Olthuis and her assistants. The response to the seminars showed that Christian schooling needed very down-to-earth, practice-oriented curriculum workshops and teacher training sessions, as well as a basic presentation and clarification of the educational principles underlying CDC work. The sessions were inspiring and rewarding, the spirit was excellent, and the participants strongly supported of each other, reported De Graaff.

In early 1974, the Association agreed to pay a subsidy to CDC of $19,000 for the year 1974–1975, though records show that CDC received just $7,600. It budgeted $30,250 for CDC for the calendar year 1975 and $32,000 for the school year 1976–77.

In 1975, an anonymous donor contributed $25,000 to CDC so that its work could develop more quickly, with the intent that this money would be matched by other donations. In 1975, after he received his master's degree from the Institute, Harry Fernhout started working three days a week to develop a distinctive Bible studies curriculum for CDC. Soon thereafter, his Institute classmate Donald Sinnema joined him in the project. For the year 1975–1976, the CDC staff included Arnold De Graaff, Jean Olthuis, Anne Tuininga, Nancy Vander Plaats, Donald Sinnema, Calvin Jongsma, Trudy Baker, Donald Vander Klok and Mary Gerritsma, most of them as part-time workers.

In 1976, CDC had deficits of $6,000 that the Association agreed to pay. But the Association had reached its limit in providing money for CDC. So in that year, the Association decided that because CDC wished to grow faster than the Association could afford, CDC should become completely independent of the Association. The Association would pay the $32,000 it had committed to CDC for 1976–1977, but each year thereafter the funding to which it would commit itself for the services CDC provided would decrease by $5,000 a year. In addition, from May to October 1976, the Association committed Harry Houtman to work at fund-raising for CDC two days a week.

In January 1977, Tom Malcolm left the employ of the Association to become Executive Secretary of CDC. In 1979, Peter Enneson joined the staff as Administrator.

CDC had a remarkable record of writing and publishing curriculum materials between 1975 and 1980. This is the list of materials it wrote and made available:

- Joy in Learning: An Integrated Curriculum for the Elementary School, edited by Arnold H. De Graaff and Jean Olthuis
- The Number and Shape of Things, by Trudy Baker and Calvin Jongsma
- Teaching with 'Joy': Implementing Integrated Education in the Classroom, by Jean Olthuis
- Reclaiming the Land: A Study of the Book of Joshua, by Donald Sinnema
- Of Kings and Prophets: A Study of the Book of Kings, by Harry Fernhout
- Japan: A Way of Life, by Arnold De Graaff, Jean Olthuis, and Anne Tuininga
- Kenya: A Way of Life, by Arnold De Graaff, Jean Olthuis, and Anne Tuininga
- Education and the Public Purpose, by Tom Malcolm and Harry Fernhout
- Promises Broken; Promise Kept: A Reader's Guide to I and II Samuel, by Harry Fernhout

The perspective underlying these materials was the CDC viewpoint that schools exist to nurture children in a Christian understanding of creation and of themselves as God's coworkers. These curriculum materials built on this basis, in both their content and pedagogy. A Christian view of the world provided the core of the curriculum, integrating learning in the key curricular areas. The materials dealt with the various parts of creation in their wholeness and in their relationships to each other and to God. The classroom activities in the materials were based on a holistic view of the child, providing for multidimensional learning (physical, emotional, intellectual, social, aesthetic, and confessional). At the same time, curriculum writers struggled with how to introduce children in a concrete and experiential way to the problem of human responsibility and sin without being simplistic, i.e., making superficial generalizations or staying with outward appearance; reductionistic, i.e., treating the technical side of certain phenomena without relating them to human responsibility and cultural formative influence; or moralistic, like merely saying "we should not pollute the land and water" without considering the religious, political, and economic motivations behind human action.

CDC's curricular materials were well received and widely used. For example, CDC invited Geoffrey and Naomi Karugu, leading educators in Kenya who were studying in the United States at the time, to review and critique the material on Kenya for them. The Karugus were so delighted with the material and with the way it portrayed the Kenyan view of life that when they returned to Kenya they used the CDC material in their teaching there.

As the materials were more widely adopted, some people began raising concerns about CDC's "integrated" approach to learning as a curricular method and its relation to the "open classroom." They questioned CDC's understanding of the nature of the learning process generally: the assumptions about the nature of the child that underlay its approach to the curricula, the nature of authority in the classroom and particularly the authority of the teacher in relation to the child, and the effects of sin on the natural eagerness of a child to learn. De Graaff countered by saying that the integrated approach was being used effectively in conventionally organized classrooms as well as those with a more open concept.

In 1978, CDC shifted its emphasis from producing teaching materials to working with teachers as they used the materials in the classroom. Agnes Struik, a highly regarded teacher and principal, joined the staff half-time, offering her consulting services. She worked in-depth with teachers in their classrooms, planning an integrally Christian learning program and handling a variety of classroom management situations. She also conducted workshops for teachers, school Board members, educational committees, parent-teacher groups, and the like, for an appropriate fee paid by the schools.

In 1980, De Graaff's position at the Institute ended and so did his services with CDC. Struik's consultation continued for several years. Schools and teachers continued to order the CDC curriculum material, but new and creative work by CDC came to an end and the organization folded in 1985. In an attempt to resurrect CDC, Harry Fernhout wrote a paper entitled *Reaffirming Educational Vision,* but nothing came out of this.

The Curriculum Development Centre had a profound effect on Christian education. Whereas in the 1970s and 1980s, "integrated units" were new and therefore suspect for some, today integration is the norm in primary education and beyond. Much of the curriculum in use in Christian day schools today starts and ends with perspective questions, such as "what is wrong" and "how do I help set things right." Also of special importance were Bible study materials written by Fernhout and Sinnema that focused on the unfolding drama of God's redemptive work in the Old Testament and that point to the climax of God's redemption in Jesus Christ.

Patmos Art Gallery

Starting in 1969, while he was a professor in Chicago, Calvin Seerveld set up an Institute for Christian Art in Chicago, a centre of young artists in full-time study and practice of the visual arts. With the help of Mary Carolyn McIntire, Mary Steenland, and Willem Hart, he brought accomplished Dutch artist Henk Krijger to Chicago to teach art part-time at Trinity Christian College and to be a master artist at the centre. The Art Institute was like a medieval guild with a Kuyperian Christian vision.

In 1971, the Institute for Christian Art moved to Toronto at the invitation of Willem Hart, who found a location for it in the downtown area. Krijger then moved to Toronto, and some of the young artists moved with him, working together in the new location. They learned from each other and from Krijger as they worked together producing contemporary artworks, including sculptures, paintings, and assemblages. They changed the name of the guild to Patmos Workshop and Gallery.

One year later, Seerveld moved from Chicago to Toronto to join the faculty of the Institute for Christian Studies. Patmos then became informally associated with the Institute for Christian Studies. After a time, Patmos opened a gallery in the downtown theatre district, and its shows were a gathering place for people interested in the arts and in promoting distinctive Christian work in the visual arts. Among Patmos artists were Matth Cupido, Ed Hagedorn, Ed Fielding, Hank Melles, Ed Kellogg, Sue Vander Weele, Dave Alexander, and John Corcoran.

One of the interesting projects of Patmos was the commitment of Krijger and the other artists to work on a common project in which each of them would create an art piece on the theme of the butterfly. Each art work was different, and the Butterfly Exhibition was one way to show the effect of Christian artists working together, each in his or her own distinctive way.

But money was always scarce and sales of the art pieces were weak. Artwork done in a modern tradition was not always popular, and many people who supported Patmos did not have the money to buy the artwork they admired. Yet Patmos with Krijger and the apprentice artists continued to define themselves as a centre for Christian visual art in the midst of a Christian community.

In 1975, Krijger decided to leave Patmos and return to the Netherlands, and the artist studio ended. James Marshall became Executive Director for one year to keep Patmos alive, paid in part with artwork. Then Joanne Salomon served as Curator of the gallery for about three years. In 1979, however, funds to support the endeavour were no longer forthcoming, and the ten-year enterprise ended, with the artistic efforts moving to other outlets.

The spirit of Patmos has continued through a legacy provided by Calvin and Inès Seerveld, called the Ruth Memorial Fund, which each year brings a noted artist to Toronto for an exhibition of distinctive Christian visual or musical art.

11

Administrative Structure and Institutional Leadership

Writings about the history of an institution of higher education rarely say much about administrative structure. The ways in which administrative work is done are usually not publicly interesting, and they remain part of an institution's unseen background. But the Association's decision-making structure has special points that make it worth looking at.

Philosophy of Administrative Leadership

In its early years, structure was a very big issue for the Association and the Institute, and it affected the Institute's early development. There were two reasons why structure became an issue. One is that the Dutch immigrants who started the school decided to adopt the dual structure of separating the academic work from its administrative support, as was the case with Dutch universities. The Institute founders did not understand clearly, though, that in the Dutch system the federal government accepted responsibility for providing the money needed to run the institution. This meant not only that fund-raising was a very minor concern, but also that the university was not very much engaged in public relations and the need to satisfy people who would donate significantly to the school so that it could pay its bills. In the European model, the academic school is nearly autonomous.

The other reason why administrative structure became a major issue was that the first professors who came to the Institute were significantly influenced by the counterculture of the 1960s. One of the key ideas of the counterculture movement was concern about "the establishment." People were not to accept blindly the authority of public and private organizations with their hierarchical structures. Freedom and fluidity were of great importance. Organizations were oppressive, and their leaders could not be trusted. This view would have ramifications for the developing Institute for Christian Studies.

People at the Institute held different views on the nature of authority. Some faculty members had a distinct fear of authority being vested in an individual. This in part was a reaction to the experience of some who saw some persons misusing authority in some schools. They rejected a hierarchical view of authority in an institution and argued that decisions should be made only with input from all persons who in one way or another would be affected by the decision. This might involve everyone from professors to office staff members. *Coordinate decentralization* was the current thinking, with a high degree of collegiality in decision making and of participation in administrative responsibilities. Coordination was the byword, and "directors" of departments now became "coordinators."

A significant vehicle articulating these ideas was the book *Insight, Authority and Power* written by Peter Schouls, long-time chair of the Institute's Board of Curators. The book argued, among other things, that to be accepted in a position of leadership, a person needs to be well qualified as well as duly appointed. Whether a leader is well qualified is to be decided by those whom the person serves as well as by those who appointed the person. The book was praised by some and lambasted by others.

One issue, for instance, was whether the head of the Institute or the Executive Director of the Association should present reports to the boards as a person with executive responsibility. Hendrik Hart, while chair of the ICS Council, argued that reports should first be approved by the staff Council, with all persons in that area having a voice. That way, if a staff member disagreed with a recommendation from the faculty or administrative staff, he or she would be able to present to the Board an alternative report and recommendation. A vertical or hierarchical way of functioning was not acceptable; no one person should be the authority at the top of a hierarchy. As a general policy, said Hart, no employee should be responsible or accountable to another (higher) employee, but only to councils, committees, and boards. Collegiality and widespread participation were required. The Institute was passionately committed to communal work, but individualism could not be put down completely.

This philosophy was carried out for the first decade in the administration of the Institute. The "Rules of the Institute," set up at Hart's initiative, identified two kinds of office at the Institute, held by what the Rules called Scholars and Administrators. Scholars included both faculty and students, and Administrators did the clerical work. The broadest body was the General Meeting, composed of all who were part of the Institute, that is, all faculty, students, and other Institute employees. The ICS Council, which served as a sort of Executive Council for internal academic decision making, was made up of all the professors and half as many students as professors. The professors sometimes also met by themselves. The Rules stated that "The academic affairs shall be conducted communally by all Scholars. . . . All other household matters affecting the Institute shall be decided by the General Meeting." In its meetings, the ICS Council handled "day to day housekeeping affairs of the Institute." The chair, secretary, and the registrar of the Institute constituted an Executive Committee. The Institute's goal was to decide all matters by consensus rather than by counting votes.

Bernard Zylstra noted some years later that a problem with this system was that assignments could be given to faculty members, but they, like professors everywhere, tend to see themselves as self-employed. A result of the Institute's system was that there was no way to hold them to account. While he was a Curator in 1978, John Olthuis said that there should be coordinate authority relations between bodies like the Curators and the ICS Council, rather than supervisory relations between Board and staff. With this reasoning, the faculty decided that decisions of the Board of Curators would be valid only after the faculty gave its consent, a view that the Curators accepted.

The Institute stated that it accepted that all administrative work and decisions pertaining to the Institute are guided by ". . . academic norms, followed by subordinate norms such as financial, technical, communicative, social, etc." The faculty seemed to view administration as something that was necessary, not as an appropriate profession with its own norms. The Institute's administration seemed to be amateur, without knowledge of practices and structures found workable in most schools. The faculty was concerned that heads of academic administration in higher education invariably dominated educational programs, functioning as boss of the academic staff.

In 1976 I presented a twenty-three-page paper to the staffs and Boards offering my ideas on a Christian basis for decision-making at the Institute and Association, the role of group process and individual leadership. I attempted to break through the hierarchical versus collegial governance pattern, using the language of "norms," which was widely used by the Institute at that time. The paper opens with these theses:

> In his creational structuring of the world, God has also provided norms for the functioning of organizations. To us these norms appear as patterns of ways things work, the ways individuals and groups interact for

maximum fruitfulness in the service of God. It is our task to discover these norms and practice them. In so doing, we build on the discoveries of our predecessors who find God's structures in the world and follow them even though they may not know or wish to obey the Lord. This means that (1) we have the obligation and privilege of learning "professional" ways of administering organizations, rather than acting non-historically by what seems intuitively good in our own eyes, and (2) we must re-form secular patterns so they will conform to the law and service of God.

In the paper I suggested this series of norms for administrative service:

1. There are different *kinds* of service in an organization like the Association.
2. The central task of administration is to *facilitate*, not to do the service for which the organization exists.
3. Administrative work may only be done by those *qualified* and *appointed*.
4. Each administrator must be held personally accountable to an identified person or group such as a Board.
5. It is normative that broader decisions of educational purpose, priorities and timing should be in the hands of a lay Board whose members do not have a vested interest in the decisions.
6. Administrative decision-making must be consultative.
7. Administrative service in an educational institution exists to bring together academic opportunities and supportive non-academic services.
8. It is normative that those called to be teachers be required to do relatively little administrative work.

Needless to say, the Institute's structure as it existed in the first years required a great deal of time and energy from everyone at the Institute. The head of the Institute at first was a faculty member who served as Chairman for one year, with the other professors serving on an annually rotating basis. A complete rotating system was set up by the faculty for its annual responsibilities for service beyond teaching and research. The rota, as it was called, included service as administrative chairperson, secretary, registrar, teacher of a summer academic course, teacher of a winter evening course, organizer of a summer academic or non-academic conference, or teacher of a January Interim course. Each faculty member had one rota assignment each year except when on sabbatical leave.

In 1974, Albert Wolters, then Director of Educational Services, reported to the Trustees that in the past six months he had been required to attend long and exhausting meetings of many staff and Council groups that had cost him a great deal of time and energy. In 1975, for example, a meeting of the ICS Council started at 9:40 A.M. and lasted until 5:30 P.M., running four hours longer than planned. An exaggerated sense of democracy tended to democratism.

In 1977, the Institute was unhappy that as Executive Director I had made arrangements for some badly needed repainting of the premises without consulting the faculty about the colours to be used. They then appointed a Building Aesthetics Committee consisting of two faculty members and a graduate student to deal with such matters.

In the late 1970s, trustee Jan de Koning wrote that some Board members complained that every decision at the Association needed to be talked about by everybody. Since so many Boards and individuals were involved, a decision was sometimes made, overturned, and remade in the course of several years because people who disagreed with a decision would use the rules to ask for a reconsideration, which could go on and on.

The trustees also had their frustrations with organizational structure. One concern expressed was that the Institute as a graduate school seemed to be a relatively autonomous unit within the Association structure. The Executive Committee of the Association had no explicit structural way of relating to the Institute, and its relation to the Board of Trustees was not clear. The Trustees were concerned that the Institute's view of making decisions meant that "what is everybody's responsibility is nobody's responsibility." Questions were raised about whether leadership and authority could be exercised in this situation.

The Board of Trustees also needed to develop its sense of appropriate matters to deal with. In the early years, the Board made many types of decisions, and as staff developed it became important that Board decisions focus on policy issues rather than administrative matters. In 1975, I culled earlier Board minutes and gave the Board a statement of policy decisions that boards had made to that point. Policy decisions generally applied to a range of future decisions, rather than being specific actions applying only to a single instance. A helpful statement was given to the Board, written in 1973 by Walter Worth, Alberta's deputy minister of education, who defined policy decisions as decisions that were "philosophically based, goal oriented directional guides for future discretionary action, parameters within which discretionary action must be contained."

Administrative Structure

In the late 1970s, a Joint Staff Council was set up for administrative service that included people from both the Institute and the Association administrative staffs. The Joint Staff Council worked on matters like policies for student financial aid, publications, financial issues, and public relations. The Council had its own committees to bring recommendations on various matters. It worked well, making use of good personal relations on both sides.

In 1975, I led a revision of Association administration that set up three departments, Development, Business and Financial Management, and Community Educational Services. This replaced the earlier three departments, which were Executive, Program and Financial Affairs, and Library. The change was helpful in setting up fund-raising and public relations as a separate entity with its own staff, since raising money had become an important need and professionally qualified persons were required for that. Christian schools always combined fund-raising with business management, but this was not satisfactory for higher education. Educational Services had a full-time director as early as 1973. The library, of course, became part of the Institute's academic program.

Harry Houtman moved to become Director of Business and Financial Management in 1975. He was followed in this position by Phil Travis and later by Rosalind Deck. In 1987, Ross Mortimer became Vice-President for Administration, a position he held with distinction until 1995. This structure separated fund-raising from the stewardly spending of funds.

Academic Leadership

After a few years, it became clear that not all the professors were good at serving as chair of the Institute, so the position was upgraded to Principal. The Board wanted to give the position of academic leadership greater public recognisability and public strength as a spokesperson for the Institute. The title seemed fitting to the practice of Canadian institutions of higher education, where it was common for the head of the school to have the title of Principal. It was agreed that a four-year term would give the Principal time to develop experience in giving strong academic leadership and to build up a place of leadership among the Institute constituency and in the academic community. Bernard Zylstra was appointed Principal to a four-year term in 1978.

The Board wanted someone in this office who had provided good research and teaching at the Institute and who had proven administrative and public relations talents. The Principal would be expected to maintain an ongoing research program and teach one course each year. At the end of four years of service, the Principal would receive a year's sabbatical leave.

The Board and the Curators did not realize how unrealistic their wishes were for the Principal; the administrative and executive leadership of the position of Principal would tend to absorb that person's time and energy because the institution was struggling to establish itself and raise money to stay afloat.

Though Zylstra was given the services of two administrative assistants, Dorothe Rogers and Kathy Vanderkloet, the range of services to be performed and of personal gifts needed made the position one that could not be carried out fully.

In defining the position, Zylstra wrote that the Principal should have no direct authority over the faculty, nor the faculty direct authority over the Principal, but that there should be cooperation and coordination with the faculty. He said that the Principal should be a scholar in the first place and an administrator in the second place.

In 1982, the Institute Council recommended to the Curators that Zylstra be reappointed as Principal, serving with two-thirds of his time in administrative work for the next four years, to 1986. The Council argued that the principalship was important for Institute academic well-being, that Zylstra was especially gifted for this service and had the full trust of the Institute.

Overall Institutional Leadership

In 1982, however, it became clear that if the Institute were to survive, it needed the legislature of Ontario to pass a bill giving it a charter to offer degrees. The government required that the school have control over all its own affairs, especially its finances, and not depend on a separate body like the Association to provide the money it needed. This meant that the Association and the Institute needed to merge into one institution. The Board agreed with this, and, in fact, had been wondering whether the dual arrangement was even helpful. Thus, the Board decided to drop the dual structure and to set up the position of President to be the chief executive officer of the whole organization. In 1982, it decided to appoint Zylstra to that position.

Zylstra found the position to be difficult for him to do as well as he wished, and in 1985, he left that position with the aim of returning to service as a professor at the Institute. But he had been bothered by health problems in recent months, and soon it was discovered that he had inoperable cancer. He died one year later.

Zylstra was a person of vigour and vision, and he was good at relating with supporters of the Institute and with leaders of other colleges and universities. He was seen as a compelling speaker, and he was an inspiring teacher who opened new vistas of Christian thinking for his students. Two of them, Jonathan Chaplin and Paul Marshall, produced a book of essays by his former students and by scholars close to Zylstra as a tribute to his work, and the Institute set up a memorial scholarship fund in Zylstra's name for Institute students.

The Search Committee for a new president was delighted to learn from Wilbur Sutherland that Dr. Clifford C. Pitt might be interested in a limited term as President. Pitt was a prominent evangelical Christian leader in Toronto and a former President of the Board of InterVarsity Christian Fellowship of Canada. He was an educational psychologist who had taught at the Ontario Institute for Studies in Education, which, in effect, was the graduate school of education for the University of Toronto, and had served as its Director, that is, as its chief executive. In his retirement, he served for five years as President of the Ontario College of Art, and, at age seventy, was willing to serve at the Institute for Christian Studies for up to five years.

Pitt was decidedly in tune with the Christian educational philosophy of the Institute, though at first not specifically informed about reformational Christian thinking, which he later came to embrace with enthusiasm. His impressive experience, the fact that he was an "outsider" to the Institute and to Dutch immigrants, his warm personal qualities, and his deep Christian faith were strongly attractive to the Board. He was fresh and exciting.

Clifford Pitt came into a situation where the academic staff was a tight-knit group of insiders, a sort of "old boys' club" who sometimes fought with each other but who never let anyone make them change. But Pitt won them over, loosening the tight grip of the faculty. Everyone liked and admired him. The Dutch immigrants who had founded and supported the Institute, who may have had problems with some of the Institute's questionable ways, loved him. He warmed their hearts by telling them what a wonderful and amazing institution they had founded.

In November 1985, after four months on the job, Pitt presented the outlines of a four-year master plan to the Trustees, which they adopted. He saw the "prime specific goal" of the Institute "to be a Christian graduate school devoted to developing and propagating biblically based, philosophically informed, Christian reformational perspectives for all areas of life." He coined the phrase, widely used, that identified the

Institute as the "graduate school with a difference." Pitt placed a strong emphasis on getting more graduate students at the Institute. Pitt worked hard to expand Institute degree offerings, and he wanted the legislature to give the Institute the right to offer the Master of Education degree, but at that he was not successful.

In the first year of Pitt's presidency, donations to the Institute went up about thirty percent from the previous years, but the financial situation was still grave. The deficit for that year was $213,000, with expenditures at $925,000.

At the time of Pitt's retirement, Stuart Williams said that Pitt was an outsider who smothered the Institute with superlatives and goaded it towards an untypical saintly assurance. Harry Fernhout said that Pitt was a man of vision, a person of whom the Bible says "Your old men shall dream dreams." He spoke of Pitt as a man of wisdom who was able to draw on his storehouse of experience and depth of understanding of the educational world to give truly wise leadership at the Institute. He retired in 1989 at age 75. He lived until 1999, ten years after he retired for the last time.

For the first two years of Pitt's presidency, Paul Marshall served as Vice-President, partly because Pitt was committed to spending with his wife the time from mid-December to mid-April in Florida each year. For the latter half of his presidency, Harry Fernhout was Vice-President.

In December 1989, Fernhout began serving as President. He grew up in Thunder Bay, Ontario, of Dutch immigrant parents. He graduated from Dordt College in 1970, after which he became a student at the Institute. He was among the first students to receive the Institute's master's degree in 1975. He then worked for the Curriculum Development Centre, located in the Institute Building, as a curriculum researcher and writer of biblical studies. He then attended the Ontario Institute for Studies in Education, from which he received the doctorate. He started his work of teaching and research at the Institute's department

Harry Fernhout

of Philosophy of Education in 1986. He was keenly aware of the Institute's need to grow in number of students and professors, financial stability, and reputation among Christians worldwide.

Fernhout's presidency was a special gift to the Institute. He had great vision for the Institute, an ability to generate solid confidence with students, faculty, and Christians everywhere. He was gentle, firm, and modest, with an ability to convince supporters and donors that the Institute is vital to a Christian understanding of scholarship and has an important educational ministry to the world in general.

Institute Membership

The general direction of the Institute is in the hands of people who become members of the Institute by signing a statement of agreement with the basis and aims of the Institute and agreeing to pay a membership fee each year.

The meaning of membership might not have been clear to the few thousand people invited to become members, so in late 1974, the Board adopted a statement that read in part:

> Membership means mutual commitment. The Association solicits and accepts membership on the basis of its stated aims and religious confessional statements, and on the strengths of the programs it conducts to carry out its aims. It pledges faithful adherence to its position statements and good stewardship in the use of resources that members provide. It promises to communicate openly with members about what it is doing, and to give careful and appropriate attention to the advice of members.
>
> Members affirm that they hold to the religious vision and the educational objectives of the Association. They pledge to support it with prayer, money, expressions of good will for the Association in their personal contacts, and constructive critique of the activities of the Association.
>
> Membership is generally considered as a family membership, including husband and wife and minor children. Each membership entitles the holder to one vote in official matters. Single adults, whether living with families or not, may hold membership on the same basis as families.
>
> To become a member a person must state in writing that he or she subscribes wholeheartedly to the Preamble, Basis and Educational Creed of the Association. During each year the member must make a financial donation to the Association whose minimum annual amount is specified by the Board of Trustees.

Members live in one of six geographical districts located in Canada and two in the United States. The members elect Board members from their district. Starting in 1980, they were also asked to ratify up to one-third as many more people nominated to serve as "at large" Board members. These nominees are identified by the Board as having special abilities for service on the Board. Some of these "at large" trustees live near Toronto so they can readily attend monthly meetings of the Executive Committee. The Board meets twice a year.

Building the Board of Trustees

In the early years, the Board of Trustees was comprised of twelve members, one or two elected to represent each of the eight geographical regions in North America in which Association members lived. This gave members in all locations a voice on the Board. A problem was that because of great distances, the Board could meet only about twice a year. So a Board of Directors was appointed by the Board of Trustees, consisting of trustees who lived near Toronto and certain other Association members who lived within commuting range of the Toronto office. This Board met monthly.

This worked reasonably well, but this Board of Directors acted rather independently of the Board of Trustees because about half of its members were not trustees and therefore did not attend trustee meetings, did not have the advantage of participating in trustee discussions, and often did not understand the reasons for certain trustee decisions.

In 1979, changes in composition of the Board of Trustees were made. Provision was made for the appointment of up to half as many trustees to the Board as were elected from the geographical regions. This permitted service of trustees who did not represent distant places, so some could be appointed who lived in the Toronto area. It also permitted service on the Board of people of certain strengths and could provide a diversified composition of the Board to include both men and women, business and professional people, farmers and city people, and so on. The selection of appointed trustees needed to be ratified by approval of the membership on a yes or no ballot. A problem arose, however, because from an area as large as a province, only the people with the highest public profiles, such as pastors, will generally be elected.

The Board of Directors was then replaced by a true Executive Committee of the Board. It was given the explicit mandate to (1) act on behalf of the Trustees between its meetings on matters on which action could not wait for the next semi-annual meeting of the Trustees, (2) carry out assignments given to it by the Trustees, (3) serve as a committee to prepare certain recommendations for forthcoming meeting of the Trustees, and (4) advise and assist the staff on matters they wished to bring to the Board. The Executive Committee was to have between five and nine members.

The importance of having a strong and able Board of Trustees is hard to overestimate. An institution is not likely to be stronger than its Board, and it is the Board that determines the quality of the work to be done. Further, a Board needs a good balance in the capabilities of its members.

Board of Curators

Until the Institute received its Charter in 1983, the Board of Curators had the task of determining the direction of curricular development and deciding and supervising the implementation of educational policy. It was called

> ... to supervise the work of the Institute in such a way that its religious direction, and the work of each staff member in the Institute, will be such as to give leadership to a biblically-directed formation of the academic enterprise in harmony with the Basis and Educational Creed of the Association. In making its decisions the Curatorium shall focus upon academic matters, that is, professional matters of learning, teaching and research for which the central criteria for decision-making shall require advanced education and pedagogical insight at the graduate level.

The Board of Curators, consisting of five to nine academicians who were also Association members, functioned as the academic advisory board to the Board of Trustees. Appointment to the Board of Curators was limited to those who could understand academic issues and judge them appropriately. Generally, Curators held the doctoral degree, and most of them were professors.

The Board of Curators reported to the Board of Trustees on the strengths and weaknesses of the academic work of the Institute. It made recommendations to the Trustees on which academic fields had priority in new faculty appointments; it interviewed and recommended to the Trustees appointments to specific persons; and it made academic policy decisions. The Curators had responsibilities that included setting the structure and direction of curricular development in consultation with the faculty. They interviewed each faculty member before recommending reappointments to the Trustees.

At times, tension developed between the Trustees and the Curators because most Curators were close friends of faculty members and strongly represented faculty viewpoints to the Trustees, viewpoints that were not always widely popular. In the earliest years of the Institute, the Trustees were relatively permissive of academic and nonacademic actions of the faculty, so the faculty largely decided how the Institute would operate.

In the later 1970s, by general assent, two prominent professors at the University of Toronto were appointed to the Board of Curators. They were Lawrence Lynch, of the College of St. Michael's University, and Richard Longenecker, a theologian at Wycliffe College. Their inside knowledge of academic policies at the University of Toronto were enormously helpful for the Institute.

Peter Schouls, a professor at the University of Alberta, chaired the Board of Curators for many years; when the Institute received its charter in 1983, he chaired its successor, the Senate. He chaired these academic boards for twenty years, until 1993. A very active and helpful member of the same boards during that period was Ed Piers, a professor at the University of British Columbia.

Master Planning

In the early 1970s, the Association and the Institute were moving forward, but there did not seem to be an overall sense of direction. There was the feeling that it was possible to move forward in a number of different ways, but communal agreement on priorities was lacking. So early in 1975, not long after I arrived in Toronto, I gave leadership to articulating a vision for the institution and a Five-Year Plan suggesting how that vision might be achieved. People in all parts of the institution participated in developing the plan, and it was accepted by the Board and staff in late 1975.

The purpose of the Institute was taken from its founding documents: "To undertake or promote scripturally directed learning and scholarly enterprise and, in particular, to establish, control and develop a Christian university and in these ways to equip men and women to bring the Word of God in all its power to bear upon the whole of life." In addition, Board action taken in 1974 directed that the Institute would be a graduate school that would not include professional training activities. It would be ". . . a continuing centre for sustained scholarly analysis, for student guidance throughout the year, for mutual discussion and for translation and original publication, all in the spirit of our Preamble and Educational Creed," words taken from the 1965 document called *Place and Task of an Institute*.

The 1975 Master Plan stated that "We wish to prepare leaders for society who will be educated people who have an encyclopaedic grasp of creational problems and a deepened historical awareness of what lies behind the contemporary situation; leaders whose gifts of Christian insight in a certain specialized area bring with it authority and, if God wills, blessing to people." Objectives of Institute research and teaching were identified as:

> 1. Outfitting graduate students with a disciplined vision, with knowledge, and with determined ability to serve academically in forming the Christian mind needed by God's people to live Christianly in our age and to serve with benefit from their having been deepened with Christian academic forming in whatever societal position they assume.
> 2. Working to develop a distillate of Christian wisdom relating to different fields of life among faculty members and Institute graduates so that semi-popular articles, books and tape recordings of an occasional nature will naturally be forthcoming to help God's people and society at large.
> 3. Publishing books, articles and pamphlets which testify to Christian scholarship in a way that confronts current professional, secular specialists with responsible directional alternatives in their fields at crucial foci, and that hints at what a non-scholastic, communal Christian philosophical perspective can mean for wise learning.

The Plan stated that the Institute expected its faculty members to exemplify Christian *academic leadership* in some area and to be able to equip the younger generation of Christ-committed graduate students, themselves becoming capable of mastering some area academically, to do likewise. The plan also stated:

> Since in North America there is no other institution doing advanced university-type studies with a cohering (reformational) Christian vision, we assume as our highest Institute working priority the task of fashioning a working community of engaged Christian scholars as a direct means to the end of providing this kind of leadership.
>
> It is *academic life* we wish to redeem, two generations working as one, and it is *long-range Christian reorientation of reflection* for cultural action with which we wish to be of service to the Lord. . . . We choose to work most vigorously at those disciplines that touch on the realities of life in our time, and do this without the pressure of solving specific practical emergencies or of graduating finished professionals trained for non-academic jobs. The Institute as such does not have responsibility to see that the fruits of its work directly apply to the problems faced by the average person. That work of taking the theoretic insights of Institute scholarship may be undertaken as the responsibility of believers outside the Institute, though at times it may also come from the professors, as with James Olthuis's 1975 book *I Pledge You My Troth.*

Limiting factors in moving forward with this plan were identified as availability of faculty qualified to carry forward the program, enough qualified and committed graduate students, money to sustain the activity, problems of welding together a team of people who could work in community with each other, and the lack of undergraduate college and university programs to prepare students for study at the Institute.

The Master Plan included the goal that the faculty would be enlarged by one new professor each year. Priorities for opening up new faculty positions were identified as follows: (1) encyclopaedic coverage of the main areas of human culture, (2) appointment of original thinkers in specialized fields able to contribute to their colleagues' work in interdisciplinary ways, and (3) complementary support in the history and theory of a definite area where special cultural emergencies require foundational investigation.

Included in the plan was a policy statement of the Board of Curators that, over the years, faculty members were expected "to fashion interdisciplinary seminars with members of the philosophy department or other colleagues on subjects that will demand professional attention to problems calling for true interdisciplinary work from specialists." Graduate students would be required to take one interdisciplinary course in the second year of their study.

The Board also adopted the Curators' recommendation that money be made available for each faculty member to attend one academic conference each academic year. Until that point, faculty members did not often attend professional meetings in their field. In later years, Institute faculty members, and also graduate students, were extraordinarily active in presenting papers to the meetings of academic societies.

The Institute looked for graduate students who would

> ... be able to study the underlying questions of philosophy, methodology, history and general theory of a field from the perspective of the biblical message of re-creation of life in Jesus Christ. They should be able to develop a field in such a way that diversity is seen to cohere internally and externally with the other sciences and the rest of life. They should be able to examine the basic questions of a field. They should explore systematically what the Christian faith means for their study and future vocation, to participate as a member of a community of scholars, to develop the ability to ask penetrating questions and detect the things that really matter, and work creatively and independently.

The plan adds, "When they leave the Institute with a degree the students should be able to take up in a meaningful manner such alternative activities as further studies in a doctoral program, do field research for publishing, or teach on any level appropriate with the education received.

They should be in a good position to fill practically-oriented jobs of administration, counselling, public service, etc., in private and public organizations."

The Master Plan projected a substantial increase in the Association's educational services outside of the Institute, as there continued to be a great need for education on a wide front showing Christian vision and behaviour from a reformational Christian perspective. The Association also accepted as one of its responsibilities the work of forming Christian students at secular universities.

The concluding part of the Master Plan gave numerous tables of numbers that show staffing needs, the costs of operating the program envisioned, how much money was needed each year and where the money could come from.

A further Master Plan was developed in 1980, and President Clifford Pitt led in developing an updated Master Plan in 1987.

The Greystone Report

In 1984, James Heynen, a consultant for non-profit ministries who was the head of The Greystone Group, was asked to "provide the Institute with a professional and confidential report that analyzes organizational problems currently faced by the Institute and recommends alternative courses of action to be taken by the Institute." The Institute had received its charter a year earlier and felt it could well receive some help in settling its structure and direction.

By means of confidential surveys of current and former staff members, Trustees, Curators, Institute fellows, Institute members, clergy, and leaders of related organizations, as well as on-site consultations, Greystone prepared a detailed report for the Institute in January 1985. Heynen said that the Institute was a movement trying to become an institution. He described the difference between the two this way:

> A movement typically criticizes extant social models; an institution seeks to create new models. A movement points out weaknesses in others; an institution builds its own strengths. A movement is measured by the power and accuracy of its theory or philosophy; an institution is measured by the potency of its practice and product. A movement is headed by informal, charismatic leadership; an institution needs formal chiefs with designated authorities and sanctioned rights or status. A movement goes up on the public platform with sizzling speeches; an institution secures its future in the quiet of private councils. A movement is characterized by its pure positions which will never be negotiated; an institution survives by the wisdom of careful accommodation.

Movements appeal to the masses through powerful and sometimes truthful rhetoric; institutions can tolerate some rhetoric, but they thrive on the productivity of steady performance.

The Institute badly needed a model for itself, said Heynen, because it was schizoid. The Institute was partly a graduate school devoted to showing graduate students how to become scholars and partly a centre for public education through popular conferences, lectures, courses, publications, and a worldview emphasis that was unique in North America and the world. You can't be two different things at the same time and be successful as an institution, said Heynen. He advised the Institute to accept the model of a school and drop its activities in public worldview education. "All functions within ICS should either support or emerge from the primary functions of recruiting, teaching, and graduating students," he wrote.

Heynen pointed out some other issues that the Institute needed to hear and address. He noted that the Institute was rich in bricks and mortar but poor in cash. He said that the agendas of various individuals had created problems of unity and coherence of the Institute and that it needed a means for resolving conflicts internally and with its supporters. He advised that the Institute should work hard to establish solid working relations with Christian schools in Canada. He pointed out that a weakness of the Institute was that it was identified with the faculty persons who served it rather than being identified as an institution. The Institute was perceived as doing what its professors did, he wrote, and thus it tended to be tossing on the sea rather than being identified with its own purpose and character.

Heynen said that the Institute badly needed planning, "solid, reliable, visionary but practical planning." This seemed to be the greatest point of need and the weakest record. The latest Master Plan, he noted, was dated 1981 and contained a vast array of proposed things to be done but almost no clear guidelines for strategy. The earlier Master Plans were visionary but not practical. Heynen said that the Institute badly needed a long-range Master Plan for the future. Where did the Institute want to go, and how did it want to develop?

Heynen also noted that the Institute had lost its close links with the elementary and secondary Christian schools that grew out of the vision of Dutch immigrants and that links with those schools should be a priority. The Institute should appoint a professor of education, a major part of whose work would be to develop and maintain very close working relations with Christian schools.

The Greystone Report was rather well received, though many thought Heynen had defined the work of a graduate school too narrowly. He had not adequately understood the unyielding desire of the Institute to give community leadership to build God's Kingdom. There was also resistance to his advice to move away from the Institute's Educational Services program, especially the ministry of extracurricular teaching of Christian perspective courses to students at nearby universities. Yet it was important for the Institute to listen to outside advice, an activity it had ignored in earlier years.

The report focused the thinking of Institute people, and in the next few years, many of the changes he suggested were adopted. The Institute slowly moved away from the mission of being a university for the people. The shortage of money led to that change, most notably with dropping the Educational Services program in 1987. The Christian community, especially that of the Dutch immigrants, was changing as the years went by, and by the late 1980s, the focus of the Institute sharpened to preparing students for Christian leadership and offering leadership through academic research faithful to the Christian vision.

12

The Rough Road of Controversy

From the very start, the Association and its Institute were a lightning rod for controversy. Some of the early controversy arose from questionable actions of the Board and staff, and some arose from people who opposed the ministry and the ways it was being conducted.

Criticisms and Controversies

There were numerous criticisms of the Institute. There were people who said that the wish to even start the Institute was foolish and unrealistic. Many Dutch immigrants had their own problems and insecurities. They were a feisty people, and for some of them, controversy was part of who they were. But early decisions by the Board were also certain to generate opposition, such as requiring three signatures for membership and setting up the Institute as a reformational institution founded on the ideas of the "Amsterdam School" of philosophy.

The Association and the Institute started with a great deal of idealism, and they were even triumphalistic in certain ways, though they could never end up being as good a place as their visionary promoters promised they would be. And, as noted earlier, the prevailing counterculture of the late 1960s affected the Institute in ways that were bound to draw criticism. Its early public criticism of other Christian institutions, including churches and Christian schools, were certain to raise hostility.

Lecturers. In December 1974, Nicholas Wolterstorff gave a well-attended public lecture in Hamilton, Ontario, and other places on the subject, "The AACS: Will it Guide Us or Divide Us?" He was very candid, and the lecture was supportive of the Association and the Institute and was well received, in part because it was objective and reasoned, which was not common in discussions about the Association in those days. He offered some critique of the AACS, including its understanding of the term *Word of God,* which he said sometimes sounded confused and blurred. He also was not happy with the "movementism" of the Institute, which led to pride, self-congratulation, defensiveness, divisiveness, and even a form of paranoia. But he agreed with the Institute's view of "sphere sovereignty" and with its having "effectively reminded us all of the cosmic scope of the obedience Christ asks of us."

Wolterstorff placed ill-tempered criticism of the Institute in the context of the wide range of different viewpoints held by Dutch Reformed people. Wolterstorff identified those whose focus is pietism, with their emphasis on personal piety and devotion; others who emphasize rational doctrinalism, who press adherence to a doctrinal system; and those who are Kuyperian and work for the reformation of all of life. Besides, he noted, each group includes people who are conservative and others who press for change within their system. All of these people are convinced that they are right and that others need to change to their position.

The lecture was printed in the December 1974 issue of *Reformed Journal*, and the March 1975 issue contained an appreciative response by Hendrik Hart. Hart wrote that the lecture was ". . . a first important attempt at critical understanding with considerable sympathy and respect" that the Institute had received. He added that ". . . your critique is generally fair . . . and we have often been guilty of the faults you point out. . . . But in the last three or four years we have become aware of most of the charges you have made and we have tried our best to be reforming. . . . You have helped us dispel certain persistently wrong accusations." Hart also wrote that the Institute was very complex, involving many different people in many different locations, that its visions and emotions were strong, and that public self-congratulation, use of jargon, and triumphalism continued to be present to some degree or other.

Also around 1974, James Houston, then Principal of Regent College in Vancouver, gave a lecture at the Institute. He said that earlier the Institute had seemed bent on throwing stones at the windows of all its neighbours, but it now seemed ready to stop that. Houston was one of the first evangelical leaders who reached out to the Institute by having Regent cosponsor with the Institute a conference titled "Affirming Creation and History" on the pertinence of the gospel of creation for Christian education, held at York University in 1975.

Magazines. Public criticism of the Institute reached the entire Christian Reformed Church membership in early 1974 when Lester De Koster, editor of *The Banner,* the weekly paper of the church, wrote seven blistering articles condemning the institution. There was enough angry response to his articles that De Koster agreed to give the Association equal time and publish in *The Banner* its own seven articles in response. It turned out that this offer was actually less generous, allowing only three or four articles. The Association Board noted that in its articles, "A warm, biblical tone is needed, as this will have a good response from our Reformed people who are confused by sophisticated word-games." The articles it wrote gave the Association the opportunity to give wide-reaching expression in positive ways about what it was trying to achieve.

A few years later, the magazine *Christian Renewal* was moved from northwest Iowa to St. Catharines, Ontario. John Hultink became its editor and, for several years, the magazine published scathing articles about the Institute.

Personnel Issues. In June 1974, Peter Schouls, chair of the Board of Curators, addressed a short paper to the Trustees about criticism of faculty members by supporters of the Association. He said that one part of the problem was that faculty members were being asked to speak on all kinds of subjects, including some in which they had no special expertise or insight. The community should not expect faculty members to be authorities on everything, he said, and faculty members should be able to refuse some kinds of speaking engagements. Further, the community did not understand that sometimes faculty members present ideas for public consideration without themselves advocating them, but hearers take such ideas as positions held by the faculty. There needed to be open discussion and weighing of ideas, not immediate and passionate rejection of them. In some cases, unfortunately, the tone of the speeches and written materials from the Institute came off as more authoritarian than it should have, admitted Schouls, and this encouraged strong rejection in some cases.

In 1975, some friends of the Association living in Iowa wrote an extended statement to the Board expressing concerns about ideas expressed by the faculty in a number of areas. They were concerned about the faculty's view of the Bible, with the Iowa writers calling for a more literal interpretation of the Bible. They questioned Institute references to three forms of the Word of God, namely, the Bible, Jesus as the incarnate Word, and God's work in the world he created. They were also concerned about the Association's view of the church, "the apparently sharp distinction almost to the point of divorce which some make between the church as God's people and the church as organization next to many other organizational structures in the present world." They raised the question ". . . of what it means to live as a Christian believer in obedience to God's will. By some you have even been put into a class with the situational ethicists." The writers spoke of the Bible as ". . . coming to us in the form of statements or propositions which are clear." The Association replied to the letter in an open and congenial way that the recipients found helpful.

Some concerns also arose about Arnold De Graaff's church relations and other matters. After he left membership in the Christian Reformed Church to become a member of Bloor Street United Church, the Board of Directors met with him in March 1978 to discuss his understanding and view of the church and how that affected the public relations work of the Association. De Graaff said he was no longer able to relate to the Christian Reformed church that served his local community. The Directors recommended that the Curators and the Trustees discuss this, since his relationship to the church was affecting the public stance of the Institute.

In 1978, the faculty discussed at one of its meetings the fact that De Graaff's marriage had broken down. They said that they found "the dissolution of such a life-commitment a terribly serious matter which compromises both Arnold's and our public witness. . . ." They said that De Graaff had acknowledged full responsibility for his share in the break and that all of us live imperfectly before the face of God. The faculty wrote in its minutes of their meeting: "The discussion with Arnold concerning his marriage breakdown brought to light a possible interrelation among a number of facets of his life, such as his personal life changes, his relationship to the church, his work in theory of psychology at the Institute, his supervision of students leading to completion of their studies, and his counselling. More than one senior member wishes to raise the question whether this interrelation has implications for the continuation of Arnold's position among us."

A further complication was that De Graaff had made some positive statements about homosexuality and began to share living quarters with a former Institute student who identified himself as homosexual.

The Board of Trustees appointed a committee to consider the situation. The committee talked with many people who had worked with De Graaff, and it heard many positive comments. But in the end, it recommended to the Trustees that De Graaff be dismissed. The faculty and the Curators disagreed with that recommendation. But at a special meeting held in King City, Ontario, in 1980, and after a thorough and difficult discussion, the Board decided to dismiss him.

At the same time, the Board was also dealing with the collapse of the marriage of Thomas McIntire. In addition, the Board was aware that

Hendrik Hart was actively promoting the acceptance of homosexual persons in the Christian church and community and that James Olthuis, who had left the Christian Reformed Church to join Bloor Street United Church, had appeared on a television panel debate with Russell Legge, President of the Canadian Council of Churches, in which Olthuis consistently referred to God as "she."

Interfaculty Strife. The faculty itself had a history of inner turmoil. During the 1980s, interpersonal conflicts consumed a certain amount of faculty energy. As unpleasant and undesirable as these tensions were, it is not surprising that they developed at a place like the Institute. The heart of its educational mission is a deeply religions vision that is not shared in the same way by all who work together to implement it, even in a group that is small and in many ways homogeneous. In fact, because the group is small, faculty members work closely with each other and differences become apparent, differences that at some distance may seem quite minor. The Institute was formed because of a vision, but any institution needs to work out what the vision means in practice. The vision is extremely dear to the hearts of those who try to work together to make it concrete. Differences in theology or Christian worldview or differences in individual temperament and personal living choices can make people feel like the other person is betraying what is dear to all of them. People who work passionately together, contributing aspects of their lives that are important to them, find tensions. Look closely at any small seminary faculty, for example, and you will find sharp tensions, though they may be carefully hidden from outside view.

The Institute was blessed with a faculty of extremely gifted and dedicated scholars. However, highly intelligent people are often very individualistic. In the early years, most of the faculty did not find it easy or natural to work closely with others. And it is often difficult for such people to be patient with members of the general public who may not easily understand what the scholars are doing. Tensions among the faculty brought tensions throughout the institution, among students, administrative staff, boards, and supporters.

In October 1979, Bernard Zylstra, as Principal, gave the Curators an extensive report on hurtful differences among the faculty members. He identified the following somewhat ideological differences as some troublesome issues: The place of authority within an institution, whether structures should be organized hierarchically or co-ordinately; the relation of the church to parachurch ministries; tradition and innovation, including whether the Institute could differ from some positions taken by Dooyeweerd; orthodoxy and ecumenism as postures in church relations; and lifestyle options in our walk of life.

Zylstra noted that the first faculty members at the Institute came directly from graduate school during the height of the counterculture and were asked to give leadership in a completely new situation. It was hard for them to learn self-discipline and self-correction. Things might have been different if the staff included one or two mature scholars with experience in leadership, he said. Close friendships led to occasional explosions with colleagues on differences of principle and strategy. All the faculty members were persons of strong personality. But they were not strong in the Christian virtue of admonishing one another in mutual compassion, understanding, and respect.

In hindsight, said Zylstra, it became clear to the Board of Trustees very early on that the faculty knew more about higher education than did Board members themselves, who were mostly pastors and business people. So the Board did not exercise the authority that would have been helpful. In the early years, the faculty often made the basic policy decisions that ran the institution.

The Institute's Responses

The Institute responded in many different ways to the controversies and conflicts that arose. The following are a description of these responses.

Spiritual Unity After Ten Years. In a notable talk given in 1977 to commemorate the Institute's opening in 1967, Hendrik Hart reflected on unity and disunity during those ten years. He demonstrated how the humanist spirit of autonomous human freedom became also the spirit of revolution. But the optimism of human freedom received a setback in World War I and the Russian Revolution, and was further smashed through World War II and Nazi fascism. When blacks revolted in American streets, many saw that the nice cultural optimism they grew up with was false. The counterculture movement arose, fed by the war in Vietnam, by Watergate, the depletion of oil resources, and much more. It was in that cultural climate that the Institute began and was given into the hands of young educated sympathisers of the counterculture.

It was not in the spirit of revolution that the counterculture took form at the Institute, said Hart. Those moving with the spirit of the counterculture felt the need to contend with the spirits in church and church-related organizations that had not understood the present times. So they struggled against the secular world of scholarship and also against what they perceived to be a blindness among fellow Christians, including those closest to them. The Institute caused division among Dutch Reformed people, a division some felt was necessary as a precondition for enlightenment. As Hart stated, "We were young, and not ready to contain the spirit of youthful enthusiasm in true sanctity. And so, in many ways, trying to be spirits of reformation, we became to many people spirits of alienation."

Hart also said, "We were taught to downplay our self-importance, to see our task in the context of many other children of the Lord doing their work in struggle and obedience. Our work could be seen in a more limited way." That statement of modesty, with its spirit of confession, spoken by people who had been seen to be arrogant was very helpful in reducing tensions between the Institute and its supporting Christian people.

Statement of Unity. In 1979, Albert Wolters and James Olthuis, whose views on some matters were quite different, wrote a Statement of Unity that all faculty members could accept. They opened the statement with these words: "In a spirit of love, frankness and good will we have explored our agreements and disagreements. On the basic matter of worldview we have substantial and wholehearted agreement. In regard to some important choices in various areas of life we have discovered wide and even serious differences."

The statement dealt with such issues as confessional affirmations; areas of agreement on Christian philosophical issues; the nature of unity in diversity; personal life and communal witness; Christian faith and emotional health; authority; tradition and innovation; church membership; marriage and divorce; homosexuality; male and female roles in church and society; and basic attitudes. The statement had a rather constructive healing effect, although it did not resolve the differences that existed.

In 1985, the Board adopted a document prepared by the staff called "Life Together at the Institute," which was helpful in articulating attitudes the faculty needed in working closely together.

Ways and Means to Improve Communication. In late 1982, the Board appointed a committee, chaired by Bert Witvoet, to make recommendations on "ways and means to communicate to our constituency the confessional stance of the Institute and the relevance of the research work of the Institute." The Board wanted to clarify how the Institute ought to function with regard to academic teaching and to cultural issues such as abortion, homosexuality, and feminism. With this mandate, the Board made clear that it expected the faculty to give public leadership in these controversial areas.

In its report, the committee pointed out that in its opinion "the Institute was not facing an acute short-term crisis in its relationship with the constituency." There was, however, evidence of a slow erosion of the support base, of a growing loss of trust in the Institute and some of its senior staff. Some critics of the Institute were raising concerns about academic issues relating to the specific biblical, theological, or philosophical leanings of one or another faculty member.

The committee pointed out that the confessional base of the Institute remained clearly expressed in the Educational Creed, which had not changed. But the committee also noted that accepted statements of confessional direction are all well and good, even essential, but they do not serve greatly as tests of practical expression in teaching, research, and publications.

For supporters of the Institute, two things were considered nonnegotiable: that all staff members demonstrate in their work and walk of life their submission to the authority of Scripture, and that they do their work from a reformational Christian perspective. The supporters deserved to see clear evidence that the work of the Institute remained faithful to its original goals and confessional outlook. "Leadership implies explanation and justification," said the report. It was considered important that the Institute show that these conditions were clearly true at the Institute.

The committee said that building the Institute had proved immensely more complex than its leaders had anticipated. In addition, the flow of popular speeches, articles, and publications that won support in the early years had decreased for good reasons. There had come to be something of a communication and credibility gap. A further problem was the tension that had developed within the faculty.

The committee report concluded that faculty members needed to be a lot more judicious about publishing their thoughts in a public setting, even though they have a right to be free in expressing them in an academic context. The faculty also needed to be extremely careful about the controversies that they started or joined. "Being controversial can be a sign of being biblically prophetic, but can also be a sign of being wrong," said the committee.

The Board and the Curators had a special meeting to deal with the committee's report. It accepted the committee's recommendation that a screening policy should be used when a faculty member was preparing to give a speech or write an article that could be divisive. The person preparing the work needed to give a draft copy of the presentation to all members of the faculty and to the Director of Development. These faculty members would then have the responsibility of suggesting to the author how the speech or article could or should be changed, and even whether it was wise to publish the article or deliver the speech at all. If there were strong differences of opinion on the matter, the faculty should meet to try to reach agreement. If they could not agree, the President would meet with the author to try to reach agreement. If agreement could not be reached, the President would report that to the Executive Committee promptly.

The Executive Committee's Response. In late 1983, the Executive Committee undertook a study of problems caused by differences within the faculty and by some public statements by faculty members. The committee was agitated because Albert Wolters, in his letter of resignation from the Institute faculty, expressed his concern that Hendrik Hart and James Olthuis each had inadequate views of Scripture. Related to that was concern about an article by Hart published in *The Banner* in which he supported thinking about God in feminine terms in some situations, as well as about an article by Olthuis in *Catalyst*, the magazine of Citizens for Public Justice, in which he suggested that Christians need not reject abortion in all circumstances. Some Institute supporters were alarmed that they were hearing what to them seemed like new and suspicious ideas.

The Executive Committee interviewed each faculty member separately and confidentially in December 1983. They reported that they had found each faculty member to be "sincere and committed Christians, and that all of them desired to be reformational." They also found that there were indeed substantial differences among them, which was more of a concern to some faculty members than to others.

The Executive Committee expressed doubt about the wisdom and responsibility of the articles by Hart and by Olthuis. They concluded that "Hart and Olthuis are sources of contention within the staff as well as within the supporting community." Some of them felt that the recent public statements by Hart and by Olthuis did not show evidence of the sensitivity and trust-creating ability that should be expected from persons in leadership positions. They recommended that the Board of Trustees interview Olthuis to "ascertain whether his present direction . . . is consistent with a teaching position at the Institute," a statement that could lead to his dismissal.

In a cover letter transmitting the report to the Trustees, Zylstra identified what steps the Institute regulations required to dismiss Olthuis from the faculty. The implication was that Zylstra favoured the dismissal of Olthuis. The faculty was shocked by Zylstra's position, which showed that he as Principal was distancing himself from a member of his faculty.

The Board of Trustees considered these matters at considerable length, and it met separately with both Olthuis and Hart. It expressed great appreciation for the contributions of them both. In the end, the Board decided to offer certain criticisms of each of them but did not dismiss them from their positions.

Maps and Compasses. Following the public problems of 1983, the Institute set up a lecture series in 1984–1985, held in nine locations, to assure supporters that it stood securely on Reformed and biblical principles. Called "Maps and Compasses," the speakers and topics were Aileen Van Ginkel on "Change in the Reformed Community 1954–84"; Hendrik Hart on "The Role of Scriptures in Charting our Course"; James Olthuis on "Growing in the Faith and Knowledge of the Lord"; Bob Goudzwaard on "Coping with Changes in Society"; and Derk Pierik on "Strategies for Dealing with Change." Especially well received was Hart's lecture, which he expanded to the book *Setting Our Sights by the Morning Star: Reflections on the Role of the Bible in Post-Modern Times*.

Perspective on the Cutting Edge. A significant factor in both internal and external criticism was that the Institute's research at the forefront of knowledge would be expected to result in varied judgments. In 1986, Carol-Ann Veenkamp wrote in *Perspective* newsletter an interview she had with Curator Peter Schouls. In the interview, he identified the nature of research at the cutting edge in which the Curators asked the faculty to engage. Veenkamp reported:

> Schouls said that by its very nature scholarship at the Institute is done at the frontiers of knowledge, which is ". . . an exhilarating as well as frightening thing to be involved in."
>
> At the cutting edge of research you are so very often (by the nature of the work) very much alone, you are alone with the demons of pride

and self-sufficiency—forces of which your own heart is not fully free. So the struggle at the cutting edge of scholarship is also often a struggle with yourself. It would be desperately lonely there if it were not for the grace of God which makes you triumphant. God's grace helps you discern what is wrong, and allows you to build new roads.

But sometimes that new road turns out to be a detour or even a blind alley. A Christian scholar needs community support so that fear turns neither into enervating panic nor self-righteous assertion. The public needs to know that when you are ". . . at the cutting edge of scholarship you have been intensely struggling with the powers of this world, with the writings of those who deny that there is any 'revelation of God in Jesus Christ' because they deny that there is a God." Then you re-enter the camp of those who in their churches are squabbling about minor issues over which they tear churches apart.

Schouls also said that "A great deal of the controversy of the past is much related to a misunderstanding of the nature and limits of leadership."

Guidelines for Dealing with Controversial Topics. In 1991, the Board of Trustees adopted a document called "Guidelines for Dealing with Controversial Topics," recognizing that there continued to be tensions between itself and the faculty on the subject. The Guidelines represented a covenant between the Board and faculty members that attempted to strike a constructive balance between the Board's trust and its control. A sense of accountability and of mutual responsibility among the faculty was assumed and mandated by the Guidelines.

The Guidelines said that faculty members were expected to regard all of their public utterances as a ministry in God's service. That implied a conscious effort to be guided by and submit to the Word and Spirit and to demonstrate respect for the body of Christ, specifically as it comes to expression in an academic community and its supporting constituency. The Board affirmed that the Institute's primary concern was not to restrict the subject matter of faculty utterances, but rather asked the faculty to consider the appropriateness of presentations with consideration of time, place, circumstances, occasion, context, and audience. The Board mandated that opinions, views, judgments, statements, and convictions expressed should be within the competence of the faculty member and be developed in a process of interaction with other members of the academic community at the Institute and beyond.

The Board acknowledged that since scholarship at the graduate level includes the requirement of critical thinking at the cutting edge, controversy would be unavoidable in the pursuit of such scholarship.

Sensitive issues exist both within the Christian community and outside it. The simple fact that some within the Institute's supporting constituency dislike discussion of a particular issue or disagree with a faculty member's view, would not itself be a sufficient reason, though it can be a factor, for judging the appropriateness of what is said or written.

The statement concluded with this important observation:

> The Board of Trustees appoints senior members to a responsible task which includes the delicate calling to be busy with front line thought on sometimes controversial issues. The Board gives senior members room to move responsibly within the guidelines set out above and pledges to uphold and defend senior members in the execution of their task within these guidelines. If and when the Board becomes involved in these matters it will exercise the same spirit of communality which is expected of senior members.

The Guidelines provided a framework within which the faculty could examine some of their generally accepted ideas that they wished to bring to the Institute's supporting community and the Christian public generally.

The Twenty-fifth Anniversary of the Institute

The twenty-fifth anniversary celebration of the Institute could be heard in many parts of the world. A major international three-day conference was held in Toronto in June 1992. It was cosponsored by the Institute, Calvin College, and the Free University, with people coming to speak from many parts of the world. The conference theme was "An Ethos of Compassion and the Integrity of Creation." The result was a very spirited conference. About 180 people attended. Among the high-profile visiting speakers were Nicholas Wolterstorff, Langdon Gilkey, Allen Verhey, Calvin DeWitt, Elaine Storkey, Bob Goudzwaard, James Skillen, Mary Stewart Van Leeuwen, Stanley Hauerwas, Myron Augsburger, Howard Van Till, and more. Institute speakers were Brian Walsh, Hendrik Hart, James Olthuis, and Calvin Seerveld. Papers and responses presented at plenary sessions were published in 1995 by the University Press of America, with the title of the book the same as the conference theme.

Creation is a concept ". . . central to the thought tradition of the Reformed branch of Christianity which gave birth to the Institute for Christian Studies," wrote President Harry Fernhout in his Introduction to the book.

This tradition understands the created world as a place lovingly and reliably ordered by God as an environment in which life can flourish. This strong emphasis on integral, life-giving order in creation provides the basis and impetus to this tradition's emphasis on the scholar's vocation; the academic pursuit of knowledge is, in fact, an investigation of the rich and reliable storehouse of creation. The theme of 'creation order' is woven into the Institute's historical understanding of its academic work.

The conference was organized to consider the strengths and limitations of this orientation to creation order. The world was changing enormously and with dazzling speed. New questions were arising from new medical discoveries, shifts in patterns of sexual relations, cultural pluralism, the New Age movement, the question of a new world order, the environmental crisis, and much more. What is lasting and "normative," and how are we to stand on the eternal verities to deal with entirely new issues?

Conference planners expected that only people with academic background would attend, and they anticipated that the speakers would have the academic freedom to bring forward some fresh ideas that might be controversial. In fact, many who attended were long-time supporters of the Institute who did not have an academic background with its understanding that controversial ideas might be brought forward to be weighed for approval or rejection. Viewpoints were presented by some of the speakers who served on the Institute faculty expressing tentative ideas that had not been spoken publicly before. Some who attended felt that the Institute was presenting a hidden agenda that would undermine its very foundation. Debate and strong differences of opinion were part of the conference.

Two presentations, those by Hart and Olthuis, created immediate controversy. Hart offered what he called a critique and refinement of creation order in the Institute's philosophical tradition. He presented serious criticism of the philosophical tradition and of some of the work of his closest colleagues. He wondered whether a static and rational set of categories could be used to show compassion to hurting people. Some who heard him felt that his style was confrontational and that he presented a one-sided characterization of the philosophical base of the reformational tradition. Some even suggested that he wanted to throw out an ethos of creation and replace it with an ethos of compassion. One of the problems was that much of the rationale for his startling statements was contained in extensive footnotes that were not read, so it seemed that his new insights lacked grounding and support as he read them.

Olthuis felt that he was given too little time to present the paper he had developed, so he gave a shortened version of his paper, delivered extemporaneously, it seemed. He suggested that Genesis 1 and 2 and Galatians 3 could be read in a way that creates room for the acceptance of committed same-sex relations as a valid response to creational and biblical norms. He argued that commitment or fidelity are keys to the relations between men and women and suggested that the Bible can be interpreted to condone long-term homosexual relations if lived in troth. His paper created a firestorm of controversy that left a mark on the conference.

President Fernhout said later that the underlying dynamic of what Hart and Olthuis wanted to do in their research is precisely at the heart of that the Institute wants to be, but that unfortunately, in these presentations, they had seriously hurt the trust the Institute needs of its people.

On the last day of the conference, Jonathan and Adrienne Dengerink Chaplin, both of whom later were to become members of the Institute faculty, summed up the activity of the conference, bringing perspective to the many ideas and strong feelings expressed. They affirmed that many people in the reformational Christian tradition accept the principle of creation order but fear that it is inattentive to the cries of the suffering. Yet what suffering people may need to experience ". . . are living examples of the fruit borne by well-ordered lives." We need to come to terms with the destructive power of sin.

The Chaplins said that "Certainly compassion must transcend human order. But in doing so it must itself be guided by God's order." The contrast between order and compassion is an ongoing challenge for the reformational tradition, they said. We need to interpret creation through Scripture and therefore "Biblical hermeneutics remains central to the task of creational hermeneutics."

Nicholas Wolterstorff, one of the speakers at the conference and a professor at Yale University Divinity School, gave a sense of perspective on the controversy that the conference raised with this appraisal: "The conference was remarkable for the way in which the Reformed tradition confronted the problems that face it and our society today with faith, intelligence and passion. I agree with Langdon Gilkey that no other faith community today is able to face major issues such as the environment, medical ethics, gender issues, and homosexuality in such a comprehensive and faith-driven way." Wolterstorff remarked that none of his colleagues at Yale would ever have the experience of a believing community wrestling together around Scripture, expressing deep divisions, and yet staying together.

After the conference, both Hart and Olthuis said they did not feel comfortable about how they handled their presentations. Both of them had brought forward ideas for consideration by their academic peers, but there were many people at the conference who were not scholars and did not take their ideas simply as viewpoints to be examined.

Because some people criticized Olthuis's presentation as exhibiting unacceptable hermeneutics, the Institute Senate sent a copy of his address to two highly regarded theologians, N. Thomas Wright and Christina Van Houten. Both reported that Olthuis's hermeneutic work was academically responsible, whether or not they agreed with his conclusions. But the Board was upset that Olthuis had not followed the Institute's Guidelines for Dealing with Controversial Topics. In reply, Olthuis said that he believed that he had met that requirement by having given this material earlier at an Institute Interdisciplinary Seminar at which no problems with his ideas were expressed.

The Board of Trustees was greatly agitated by the two presentations and the controversy they raised, feeling that both had displayed a serious lack of wisdom. So they appointed a high-profile committee to advise it. The committee worked long and hard at the task it had received. On the basis of the committee's report, in May 1993, the Board decided not to dismiss Hart and Olthuis as some had demanded. The Board's lengthy report concluded with the statement:

> The Board reaffirms, with the other components of the Institute, the task of on-going reformation in scholarship. The Board accepts that this task involves addressing unsettling and difficult questions and affirms the importance of a proactive rather than a reactive approach to these matters.

13

Development for the Institute

The work of development at a non-profit institution includes that of building its reputation and goodwill among people who might support it, raising money to keep it viable, and, in private schools, recruiting students.

Development work is a ministry in the name of Christ. In the case of the Institute, this means presenting the biblical worldview and philosophy of education through which the Institute wishes to be a blessing. The work of fund-raising is itself a blessing to people as it helps them offer some of their resources to the ministry of God's Kingdom.

In 1979, the Association took a clear look at its need for development, to be sure it had a good focus on the broad educational program for which resources were needed. It saw its calling as an institution to work at ". . . the promotion of scripturally directed higher learning." The core of this was the foundational research of the Institute and the teaching program in Toronto. From these grew the educational outreach ministry of the Association. The prominent, distinct features of this ministry were:

1. Institute research, aimed at fresh thinking at the roots, lest the education be derivative, needing to rely entirely on the scholarly findings of others. The Institute is one of very few Christian institutions structured to permit foundational research as a significant activity.
2. Institute teaching of students based in its Toronto classrooms and offices. The sustained teaching and learning of full time students is necessary in order to educate coming generations of students so they will in turn be able to carry on research of their own, and so that they can take positions of formative leadership in many areas of life.
3. Institute external teaching like short courses for the public, teaching of students like those of the Coalition for Christian Outreach, teaching January Interim courses, and various lecture series; external teaching gives wider spread to the work and gives Institute faculty a response to its research from a larger and more diverse group than its students in Toronto.
4. Ministry to students on secular university campuses.

5. Education of the general public, the non-academic education which gives vision for life and is carried out through writings, conferences for the public and public lectures.

Promotional service informs people of this work with a view to eliciting their support. Promotion itself includes a large element of education. An essential part of development work is appealing to people who have seen the Institute's educational vision, who are asked to join in to keep it alive.

The Difficulties of Development

The ministry of development is more difficult at the Institute than it is at most Christian institutions. The faculty is asked to deal in deep Christian ways with major issues in our culture that other Christians may not wish to think about, issues that may be controversial.

Raising enough money for the Institute seems almost impossible. The most common ways of raising money for colleges and universities are not very helpful for the Institute, namely government support, tuition income, and significant church donations. Governments rarely support schools for religious teaching and research. Tuition fees are necessarily low at the Institute because students have already paid for an education through a bachelor's degree and have often accumulated significant educational debt. In addition, their parents may feel that the students are finally old enough to support themselves. Besides, the number of students a professor at the graduate school level teaches is rather low because much individual attention is needed. Churches do not generally support graduate education significantly because churches have their own ecclesiastical ministries and financial needs. And the Institute is not even a church college.

Graduate education is rather far removed from the concerns of most people. Their own children probably do not attend a graduate school, nor the children of their friends. Research at the Institute centres on theory, on foundational issues, which people in the general public may not understand and which seems to them not to affect their lives. Graduate education is thus not a priority item in their charitable giving.

What people mostly know is that the Institute comes up with new ideas and brings up problems they don't really want to deal with. Because these are Christian ideas, the scholars will relate them to biblical teachings; if people do not like the answers scholars suggest, people wonder if the scholars use the Bible in good ways.

Development staff members need to communicate that the issues the Institute deals with will set up the atmosphere in which we all live, and they should be dealt with in a deep and sensitive biblical way. In 1976, the Institute's Albert Wolters made this point vividly in a speech he gave for the Christian Labour Association of Canada called "Ideas Have Legs," which in 1978 was published in the book *A Christian Union in Labour's Wasteland*. Wolters said, "In the context of philosophy and spiritual warfare I think that ideas have legs in the sense that they are not the disembodied abstractions of some ivory-tower academic theorist, but are real spiritual forces that go somewhere, that are on the march in somebody's army, and have a widespread effect on our practical, everyday lives." He quoted John Maynard Keynes: "The ideas of economists and political philosophers, both when they are right and when they are wrong, are more powerful than is commonly understood. Indeed the world is ruled by little else." Wolters concluded that "The conviction of the Institute for Christian Studies is that all of education needs to be aware of the philosophical ideas that underlie culture if we are to have education that advances the Kingdom of God."

Initial Development Work

Development work started as soon as the founders had the idea of starting the Association and the Institute. They wanted people to hear about these ideas and support them. The earliest work, which included travel of short distances to meetings and some mailings, was paid for by the people who did them. Later, people were asked by mail to make donations. At first, the Board adopted the policy of "promotion through services," that services like public lectures should show people the good ideas and intentions of the ministry. But soon the money the services generated was not enough. A system of membership dues was started, and local Chapters were expected to receive dues payments and to some extent raise donations.

When John Vander Stelt and Fred Cupido left their development services for the Association in 1968, John Hultink was appointed Director of Development. His assignment, like that of his predecessors, was to organize Chapters and work with them, gain new members, and solicit donations. In 1970, Robert Carvill was appointed half-time as Director of Communications to broaden the outreach of the Association and the Institute through mailings and written articles. One year later, when Carvill moved to become Editor and Executive Director of Wedge Publishing Foundation, Harry Houtman became Associate Director of Development, and James Visser became part-time Director of

> **John Hultink** was set on fire as a student of Evan Runner in Michigan, and already as a student worked hard to gain support for the Institute. He was extremely good at fund-raising and marketing; after his graduation from Calvin College, he turned these skills to good use at the Institute. He was highly successful and became a hero at the Institute at that time.
>
> Hultink had an almost ideological obsession with the ideas of Herman Dooyeweerd, and in some ways even appeared fanatical. His sharpness offended many people, and he was hard to tone down. He was unpredictable and never let go of an issue. He was very effective in translating excellent Dutch books into English. He organized the start of Wedge Publishing Foundation and later left his work for the Institute to build Wedge.

Development for service in western Canada. In 1972, Hultink left the Association for full-time service with Wedge. Sylvan Gerritsma became Associate Director of Development, John Horner was appointed to part-time service in development in the eastern United States, and Marcia Hollingsworth became Assistant to Executive Director John Olthuis.

Approaches to Development

In the early 1970s, money was solicited mainly by letters, an activity that grew in intensity. Regional development staff asked for donations from people they visited. In 1973, the Association advertised for a Director of Financial Planning, but none was found. In 1974, the Canadian government increased the family allowance it paid from eight dollars to twenty dollars a month, so the Association urged people with children to send part of that extra money as donations or loans for the work of the Institute. The Association was paying thirteen percent interest on a mortgage loan from the bank, so it offered to pay six percent interest on loans to help it pay off some of the high-interest mortgage. The Association also ran a campaign called Everyone One, asking each member to recruit another person to become a member. Its success was modest.

Very helpful for development work for the Association and the Institute was a determined shift around 1973 by faculty members away from aggressive criticism of Dutch Reformed churches, schools, and parachurch ministries. The new approach was to recognize that, though improvements in these groups were needed, there was much that was good and much that the Association and Institute could work with. One of the first things I did when I arrived as Executive Director in 1974 was to attend all classis meetings, that is, regional meetings of pastors and elders of Christian Reformed churches in southern Ontario, to say that there was a new emphasis at the Institute, a commitment to work with churches and to ask for their prayers and support.

The concept of professionally oriented development did not arise until 1975, when the Association invited two development consultants, Robert Fraley and Robert den Dulk, to visit the Institute separately and offer advice. In the following years, David Steen, Marcia Hollingsworth, Nick Loenen, and I each separately attended Fraley's annual workshop on development held in Tulsa, Oklahoma.

When the Association staff was reorganized in 1975, a Development Department was created. Harry Houtman was offered the position, but he decided not to take it, serving instead as Director of Business and Finance. David Steen, a graphic artist, became Director of Development. Steen served for about a year and then returned to the work of graphic arts. He was succeeded as Director of Development by Marcia Hollingsworth, who had started work for the Association in 1972 as executive assistant to John Olthuis.

The crying need for the Development Department was always to raise enough money to pay the bills. The real heroes of the Association and the Institute are the people who were doing the work of fund-raising. Those based in Toronto who took this responsibility were John Olthuis, John Hultink, Harry Houtman, David Steen, Marcia Hollingsworth, Aileen Van Ginkel, Adrianna Pierik, Harry Kits, Mike Den Haan, and John Meiboom. Those who were based in other locations were James Van Oosterom, Fred Cupido, John Horner, Sylvan Gerritsma, James Visser, Nick Loenen, Nicholas Terpstra, and Reinder Klein. Because the geographical area served by the Institute was so large, and because its ministry seemed removed from the daily experience of people, face-to-face contact was of special importance. The service of these development staff people is beyond measure.

Of special mention is the service of Marcia Hollingsworth. She served as Director of Development from January 1977 until September 1981, and she was the heart and mainstay of the administrative staff for nine years. She worked with great energy and insight and related well with everyone. In the end, she was worn out by the stress of the position. With all the bickering and differing views within the faculty, she found it hard to communicate the Institute's message positively during the years when goodwill toward the Institute and money to pay the bills were in short supply.

Outstanding service was also given by John Meiboom, who worked tirelessly from 1989 to 2007 to build a climate of appreciation for the Institute and to draw the donation income that was needed. Working with him was President Harry Fernhout, whose manner and integrity built trust and drew financial support. The value of their services cannot be overstated. In 1995, when Ross Mortimer retired from the Institute, Meiboom combined administrative leadership with development and was given the title Vice-President for Administration and Development.

Deferred Giving. In 1974, Harry Houtman began setting up a deferred giving program for the Association. From this work, he developed the idea, modelled after the Mennonite Mutual Aid Association, for an organization that would be a means for Christian people to plan their long-term stewardship of the assets God had given them and to offer them the opportunity to consider significant contributions, especially from assets, to Christian causes. Important parts of this include a Registered Retirement Savings Plan and Charitable Gift Annuity programs in which the money could be invested in churches and Christian schools.

A committee of Dutch Reformed people examined the idea, and they incorporated it as Christian Stewardship Services in 1976. Their search for a staff person led them to Houtman himself. He was somewhat embarrassed when he was appointed, but in the end, he accepted the position. The organization has flourished and has been a blessing to the Institute in many ways. Harry Vander Velde succeeded Houtman in 1977 as Director of Business and Finance for the Association.

The AACS Foundation. In 1971, some American supporters, led by Glenn Andreas, set up the AACS Foundation through which American donors could donate to the Association and the Institute and also receive income tax credit for their donations. At first, the Foundation could only send money by passing a formal motion to support specific projects, but in 1979, it became possible for the Foundation to make a "continuing grant" to the Canadian ministry. The conditions included the requirement that the Association and Institute send to the Foundation all nonconfidential materials the Association produced; in return, the Association received all minutes of Foundation Board meetings.

Western Development with Nick Loenen. Nick Loenen worked with great energy and creativeness as Development Associate in western Canada for seven years, starting in 1977. His service included fund-raising among Association members and donors; prospecting for new donors and members; working at deferred giving; providing educational services to include local initiative in organizing lectures, conferences and the like; and keeping Association staff members in Toronto informed of western Canadian needs and interests. Loenen's campus outreach included working with Christian professors and students at universities, seeing about offering Christian Perspective courses at universities, establishing good relations at Regent College and Trinity Western University, and recruiting students to the Institute.

Loenen worked in British Columbia, Alberta, and northern Washington, with a primary emphasis on the British Columbia lower mainland. He and his wife Jayne ran a book service and, in a great variety of ways, showed people in the West that the Institute could serve them and that they were valued participants in its programs. He had strengths in personal relations and was very effective in building confidence in the Association and the Institute.

Peter Steen in Pennsylvania. Peter Steen was a powerhouse for the Institute in western Pennsylvania. He worked with college and university students and was tireless in recommending that the students he met spend some time in study at the Institute. Starting in March 1979, the Institute put Steen on a retainer of $2,500 a year, plus his expenses to visit the Institute periodically. A considerable number of his students studied at the Institute in the 1970s and 1980s. When he died of cancer in 1984, the Institute set up a scholarship fund to keep before the Institute his special ministry. It was aimed especially to support students from the tristate area around Pittsburgh where he worked.

Other Development Issues. A report in December 1976 said that development had become the largest area of work at the Association, second only to the academic work of the Institute itself, with all aspects of development together costing about $100,000 a year. The Association and the Institute were small, but even a small private school is surprisingly complex. The list of necessary development activities was quite long.

By 1978, it seemed painfully clear that Association's programs had developed to a scale where it did not have the ability to draw enough money to finance them, at least not with the current effective and hardworking staff. One problem was that the Association was often trying to communicate advanced academic ideas to people who did not have the education to know what it was talking about nor to know how it affected them, their families, and their churches. Internal problems at the Institute were always a drawback. In addition, people saw that the Institute enrolment was not very large, and they wondered whether all the work and money were worth it. And the Institute was usually seen by evangelical Christians as a Dutch, Christian Reformed institution that did not affect them.

Pastor Survey and Long-Range Planning

In 1982, a survey was made of Christian Reformed pastors in Canada asking how the Institute could improve its service to the Christian community. The most common answers called for publications that were less academic and for improvement in the public image so that people would trust the Institute again. Most of the eighty-five pastors who responded said that, in general, their members seemed indifferent to the Institute.

A concern in fund-raising for the Institute was that the pool of potential donors consisted of people who supported many other Christian service organizations as well. In a sense, there was competition among Christian fund-raisers for the same dollars. In 1983, the Institute invited people from other Christian organizations to a day-long discussion of this issue at the Institute. A person from each organization was asked to identify how they undertook fund-raising and how much money they needed to raise through donations each year. There were no challenges, simply the exchange of information on an issue in which all were interested. There was an excellent spirit and such a good acceptance of each other among the Christian organizations that a decision was made to have a similar meeting a year later, which also proved to be helpful.

Also in 1982, the Board appointed a Long-Range Financial Planning Committee to (a) identify and assess the short-term and long-term financial problems of the Association and the Institute; (b) identify indicators that would enable ICS on a continuing basis to monitor its financial situation and changes in it; and (c) recommend to the Board of Trustees short-term and long-term actions to solve the financial problems, giving consideration to the possible need for structural and program changes to maintain institutional viability.

The problem was that the income of the institution was too low to maintain the services already in place. It was a matter of raising more financial support or cutting expenses. The largest cost in the institution was salaries, but the salaries of professors were already rock-bottom low and could hardly be cut very much. Programs could be cut, but cutting teaching positions seemed out of the question in so small a school.

In the end, some non-Institute programs were cut, salaries were frozen, and a plan was put in place to add to the fund-raising staff. Special solicitations were made to Christian Reformed churches, and small and rather ineffective efforts were put forth to draw more financial support from evangelical Christians. Supporters had reason to hope that the Institute could benefit from revised allocations of funds for higher education from the Christian Reformed Church. There was serious consideration that the Institute should sell its building, but that did not happen. Some years later, the Institute did enter a partnership for joint ownership of the building with a supporting friend of the Institute, which provided some financial help. Although these efforts were only moderately successful, they did permit the Institute to continue. In 1987, however, the Board of Trustees reluctantly decided to drop the Educational Services program to save some money on salaries, though it lost services that were attractive and helpful to many nonacademic people.

Ontario Summer Conferences for the Public

One of the most effective public relations efforts by the Institute was the annual summer conferences for the general public. The conferences arose from the summer conferences for students started in 1959. In later years, families came and many of them camped together. Held for many years on the Ontario August holiday weekend, the conferences featured keynote speakers, workshops, sports activities, children's programs, spirited singing, and inspiring worship. In 1970, the total attendance at the seven summer conferences held in different locations was over 1,500. In the 1980s, the Ontario conference alone drew over one thousand people each year. The conferences brought together the leaders of the Reformed Christian community. These conferences ran for over forty years.

An unforgettable address was given by Calvin Seerveld at the twentieth annual summer conference in 1977. He gave the rationale for the Institute, drawing heavily on Psalm 78 and Malachi 3. He affirmed the importance of the Institute for Christian life in the latter twentieth century. He said that the Institute dealt largely with philosophical research that did not deal with vague generalities, as many people might think. "The Institute in Toronto exists to thank God with scholarship," he said. "The Institute exists to wed an older and younger generation to scholarly praise of the Lord, and so to build up God's people. We want to get the leading ideas in academic disciplines conformed not to human traditions but to the will of God."

Summer weekend conferences for the public were also held for many years in other places like Alberta, British Columbia, and various parts of the United States. They were festive occasions focused on enhancing Christian living rooted in the vision of the Institute. They were important occasions that brought Institute supporters together for learning and worshipping activities in an outdoor social setting.

Twenty-fifth Anniversary Celebrations

In 1982, the Association celebrated the twenty-fifth anniversary of its activities to give thanks for its founding in 1957. The theme "Let's Build the House" conveyed the idea that the foundation had been laid and it was now time to build the superstructure. Biblical guides were from three texts, 1 Corinthians 3:11: "No one can lay any foundation other than the one already laid, which is in Jesus Christ"; Proverbs 24:3, "By wisdom a house is built, and through understanding it is established"; and from Psalm 127:1, "Unless the Lord builds the house, its builders labour in vain."

Hostess suppers of celebration were held in about twenty-five communities. Much attention was given to promotion in Christian Reformed churches, which had special prayers and offerings. Bert Witvoet wrote articles in *Christian Courier* (formerly called *Calvinist Contact*). Strong attention was given to attractive printed materials. Many volunteers participated in the event, and the result was that the Institute had a high profile. A wonderful three-day event was held in Toronto, culminating in a worship service on Sunday. It was a time of celebration and thanksgiving for the blessings of God.

The anniversary also included a financial drive, which brought in $330,000, less than the $500,000 goal but more than the Association had received in any previous financial appeal. More than 600 donations were given, 250 coming from British Columbia alone through the tireless efforts of Nick Loenen.

The drive was held under difficult circumstances. There was no Director of Development to lead it, since Marcia Hollingsworth had left a year earlier and a replacement had not yet been found. Canada was experiencing its worst recession for many years, and the government of Ontario had just introduced a massive change in income tax policy that cost patrons of Ontario's Christian schools dearly. In addition, two new colleges sponsored largely by Christian Reformed people, The King's University College in Edmonton and Redeemer University College in Ancaster, Ontario, were just starting up.

In 1992, the Institute celebrated its twenty-fifth anniversary as a graduate school. In addition to the gala event, the international conference described in the previous chapter, a major fund-raising campaign was set up. The goal of $2.5 million was achieved, in part because of a donation of $1 million (American). The intent of the campaign was to bolster the field of theology at Institute, which resulted in the appointment of Sylvia Keesmaat in Biblical Studies and Hermeneutics. Marcille Frederick was now able to work full-time as Librarian and Wanda Coffey Bailey full-time in Student Services and Recruitment.

In the years 1982 to 1984, Nicholas Terpstra spent two-thirds of his time as Development Associate in eastern Ontario. His aim was to bring the ministry of the Institute close to Dutch Reformed people there and especially to develop contacts and support among evangelical Christians in that area. He focused on Peterborough, Kingston, Ottawa, and Montreal. He represented the Institute at a L'Abri conference in Rochester, Minnesota; at a meeting in Ottawa of the World Alliance of Reformed Churches; and at a Presbyterian Church Congress in Toronto.

Student Recruitment

In the early years, students came to study at the Institute because they had heard about it from someone or had seen advertisements like those developed by John Hultink and Robert Carvill. In the mid-1970s, recruitment was moved from the Institute itself and became part of the Association's work of Educational Services. Recent Institute graduates recruited students and, at the same time, were leaders in the Association's campus ministry program and other educational outreach.

A problem with recruiting students was that potential sources of students were dispersed, even worldwide. Some students came from certain undergraduate colleges, but mostly students needed to contact the Institute first. On a first contact, prospective students usually identified the area they wished to study, and the response was to send information about the Institute and a list of readings in their area of interest. Correspondence usually continued for some time, sometimes with face-to-face contact, and often included direct contact with the professor in the field of interest.

Many times, a prospective student came across material about the Institute and read some books by Institute people in the field of interest. The time between a first contact and the student coming to study was frequently a period of two to three years. It proved important for students to understand the Institute's distinctive characteristics before making the decision to attend.

A factor in student recruitment is that study at the Institute basically centres on philosophy. The programs of concentration are either philosophy proper or the philosophy of a given subject, like theology, art, education, political theory, history, economics, psychology, or technology. It is a solidly academic program aimed at producing scholars, people who will reflect seriously about their work, whether or not they become a professor. There is a worldwide market of potential students, though it is not very large, from which to recruit Christian young people to use philosophy as a means to Christian thinking, living, and professional service. More recently, the Institute's program in Worldview Studies has brought students who wish to study for a year or two to develop their Christian insight on life and vocational service. In most evangelical Christian communities, though, the route to Christian thinking is through theology, not philosophy.

In its annual poster prepared for prospective students, the Institute identified itself, as in this text from 1984:

> At the Institute for Christian Studies, Toronto, we specialize in the study of the interpenetration of religion, philosophy and the special academic fields. This entails our examining questions and problems which underlie various academic disciplines and serve as points of communication among them. These basic matters pertain to the philosophy, the methodology, the general theory, and the history of the different fields of study. Put in different words, our special task is interdisciplinary, foundational studies.
>
> Our aim is to understand how a Christian perspective may help shape the categories and the framework within which academic study is undertaken. We seek a religiously integrated view of learning and of the relation of learning to life as a whole. Through interactions with important secular scholars we wish to explore the implications of a Christian view of such topics as human personality, the creation, evil and salvation, culture and society, aesthetic life, justice and stewardship.
>
> We are an inter-denominational independent Christian community working together on the basis of a shared biblically founded worldview. We provide service to scholars, students and the general Christian community by a variety of means which include sponsoring academic conferences, lecture programs, non-credit courses and publications.

The Institute faced the dilemma of wanting to educate scholars in the foundations of learning but also to serve students with Christian academic insight who were seeking other kinds of professional work. To do this with such an extremely small faculty seemed out of the question. It led Hendrik Hart to offer his one-year Worldview Studies program, and later the Institute set up a Christian Worldview program with Brian Walsh that led to a Master of Worldview Studies degree that was approved by the Ontario legislature. That program was highly successful, and when Walsh left the Institute in 1994, Carroll Guen Hart took it over.

In 1976, Tom Malcolm reported that the mood of college and university students had swung remarkably away from the earlier countercultural outlook. Most of them, he said ". . . have given up on any fundamental critique of the positivistic view of science they are getting in the classroom, the view which believes that dismantling the creation and reconstructing it according to scientific models is the beginning of all wisdom." Students are very pragmatic, wanting education to get a job. Many university students, he said, are committed to specialism, expert knowledge of a small corner of reality.

An interesting and surprising fact of student recruitment is that the Institute has always drawn a considerable portion of its students from overseas, from people of cultures very different from that of Canada. In the early years, students came from Lebanon and Cyprus, and others soon followed from Japan, Australia, New Zealand, Europe, Africa, and parts of Asia. They were attracted by the Institute's Christian philosophical approach and its critique of secular society. Many needed financial assistance, and the Institute provided special grants that helped meet their needs.

Attractiveness to Other Church Communities

In 1987, a planning committee appointed by the Board reported on possibilities for Institute support from various church groups in Canada. The conclusions were not hopeful. The report of the committee said that the Christians nearest to the Institute in theology and worldview were identified as Irish Protestants in Ontario, in comparison with whom ". . . there is no more conservative or defensive constituency." The committee noted that "In Atlantic Canada the evangelical community is either highly revivalistic or highly traditional, and in either case intensely regional. It would be very difficult for such a constituency to comprehend what the Institute is trying to do. On the Prairies an extreme pietism of ethnic continental European origin predominates, and it would be difficult to imagine anything with an agenda further from the Institute."

The report also stated: "Liberal Protestantism with a Social Gospel lineage finds the theological presuppositions of the Institute unacceptable and intolerable. . . . Mainstream Protestantism does not sympathize with the alternate structural approach of the Institute. It does appreciate Institute intelligence and may write well-meaning letters of support, but it cannot commit itself to the Institute either theologically or culturally. . . . There is, however, a new evangelical mainstream emerging across Canada which may have some openness because it senses some responsibility for Canadian society and may be open to the deeper cultural issues that the Institute is addressing. This includes the Mennonite Brethren and the Pentecostal Assemblies of Canada."

The report said that grassroots Baptists throughout Canada could be quite sympathetic. Its most positive assessment for relations with the Institute was considered to be the burgeoning Chinese Christian population. The report said that "The new ethnic Christian Chinese communities might have the greatest possibility. They include intelligent, thoughtful and well-educated Christians who are able to comprehend what the Institute is all about. Their congregations are filled with successful entrepreneurs and professionals. These communities might well be the leaders of Ontario Christianity in the next generation."

A strength of the Institute is that it fosters an ethos of open debate and is prepared to scrutinize and challenge cherished Christian assumptions in pursuit of the goal of allowing biblical wisdom to guide Christian academic activity. But a major problem and weakness of the Institute is its difficulty in winning trust and recruiting more students from the wider evangelical world, which is by far its largest potential market. Another problem is that all Christians have limits to which ideas they are prepared to see fundamentally questioned, and a large number of evangelical Christians operate with a different range of limits than those of the Institute.

While there is a growing recognition in the evangelical world of the need for integrated Christian scholarship, and an increasing respect in some evangelical and Reformed circles for the quality of Institute work, this does not produce very many students from Canadian evangelical communities, nor does it provide much money for the Institute. One problem may be that the Institute is identified with a particular theological and philosophical tradition (reformational, Dooyeweerdian, etc.) which is seen by many evangelicals as dubiously founded, parochial, and even eccentric. Regent College, for example, has a breadth of trust among evangelicals that the Institute does not have. It is true that some evangelical Christian academics do deal seriously with difficult questions. But new promotional strategies will not change the perceptions of most evangelical Christians about the Institute very much.

14

Finances

One way to understand that the Institute is a ministry approved by God is to know that it has always been able to pay its bills. As a faith ministry, the Institute has all the financial problems that other faith ministries have. In addition, a person who takes a calm and rational look at what the Institute has set out to do will be astonished that it has always paid its bills and still exists.

The Institute founders did not realize that you cannot finance an independent graduate school from the small donations of God's people. They did know, however, that small, faithful acts could be blessed. A moving example of this was the Penny-A-Day Banks set up by devoted women who wanted to do their part, small though it might be. Further, the founders did not know that independent schools of higher education, not controlled and financed by governments, had no room for existence in the British system of higher education that Canada adopted.

Yet the Institute for Christian Studies has existed for some decades. And the strange truth is that, for most of the years of its existence, the Institute's expenses have been greater than its income.

How has that been possible? This chapter shows how it happened, though the financial details are condensed.

The Beginning

In the 1960s, the Association's costs were low, largely limited to the half-time salary of an Executive Director plus secretarial staff. A big financial moment came in 1967 with the purchase of the large house at 141 Lyndhurst Avenue to accommodate the Institute, plus the expectation of the coming full-time salaries of faculty members. A campaign was set up to raise $100,000 for the purchase and renovation of the building. Enough money was raised for the downpayment, but two efforts to raise the money for that shows how difficult a task it was and how inexperienced the staff was with fund-raising.

With great faith, the Board's treasurer Jan de Koning stated in 1969, "The Lord provides." The Lord did provide, but just barely. In 1963, the income of $10,666 slightly exceeded expenses, and in 1966, the income of $34,465 was also enough. In the year 1967, income was $36,010 and expenses $40,460. For the year ending August 31, 1969, income was reported to be $72,832 and expenses were $81,917. For the year ending August 31, 1970, income rose to $112,500 but expenses were again a bit higher at $129,700.

Various means were tried to raise money. For example, the Association had a Publication Fund from which it drew money for the production costs of the books it published. In 1968, six of its books needed to be reprinted and six more new books were ready to be published, but the cupboard was bare. Urgent requests for the books were coming from friends in Canada, but also from distant places like Korea, Argentina, Japan, and Switzerland. A mail campaign tried to raise $20,000 for the Publication Fund, but little money was received.

Property Ownership

The Association paid $83,000 for its building on Lyndhurst Avenue, and the equity from its sale in 1972 helped provide an initial payment for its $550,000 purchase of the six-storey building at 229 College Street. The purchase of this large building was the means God used to enable the Association to pay its bills long into the future.

A special friend of the Institute pledged to pay over a period of some years half of the money needed to buy the building, which was an enormous blessing. The seller of the building, the International Order of Odd Fellows, took back a second mortgage of $300,000, and the bank provided the rest. The market value of the building rose dramatically, so that seventeen years later it could have been sold for $5.5 million. In the 1970s and early 1980s, the Association's expenses were greater than its income each year by amounts between $20,000 and $50,000 each year. The solution was to borrow money against the increased equity of the building. Much of the money was borrowed from friends of the Association, who, in 1974, for instance, were receiving eight percent interest from the Association while the bank's mortgage rate was eleven and a half percent. This was an unstable situation, of course, and in the mid-1980s the Institute had a very high equity in the building but also very high liabilities because of its borrowing.

When the Association bought the building, most of its space was rented. The Association used one floor of the building, with the Toronto

Public Library renting most of the rest of the building, using the space as an annex to its main building across the street. But the city had decided to build a new library building, so the Association knew that in a few years the library would be moving out. When this happened in 1977, the Association lost about $100,000 a year in rent, and it needed another $100,000 to refit the building for other tenants. Rental rates were rising rapidly, so the prospects were good.

Shortly after the library moved out, the Association was approached by Cosmopolitan College to rent a small amount of space. This college was a private high school operated by Chinese people who prepared students from China for entry to university. The college grew steadily; in a few years, it occupied nearly half of the available rental space, which was a great help to the Association. Later, its enrolment gradually declined and it was using less space. In the winter of 1985, the Institute staff arrived for work one Monday morning to find that the college had simply disappeared, having moved out over the weekend. It was never seen or heard from after that. It also owed the Association $35,000 rent, which was never recovered.

By the summer of 1979, all the available space in the building was rented again, thanks to the excellent services of Harry Vander Velde in making arrangements with tenants. But the Institute continued to have such great financial problems that, in 1985, the Board of Trustees stated that it was ready to mortgage the building to the highest possible amount so that the bills could be paid. It was also ready to sell the building, having received an offer of $2.7 million. But the Property and Finance Committee argued that selling the building would not solve the Institute's long-term financial problems. During the last six months of 1986, the building provided the Institute a net income of $8,400 plus its own free use of space, but its debt against the building was $977,000.

In June 1988, the Board decided to sell a partnership in the building to a group of Institute supporters for $3.5 million, with the Institute as the major partner. Later, it became clear that the building needed major retrofitting, especially to improve the antiquated heating, plumbing, and electrical services. The leases of nearly all the tenants were not renewed, and the building was virtually gutted. New tenants were readily found at increased rental rates, though the net income from tenants was less than expected. In 1989, the Institute was paying $6,000 a month to the partnership due to a decrease in equity in the building.

On June 30, 1988, the auditor reported that the Institute had liabilities of $1,208,500. Income from selling the building was allocated as follows: $1,250,000 paid for loans and mortgages that had been secured by the building, $100,000 deposited with Christian Stewardship Services, and the rest distributed at the Bank of Montreal, DUCA Credit Union, and the building partnership. The interest received from the financial institutions varied between ten and twelve and three-quarters percent in this time of high interest rates.

In 1990, the Institute's building was sold by the partners at a higher price, this time with equity of seventy-three percent going to one person who was a supporter of the Institute. Seven percent was retained by another supporter, with twenty percent being held by the Institute, which also received a fifty percent voting share in the partnership.

Benefits

The Board considered the prospect of its valued staff living in poverty after retirement to be unconscionable. So in 1975, the Association set up a matching retirement program for its long-term staff consisting of five percent of gross salary payments, matched by an equal payment from the Association in a Registered Retirement Savings Plan.

At the same time, the staff and Board clearly recognized that new appointments to the faculty would be limited to persons at or near the start of their careers because salaries were low and top Institute salaries were not competitive with those offered at other colleges and universities. In those years, the faculty insisted that its salaries be kept low to fit the Institute's financial capabilities and that, as Hendrik Hart stated later, ". . . a salary the faculty would have would not wake you up at night with either guilt or worry."

In 1975, the Board saw that the cost of buying a house was quite high in Toronto and rising with high inflation, which would make it difficult for new professors to buy a house. So it adopted the policy that if a staff member purchased the house in which he or she lived, the Association would pay half the amount by which the costs of principal and interest of the mortgage exceeded twenty percent of the person's gross salary. In doing this, the Board accepted studies made in Toronto that if housing costs exceeded twenty percent of income, especially if the income were not very high, the family carried an untoward financial burden. By paying only half of the amount above twenty percent, however, it was felt that the staff member would be deterred from buying a highly expensive house.

Annual Pluses and Minuses

In 1973, John Olthuis reported that, in the five years from 1967 to 1972, the staff increased from three people to thirteen and the budget increased from $26,000 a year to $250,000. He said that a great deal had been achieved in those years, but that some mistakes had been made and some misunderstandings provoked a climate of suspicion. The Institute had introduced some new ideas for which the potential supporting community was not ready, and trust had not developed.

In the 1970s, there were 1,700 to 1,800 donors, most of whom were members of the Association. Annual yearly donations increased from $130,000 in 1973 to $274,000 in 1978. During the same years, contributions from Christian Reformed churches increased from $8,500 in 1973 to $18,000 in 1977, with a big jump to $46,200 in 1978. By 1981, the total donation income for the Association was about $250,000, about the same as it was four years earlier, in spite of high inflation in Canada.

In July 1977, I made the following observation to the Board, faculty, and staff as part of a proposed program for the coming year:

> In our planning and budgeting for 1978, we will certainly need to deal effectively with a financial situation which has almost gotten out of hand. The rate at which we are spending money is appreciably higher than the rate at which we are receiving it or have reasonable hopes of receiving it. Precisely what the extent of changes in present operations will need to be for 1978 in order to deal effectively with this situation is not entirely clear at this point. They will become more clear as we work with the numbers which need to follow this verbal plan. In order to pay our bills and salaries currently we are borrowing a substantial amount of money, and our planning for 1978 and beyond will need also to deal with the matter of the rate of repayment of this borrowing together with other long-term indebtedness.

The Association finances were in desperate shape. It depended too heavily on rather modest donations from a wide range of people. It had no financial reserves, so it depended each year on the income received that year. In 1977, the faculty offered to take a salary cut of twenty-five percent.

In 1978, finances were so tight that faculty salaries were temporarily reduced, contributions to the matching retirement program were cancelled for six months, and payments to the Curriculum Development Centre were reduced. There were now nine faculty members, and it was almost impossible to provide for that large a faculty.

A University for the People

In 1979, the Association developed deferred giving programs with Harry Houtman at Christian Stewardship Services, but significant income from that source was slow in developing because many people felt unsure about the long-term prospects of the Institute.

The Association received nearly all of its income through the mail, so it was a minor disaster when the Canadian postal system went on strike for six weeks in the summer of 1981. The Association needed to borrow $40,000 from the bank on a short-term basis to pay its bills at a time when the annual interest rate was close to twenty-five percent.

The year 1982 brought new major financial problems, so the Institute and senior administrative staff agreed to accept a fifteen percent cut in salaries. One problem was that the Association was paying seventeen percent interest on one loan, which was considered a favourable rate negotiated with the help of Wietse Posthumus, and it paid a below-market rate of thirteen percent on a loan from the Christian Reformed Church Extension Fund.

Once you have met **Wietse Posthumus**, you will never forget him. He's an unrepentant Frisian who never considered Anglicizing his first name. The front of his house declares that this domicile is *Ú's Honk*—Frisian for "Our Home." Wietse has an innate desire to be the devil's advocate. If you think 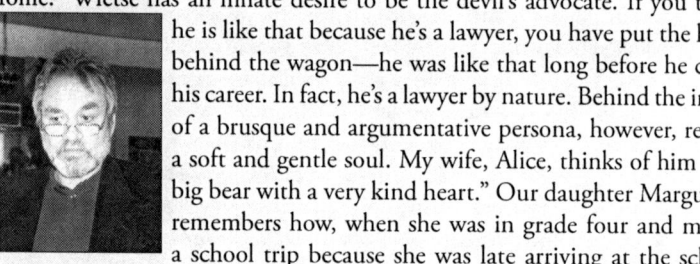 he is like that because he's a lawyer, you have put the horse behind the wagon—he was like that long before he chose his career. In fact, he's a lawyer by nature. Behind the image of a brusque and argumentative persona, however, resides a soft and gentle soul. My wife, Alice, thinks of him as "a big bear with a very kind heart." Our daughter Marguerite remembers how, when she was in grade four and missed a school trip because she was late arriving at the school, Wietse drove her all the way to the Science Centre. You can't have a better friend when you're in need. But you have to be brutally honest with him.

Wietse married fellow Calvin College student Kathryn Joustra from Paterson, New Jersey, more than forty years ago, probably because she is also from Frisian stock and can stand up to him. The two make for a most interesting couple. Their sizable house in Toronto is a coffee-kletz and party haven for all kinds of artists, professionals, and derelicts.

Wietse has served the Christian Reformed Church in Canada as its legal advisor; he has been an elder in Toronto's First Christian Reformed Church; and he has been a member of the Institute's Board of Trustees and Executive Committee for many years. But the thing he loves most is challenging aspects of the faith that he adheres to. Just because theologians have said this or that for centuries does not mean it's gospel truth. Authenticity is pretty high up on the list of characteristics that Wietse prizes.

—Bert Witvoet

In 1982, the Board appointed a Task Force to study the continued financial problems of the Association. It was running deficits each year and ways needed to be found to turn that around. At the committee's recommendation, the Board cut staff support services in some programs, cut faculty salaries twenty-five percent, and froze other salaries. A plan was put into place to add to the fund-raising staff. Special solicitations were made to Christian Reformed churches, and small and rather ineffective efforts were made to draw more financial support from evangelical Christians. There was serious talk of selling the Institute's building.

The Institute was paying twelve percent interest to its members for loans, instead of paying higher rates for borrowing from commercial loan makers. The annual rate of inflation in 1982 was around eighteen percent. This meant that donation income needed to increase at eighteen percent just to maintain programs. The next year, staff salaries were not increased, which in effect was a decrease in salary given the high inflation rate.

In 1986, the Institute had 805 members whose membership dues were paid up and 732 who were somewhat behind in the payment of dues. There were also 641 donors who were not members. In 1993, President Fernhout reported that about 1,500 individuals and families made donations to the Institute each year, some of quite small amounts and some of very large amounts. The trend over the years had been for the Institute to have a smaller number of donors each year but for the average size of donation to increase.

In 1989, John Meiboom became Director of Development, succeeding Adriana Pierik. In 1995, he said that development problems for the Institute included decreasing numbers of Institute members, aging constituency, minimal growth of donations apart from large donations, difficulty in getting support outside the Reformed Christian community, and need for greater visibility in the constituency. In the same year, Fernhout noted that, for most of its history, the Institute has lived on the edge of a financial abyss. In addition to emergency salary cuts, in some years, it was not unusual for staff to be told not to cash their paycheques for a few days or weeks. When Clifford Pitt became president, he was deeply worried that the Institute did not have sufficient assets to cover its many debts, especially to repay loans from Institute members.

In 1989–1990, the deficit for the year was $102,300, and the next year it was $82,000. The deficit for 1992–1993 was $213,000. Because of this annual problem of deficits, the Board of Trustees decided to approach donors to the 1992 Anniversary Financial Campaign to ask them if the Institute could use some of the money they donated in order to pay current bills instead of using it all for special projects, and this was accepted. It had become clear that annual donations to the Institute were no longer able to pay the costs of operating the Institute.

At that time, too, Canada experienced a significant financial depression so that real estate values had dropped considerably. Tenants in the Institute building had difficulty paying their rents. The result was serious losses in the value of the Institute building partnership so that it could no longer collect the mortgage of $1.4 million owed to the Institute when the partnership later sold the building. Necessary expenditures grew to the point that, for the year 2002–2003, the Institute's annual budget for expenditures stood at $1.35 million.

Capital Campaigns

In the 1990s, the Institute badly needed money for new programs and ways to give a firmer financial foundation for vital activities that could not be supported from annual giving. So the Institute began making special appeals for capital funds projects for which donations would be pledged for five years. These appeals asked for reasonable, even modest, sums of money and were a great help in stabilizing ICS finances. For example, in 2004, under the name of "reGeneration! The Campaign for ICS," the goal was $5 million, which covered these projects: $3 million for endowed faculty chairs, $1 million for scholarship funds for students, $600,000 for distributed learning to send ICS courses overseas on the Internet, and $400,00 for a Faith and Learning Network of written materials that address the role of Christian faith in learning to be made available on the Internet. These special appeals have drawn funds not otherwise available to the Institute and provided fresh ways to develop the Institute's service.

15

Accreditation and Relations with Other Schools

It is not possible just to start a new college or university in Canada and give courses and degrees in the same way as can be done in the United States. For one thing, the government needs to know that real education takes place so that the credits and degrees given are not a fraud. Other colleges and universities want to know that the academic work is as good as what they offer or else they will not accept credit from students nor recognize degrees.

In its earliest years, the Institute offered instruction but not regular courses for which students received academic credit. But as the instruction became more organized and students wanted course credits, it was necessary for the Institute to receive official status.

In Ontario, the provincial government keeps a tight hold on higher education. There are two ways for a school offering postsecondary liberal arts education to be officially recognized. One is to have the provincial Legislature pass a bill that grants a charter to operate. The other is to become affiliated with a university that already has its charter from the Legislature, under arrangements in which the university grants the degree and oversees the program of the affiliated institution.

The Quest to Grant Degrees

John Olthuis started seeking public recognition in 1973. As a lawyer, he first made inquiries at the Legislature about steps to obtain a charter, and he also learned what was involved in becoming affiliated with a university. The charter route seemed more attractive because it would give the Institute the most independence and flexibility. In 1974, he prepared a draft charter for action by the Ontario Legislature, but it was never acted on.

In February 1975, Olthuis and I arranged a visit with the Minister of Colleges and Universities, James Auld. He told us that it would not be possible for the Institute to receive a charter and that the only way for new institutions to start was by affiliation with one of Ontario's fifteen chartered universities. He did not tell us that in the early 1970s the Ontario government had promised its universities that it would not give out any more degree-granting charters. He did say that he could help us with gaining affiliation if we wished.

Possible Affiliations

After this meeting, I wrote to eight of the Ontario universities nearest us, and I visited and talked with the presidents of five of these universities. Each answer was a polite "not interested." One of the complications was that the government had placed a moratorium on the start of new graduate study programs. If a university affiliated with the Institute, the Institute's graduate programs would become part of the university's course offerings, which the government would not permit. The University of Toronto, for example, sent a letter from vice-president J. H. Sword saying that even if the university wanted to affiliate with the Institute, the government would not permit it because of its moratorium on new courses.

The Institute reported to the Ministry that its efforts to gain affiliation met only negative response, and the Ministry again said that it would help. Some weeks later, the Institute received a phone call from the Ministry saying that the University of Waterloo, which already had four affiliated undergraduate Christian colleges, would be glad to talk with Institute representatives. So Bernard Zylstra and I made an appointment at which Waterloo's President Burt Matthews did nothing but lecture us on why Institute affiliation with the university was impossible.

In February 1975, Institute representatives met with professor G. A. B. Wilson, a key person in the University of Toronto's Graduate Centre for Religious Studies. Because it was so new, the Centre was not in a position to undertake affiliation, but Wilson alerted the Institute that at universities the study of religion is not considered to be academically sound. It was believed that religious studies dealt with devotion and faith, which could not be considered academic matters. Consequently Religious Studies were required to be taught in a completely secular, noncommitted way, certainly not from a committed Christian viewpoint. He said that the feeling was that studies that were religious were nonacademic, and academic studies were not religious.

In addition, University of Toronto professors of higher education E. E. Sheffield and Robin S. Harris told the Institute that a graduate school would be harder to affiliate with a university than an undergraduate institution. A reason they gave is that students of an affiliated college normally take just one or two courses a year at the college and the rest from the broader offerings of the university. That, of course, would not suit the Institute.

The Institute contacted the American Association of Theological Schools to see whether accreditation by this body would be of help. An official of the organization visited the Institute while he was in Toronto for another meeting. But he said that the organization could not grant professional accreditation to the Institute because the association required its members to have a program to train pastors, which the Institute did not have.

The Institute did have a cordial reception from Brock University in St. Catharines. The initial contact was by Albert Wolters with philosophy professor John Nota, a Dutch Jesuit. Institute people met with the head of the philosophy department John Mayer and with President Alan Earp, both of whom looked favourably on affiliation with the Institute. A factor in the Institute's favour was that the philosophy department at Brock was strongly committed to phenomenological philosophy rather than to philosophy oriented to logical positivism. However, Brock did not offer doctoral degrees in philosophy and the Institute would need to move to the Brock campus in St. Catharines to become affiliated, so this approach was abandoned.

In 1977, James Olthuis and I met with Dr. John Meagher of the graduate Institute for Christian Thought at St. Michael's University of the University of Toronto, who suggested that we try to affiliate with the Toronto School of Theology rather than with the Institute for Christian Thought at St. Michael's. We had received that advice also from University of Toronto President John Evans, who said that the university had so many affiliated and associated colleges and institutes that it would not be willing to add more to the university's complexity. The Toronto School of Theology had recently been formed by the theological colleges affiliated with the university. TST's initial relationship with the university was not very secure, and the Institute was not welcomed by TST because it did not have a charter.

In the late 1970s, when he was chair of the Institute faculty, Thomas McIntire met with a considerable number of University of Toronto officials and professors, many of whom were theologians. They told him that they considered the Institute to be academically very strong, but also very small and isolated from the academic world. Some said that a weakness was that it did not have on its faculty a biblical scholar, someone qualified in Old or New Testament theology, to anchor its emphasis on biblical foundations.

In 1982, the Institute tried again to become part of the Toronto School of Theology. In July of that year, Iain G. Nicol, Director of TST, wrote a letter to Thomas McIntire reporting that the heads of its member colleges discussed at some length the Institute's overture to closer relations, and possibly membership in TST. He summarized the results of their discussion as follows:

> 1. We had some difficulty in defining the "philosophical" position of ICS and it was generally felt that the basic problem lies at this level. The ICS Bulletin refers to the fact that the overall program of the Institute is philosophical rather than religious or theological, yet some would question whether it is philosophical in any generally accepted sense.
> 2. Your letter also refers to the aim of undertaking to ". . . promote scripturally directed learning." In this connection it was pointed out that the Institute does not have a faculty member whose competence is in the biblical field.

The Institute also met with Dr. Stephan Dupré, chair of the Ontario Council on University Affairs. This body had been newly chartered by the Ontario government to advise it on university matters. He advised the Institute to try to relate with the Pontifical Institute for Medieval Studies at the University of Toronto, which was similar to the Institute in some ways, but this proved unworkable.

An Unrecognized Degree. In March 1975, James Olthuis and I went to see the Minister of Colleges and Universities, who was now Harry Parrott, to report that affiliation was a dead end. At the meeting, the top two deputies in the Ministry were also present. There appeared to be an impasse: affiliation could not work, and the government refused to grant a charter. Then Parrott said that there seemed to be no reason why we could not give the degree that we wanted, though the degree would be recognized only by those who chose to recognize it. He asked his deputies if that were not true, and they both nodded their assent, though that must have been done with gritted teeth. Parrott and his deputy ministers admitted freely, if with some chagrin, that the university system was monolithic and new schools needed to fit their system.

It seemed strange to the Institute that it could give a degree with no legal hindrance. John Olthuis checked with lawyers and they could find no law forbidding it. Professor Delwin McCormack Smyth of York University told us that a very high official in the Ministry of College and Universities had written a doctoral dissertation in which he stated that there was no law forbidding a new freestanding college or university from granting degrees, but it was common practice, a sort of gentleman's agreement, that this would not be done. The Institute checked and found that to be true.

The Institute had nowhere else to go. So in 1975 it granted its first Master of Philosophy degrees. In April 1976, I wrote to the Minister of Higher Education that the Institute had started to offer the degree called Master of Philosophy. But that seriously upset the Ministry. We promptly received a letter from the Minister's office saying, "Without Legislative authority, the Institute has no power to grant degrees. Therefore, if the Institute persists in conferring degrees without any express power to do so, the Ministry will be forced to take appropriate measures to prevent the Institute from continuing such practice."

Knowing that the Institute had the law on its side, it was not intimidated. From 1975 to 1983, it continued to give the Master of Philosophy degree. During those years, Institute representatives met with a considerable number of University of Toronto administrators, but there seemed to be no way the Institute could affiliate with the university. The administrators were rather impressed by the Institute, so the contacts were useful in opening their eyes that some good graduate education was taking place independently across the street from the university. Those contacts, plus the fact that university professors were now invited to take part in nearly all of the oral examinations of Institute students applying for the master's degree, led many university professors to have a favourable impression of the Institute.

In 1982, the Institute tried to get the government to grant it a charter that would allow it "to grant the degrees of Master of Arts and Master of Philosophy in foundational, philosophical studies in the arts, humanities and sciences," but the government did not accept that request.

Evaluations. In January 1976, Dr. H. H. Yates, executive vice-chairman of the Ontario Council of Graduate Studies, wrote the Institute agreeing to help set up an outside evaluation of Institute work. The Institute accepted the offer, but the help never came through.

Also in January 1976, the Institute contacted the Council of Ontario Universities, a body formed by Ontario universities to present their requests with a united voice to the Ministry of Higher Education.

This council, which sent teams to university academic departments to assess their strengths, offered to help the Institute with this. In the end, however, they said that they were limited to assessing individual graduate department programs only, not to broader institutional evaluation, which it seemed to them to be what the Institute was seeking and needing. The fact that the Institute was dealing with the question of whether it constituted several academic departments or was really a single "department" of foundational and interdisciplinary studies of various areas did not permit the Council to be of help.

The Institute knew that positive assessments would be a great asset as it sought public academic recognition, but the Council could not provide that because the Institute was outside of the university system. This led the Institute to set up a number of academic evaluations by recognized scholars between 1979 and 1981. These included overall evaluations of the Institute as a school by Abraham Rotstein of the University of Toronto, J. William Kamphuis of Queen's University, and Nicholas Wolterstorff of Yale University. David Jeffries of the University of Ottawa and Francis Sparshott of the University of Toronto evaluated the Institute's work in aesthetics; Michael Sheehan of the University of Toronto (St. Michael's University) and Robert Swierenga of Kent State University evaluated the work in history; Mary Vander Goot of Calvin College and Donald Moncrieff of Christian Counselling Services evaluated psychology; Oliver O'Donovan of the University of Toronto (Wycliffe College) evaluated theology; and Joan Lockwood of the University of Toronto evaluated the work in political theory. Each of these examinations was done separately, and each examiner gave a detailed and favourable written report.

Other Orphan Colleges and Universities in Toronto

In 1977, James Olthuis and I visited George Korey, who at the time was academic vice-president of Ryerson University in downtown Toronto. Korey had bypassed the Ontario government to obtain a charter from the federal government for his own school, Northland Open University, which would offer instruction in the Yukon and Northwest Territories. Korey was wily enough to have added to the federal charter that its instruction could also be offered ". . . elsewhere in Canada." So he rented rooms in the building of the Ontario Institute for Studies in Education in downtown Toronto and began to offer courses in evenings and weekends. This instruction continued until 1983 when the government passed a bill that closed the school.

A Christian institution offering degrees was Richmond College, located in Toronto. Its president, Rev. Elmer McVety, had received a charter to start a college in Manitoba, on the basis of which he set up his college in Toronto. The Ontario government could not stop this any more than it could stop the Institute's granting of a master's degree. The college continues because in 1983 the Legislature's bill closing all post-secondary schools without a charter made an exemption for explicitly religious schools.

Knowing that non-chartered institutions of higher education in Canada could not be accredited, Korey tried to set up a Canadian Association of Independent Universities, Colleges and Institutes to act as an accrediting agency outside of the government. He tried to get membership from across Canada, and the Institute considered participation but in the end decided against it. The organization was never set up.

In addition to the initiatives of Korey and McVety, some American degree mills, which offered degrees for a fee but with little or no requirement of academic study, were moving into Ontario because they found that Ontario law did not require that they have a charter.

The Granting of Degrees

The Ontario government saw a loophole in its laws forbidding the operation of unauthorized schools of higher education, so it felt the need to act. In 1980, the government introduced to the Legislature a bill to shut down all postsecondary schools that did not have a charter from the Ontario government. It was known as Bill 4 and had the title "An act to regulate the granting of degrees." The bill stated that

> No person shall directly or indirectly (a) operate or maintain a university; (b) use or be known by a name of a university or any derivation or abbreviation thereof; (c) hold himself out to be a university; (d) make use of, in any advertising relating to an educational institution, the word university or any derivation or abbreviation thereof, unless the person (e) is by a special Act of the Assembly incorporated as a university; (f) on the day this Act comes into force, is a person who has by a special Act of the Assembly been incorporated as a university or has by a special Act of the Assembly been confirmed as a university; (g) is a university established in Canada and listed in the Schedule; or (h) is a university established outside Canada and has the written consent of the Minister.

It added that postsecondary course credit and degrees could only be given by an institution that had a charter from the Legislature, and then it laid out all the steps required to apply for the charter. What it did not say was that the government had decided earlier it would not grant any new charters. The bill showed a road going nowhere.

This bill clearly would have closed down the Institute. The Legislature considered this bill to be of little public interest, so it wanted to fast-track its passage without having a committee hearing, in contrast to the usual procedure for significant legislation. The Institute, hearing of this, quickly alerted its Ontario supporters, who flooded their legislators with complaints, and a committee hearing was scheduled. Then the Ministry of Higher Education learned that the way the bill had been written, all Bible colleges and seminaries would need to close, too, so the bill was modified so that it would not apply to those institutions. The government hoped that this change would satisfy the Institute, but it did not.

The legislators received such a barrage of objections to the bill from supporters of the Institute and others that the bill was put on the back burner and was allowed to die when the next election was called. In the meantime, about fifty highly recognized scholars wrote to the Ministry of Higher Education of their very high regard for the Institute, urging that it not be closed. It became clear to the government that it would be politically dangerous to close the Institute.

The bill was reintroduced to the new Legislature as Bill 137. The Minister of Colleges and Universities, Dr. Bette Stephensen, invited the Institute to meet with her to find a way to protect the Institute. The Minister wanted the Institute to accept the degree designation of Master of Christian Studies, which, she said, would fit well with its name, the Institute for Christian Studies. The Ministry wanted a degree that showed in its title that it was based on study that was specifically religious. That was the way that the government gave special room to seminaries and Bible colleges, which then could not then be mistaken as being part of the government-sanctioned secular university system.

But the Institute refused, knowing that such a degree would identify the Institute as a religious school like a seminary or Bible college. It carefully explained to the Minister that Institute instruction was in subjects like history, philosophy, education, aesthetics, economics, political theory, and theology, in all of which education was informed by the revelation of God in the Bible. It insisted that a general university education was offered, not Bible studies. The education was undertaken in an interdisciplinary and foundational way undergirded by philosophy. Finally, a compromise was reached. The degree would be the Master of Philosophical Foundations. The Institute saw that this degree designation, awkward though it was, would safeguard its academic standing and accurately express what kind of education it offered. Presumably, the government was satisfied that at least no university would grant a degree with such a strange title. The bill was finally passed by the Legislature on October 25, 1983.

The Institute charter stated that the objects and purposes of the Institute were:

> (a) to operate and maintain an institution for post-secondary education and research in all areas of learning based on the Scriptures of the Old and New Testaments and consistent with the Basis and Educational Creed of the Institute.
> (b) to advance scholarship in all areas of learning so as to exhibit the coherence of all reality in Christ and in this way equip people to direct their lives by the Gospel; and
> (c) to sponsor at other institutions lectureships, courses, teaching programs and research projects.

The Institute for Christian Studies Act is different from other university charters in that it permits two members of the Board of Trustees to be American citizens living in the United States, since the Institute receives significant support from Americans. Ontario's standard practice is to restrict university Board membership to Canadian citizens.

After it had given a charter to the Institute, the Legislature of Ontario in late 1983 passed Bill 41, titled "An act to regulate the granting of degrees," which included these words:

> No person shall directly or indirectly,
> (a) grant a degree;
> (b) provide a program of post-secondary study offered in Ontario leading to a degree to be conferred by a person in or outside Ontario;
> (c) advertise a program of post-secondary study offered in Ontario; or
> (d) sell, offer for sale, or provide by agreement for a fee, reward or other remuneration, a diploma, certificate, document or other material that is, or indicates or implies the granting or conferring of, a degree,
> unless the person,
> (e) is by an Act of the Assembly authorized to grant the degree; or
> (f) is a degree granting institution established outside Ontario and has the written consent of the Minister.

When the Institute received its charter, a reorganization of its structure was needed. The Association ceased to exist. A Senate replaced the Board of Curators, and Senate membership included some Institute faculty members and one or two of its graduate students. The responsibilities of the Board of Trustees remained much as they had been earlier.

The earlier dual structure of the Association and the Institute had brought its own problems. But all the things that the Association had been doing outside the Institute were really activities that were properly part of a university. Fund-raising, student recruitment, financial aid, educational services to the general public outside of degree work—all these and more are regularly done by universities. The new structure simplified and made clear the responsibilities within the organization, and the Institute experienced some relief with the formation of the new unitary structure.

In 1993, the Institute received a modification in its charter permitting it to offer the degree of Master of Worldview Studies. It was publicly stated that the program ". . . is designed to help professionals develop a Christian approach to their vocations so that their relationship with God is not only personally engaging but culturally relevant as well. The program is directed to people in various professions who already have an undergraduate degree but want to develop their Christian perspective in their work."

In 2005, the Ontario government passed legislation permitting the Institute to offer the Master of Arts (Philosophy) and the Ph.D., as described in Chapter 17.

Institutional Relations

Though the Institute was not able to form supportive working relations with churches other than the Christian Reformed Church, it did have mutually supportive relations with universities and other educational institutions. Its roots were in the Netherlands, of course, so these relations included reformational Christians and their organizations in Holland. Its connections with the Free University were most evident in that university's readiness to support the Institute's educational program and especially its Ph.D.

Also of importance in the Netherlands was the Association for Calvinistic Philosophy, which had a very similar Christian educational vision to that of the Institute. Its basis states that

> The Association, convinced that all philosophy is religiously determined by its point of departure, direction and elaboration, and that

therefore neutrality in this area is precluded, confesses the Christ of Scriptures, the Redeemer of our entire life, to be also the new Root of theoretic thought. Accordingly, it desires to pursue philosophy solely by the light of Scripture . . . while repudiating every synthesis with any thought which does not place itself under the direct sovereignty of God over all created reality, fails to acknowledge his law as the boundary between the Creator and his cosmos subject to this ordinance, and rejects the kingship of Christ over scholarship. The purpose of the Association is to pursue and stimulate philosophical study and discussion and to make such study and discussion fruitful for practical life."

Clearly, this would resonate with the founders of the Institute.

The Institute is nearly the only independent graduate school in North America that is not structurally part of undergraduate education offering one or more bachelor's degrees. In the second half of the twentieth century, two other Christian academic institutions began offering instruction only at the graduate level, and they continue to the present. One is Regent College in Vancouver, set up to offer advanced education as an alternative to seminary education for people who want Christian postsecondary education to help them serve in their chosen vocation in deeper Christian ways. Regent eventually found that it would gain greater stability and have a greater outreach by adding seminary education. It is also blessed by some funding from the government of British Columbia.

The other freestanding graduate school is Regent University, established in Virginia Beach, Virginia. It was founded by the Christian television broadcaster Pat Robertson, and Regent University benefits financially and in other ways from his television ministry.

Other organizations with which the Institute has had warm relationships and in many cases to which it has provided materials include L'Abri Fellowship, New College (Berkeley), St. Stephen's University (New Brunswick), Christian College Coalition, Institute for Christian Leadership and Renewal (Portland, Oregon), The Julian Center (Julian, CA), The Carolina Study Project (North Carolina), Universities and Colleges Christian Fellowship (Leicester, England), Christian Study Centre (Pakistan), Zadok Institute for Christianity and Society (Australia), The Christian Faith and Action Trust (New Zealand), and Christian Impact (London, England).

In Canada, the Institute became a member of the Evangelical Fellowship of Canada and the Canadian Council of Christian Charities. Institute people often attended and spoke at meetings of the Christian Labour Association of Canada, the International Association for the

Promotion of Christian Higher Education, and the International Association for Reformed Faith and Action. In 1968, the Christian Reformed Church accepted the Association as an "affiliated educational agency," which was its way of recommending the Association for support.

In 1976, the Institute faculty traveled to Syracuse, New York, for a one-day consultation with the faculty of Westminster Theological Seminary, located in Philadelphia. The Institute held much the same theological and philosophical views as did Westminster, though there were some differences in areas like hermeneutics that seemed important to institutions whose viewpoints were in most respects quite close.

The Institute never felt that it had the strength to add an undergraduate program to its educational ministry. At the same time that it gained greater stability, that need began to be adequately served by undergraduate Christian colleges started and governed by Dutch Reformed people, especially by Redeemer University College and The King's University College.

But the Institute felt much alone as a freestanding graduate school. It drew students from colleges and universities all over the world, but it had no undergraduate institution of its own on which it could rely for students. Although in 1983, the Institute received a charter to operate from the Ontario government, it did not have the minimum of two hundred students needed at that time to be accredited by the Association of Universities and Colleges of Canada. That lack prevented the Institute from public recognition by Canadian universities and the benefits allotted to them as well as preventing membership in the American-based Council of Christian Colleges and Universities, which required accreditation. As the years went by, however, Institute professors and graduate students became very active in participation in the academic professional societies of Canada, popularly called "the Learneds." They gave a significant number of academic papers at each annual meeting.

International Association for the Promotion of Christian Higher Institutions (IAPCHE)

In 1975, Potchefstroom University of Christian Higher Education organized a major conference at its campus in South Africa. It invited representatives of Christian institutions of postsecondary education worldwide to discuss issues that could promote their educational ministries. The conference was a success, and the papers were published in the book *Christian Higher Education: The Contemporary Challenge*. Potchefstroom

University sought international connections because Christian scholars in other parts of the world tended to isolate it because of its perceived complicity with the South African social policy of apartheid. The Institute was a charter member of the organization that was formed as a result of the conference, called the International Association for the Promotion of Christian Higher Education (IAPCHE).

At first, IAPCHE was centered at Potchefstroom, led by Bennie van der Walt, but later it was moved to Dordt College in Iowa, where Dordt professor John Vander Stelt served as its Executive Director for many years. IAPCHE grew over the years and has sponsored many international and also regional conferences that have been especially helpful for emerging Christian schools of higher education throughout the world. John Hulst succeeded Vander Stelt as director, and Nick Lantinga is its current director. The office and leadership continue to be located at Dordt College. The Institute has continued to be a leading member of this association, and Harry Fernhout served on its Board for many years.

In cooperation with IAPCHE, the Institute set about the development of a Faith and Learning Network. The Network is a comprehensive database of resources for the understanding of a Christian worldview in academic work. It incorporates materials produced by scholars whose academic work is rooted in their Christian faith, materials that explicitly address the role of faith in learning, and materials resulting from the scholarly study of Christians. Many of these materials are held in the Institute library. The books and articles are available to scholars in North America through interlibrary loans, and document delivery is also available internationally. As part of the Network, the Institute is developing a database of Christian scholars whose work is included in the bibliography.

Association of Reformed Institutions of Higher Education (ARIHE)

At the initiative of Calvin College and of Derk Pierik, chair of the ICS Board of Trustees and a member of the Calvin College Board, a discussion and planning group started in the 1980s to pull together representatives of Reformed Christian higher educational institutions in North America. Under the name of Reformed University of North America (RUNA), it met regularly to explore the possibility of developing a Reformed university with a full range of graduate degree programs. As the only graduate school in the group of participating institutions, the Institute had a special role.

The grand idea could never get off the ground, in spite of great interest in making it work. After years of meetings, Robert Andringa of the Council for Christian Colleges and Universities helped the group to focus on a clearer understanding of priorities. The result was that the group transformed itself and became the Association of Reformed Institutions in Higher Education (ARIHE). Cooperation in graduate studies became one of its projects. In 2003, it started a visiting lectureship in which a professor could give the same lecture at various member colleges to stimulate a common discussion on issues of the development of Christian higher education. The early lecturers were people closely associated with the Institute.

ARIHE made the transition from high level talking in rather abstract ways about a Reformed university to a group that talks much more about small-scale issues but at a concrete level, with a focus on faculty development. The good rapport that developed among the participating Reformed colleges was very important to the Institute. The Institute played a major role in the development of AIRHE, and Harry Fernhout chaired its Board until 2004.

The Free University in Amsterdam

The Institute's closest links in the early years were with the Philosophy Department of the Free University in Amsterdam. Besides the close religious and philosophical kinship, a number of the Institute's early faculty members had received their doctorates from the Free University. The Institute received major encouragement and academic support from Free University professors like Herman Dooyeweerd, Dirk Vollenhoven, Johan van der Hoeven, Hendrik van Riessen, Bob Goudzwaard, Egbert Schuurman, and Jacob Klapwijk. The Institute also received encouragement and assistance from the central administration of the university.

Institutional links were very not strong, however, for various reasons. The Free University's North American relations were focused primarily on Calvin College, and the Institute related only with the segment of the Free University that was interested in reformational philosophy.

But in 1979, the Free University and Calvin College invited the Institute to be part of an informal "tripartite" relationship in which the three institutions would cosponsor some international academic conferences, copublish some books, and potentially cooperate in some research programs. For the Institute, this meant enhanced recognition for its work on a worldwide scale. There were indeed various international conferences jointly sponsored by the three institutions, including the conference in Toronto in 1992 celebrating the twenty-fifth anniversary of the start of the Institute. From this tripartite activity, the Free University stepped forward to work with the Institute in its studies and research for the Institute's doctoral degree, which was actually awarded by the Free University.

The "aloneness" of the Institute was a major issue for Harry Fernhout when he became President of the Institute in December 1989. In his inaugural address, Fernhout asked, "Is the Institute's present structure best suited to the task at hand?. . . Is this the best way to go or is it time to re-examine this?. . . Should we consider, for example, a closer institutional alignment with one or more of our kindred institutions? To me, this is an open question. I believe that every institution should from time to time examine whether its structure still best suits its purposes."

In 1989, there was serious discussion with leading officials at Calvin College about some sort of merger of the two institutions. But the overall picture looked like a friendly takeover of the Institute by Calvin, which was not attractive to the Institute. Program-by-program cooperation with Calvin offered more promise, especially in the development of distance education via the Internet. But this kind of cooperation was not implemented.

In the 1980s, the Institute made a serious effort to develop a close working relation with Redeemer College, located an hour's drive away in a suburb of Hamilton, Ontario. In 1987, Board chair Fred Reinders and President Clifford Pitt met with Redeemer College President Henry De Bolster and Board chair John Zantingh to discuss closer relations. In the early 1990s, Fernhout met with De Bolster to explore an affiliation arrangement. The Institute Board then asked the Redeemer Board to meet with it to explore close working relations, but the Redeemer Board thought such a meeting would not be productive. The presidents of the two institutions continued to have congenial meetings, but the Redeemer people chose to keep a distance from the Institute, wanting to be free from the controversies that had embroiled the Institute in earlier years. Redeemer wanted to make sure it did not ruffle the feathers of its supporters, some of whom had been alienated by the Institute. Redeemer was also more connected than the Institute to the Christian Reformed Church, to which Redeemer looked for significant financial support. Relations between the two schools in Redeemer's early years were not strained, but neither were they warmly cordial.

The King's University College

In the early 1990s, President Fernhout had a number of informal conversations with The King's President Henk Van Andel about institutional relations. Both felt that an affiliation of the two institutions could offer great advantages to both of them and to all people interested in Christian higher education. In August 1996, the Institute Board's Executive Committee sent a letter to the Board of The King's indicating that it wished ". . . to initiate a conversation about the possibility of an affiliation between our two institutions, with the goal of creating a small Christian University." The Executive Committee of the Board of The King's responded by appointing a small ad hoc committee to meet with counterparts from the Institute for an exploratory discussion.

In September 1996, the Institute sent a six-page proposal to The King's as the basis for discussions about affiliation. The proposal included this quotation from the Institute academic bulletin regarding the philosophical, foundational, and interdisciplinary nature of the Institute's programs:

> Our method of developing a Christian perspective in academic studies is to concentrate on pivotal direction-setting issues in various fields of study. We focus on fundamental philosophical and methodological issues which underlie scholarship in various disciplines; studies at ICS focus on the philosophical and worldview *foundations* of scholarship. These crucial issues in one field tend to connect with similar concerns in other fields; consequently studies at ICS are *interdisciplinary* in nature.

A vital part of the plan would be for the Institute to move to Edmonton, because physical closeness was essential for the affiliation to be effective. The King's owned and occupied a large and attractive building in which the Institute could be comfortably housed. The Institute was hopeful that the Alberta Legislature would grant full accreditation for its graduate program. It had grown frustrated by the cold shoulder it constantly received from the Legislature of Ontario and had good hopes of a better relation with the Alberta Legislature. A crucial question was the ability and willingness of the Institute faculty and staff to move to Edmonton.

Task forces from each school met together four times for full-day meetings between November 1997 and April 1998. In addition, the two presidents met twice to work on aspects of an integrated model of affiliation.

It was agreed that the Institute would be able to contribute an established graduate faculty with a strong international reputation in research, publication, and teaching; more than thirty years of experience in graduate education and well-established and proven master's degree programs; a unique program of doctoral studies leading to the Ph.D. granted by the Free University in Amsterdam; and a foundational/ interdisciplinary thrust strongly oriented to the inner reformation of scholarship, which contributes to an overall creative intellectual climate.

The King's could contribute a larger institutional context, providing the atmosphere of a university; formal and informal interaction with The King's faculty consisting of thirty qualified people with doctoral degrees in over fifteen disciplines; participation of some of its faculty members in graduate education and research; support in securing program accreditation and offering standard degrees, possibly including the Institute's Ph.D. in philosophy; online access to twenty libraries; excellent institutional ties and a strong academic reputation among universities and Christian colleges in Canada; strong administrative and technical infrastructures that would enable the Institute to take better advantage of innovations in information technology and distance education; and a bright, cheerful and physically attractive campus.

Some members of The King's faculty would be able to offer courses in the graduate program of the Institute, and advanced Institute graduate students could serve as teaching assistants and sessional lecturers for The King's. The two libraries would be merged, providing an exceptional library that included an emphasis on Reformed Christian materials.

Overall, the affiliation would represent better Christian stewardship of resources and an enhanced reputation for both schools, plus better service to both constituencies. Further, offering education to high school graduates for bachelor's degrees through the Ph.D. would make the institution very exciting for Christian people in North America. The proposed affiliation was driven by vision, not by more practical needs, though there were indeed practical advantages.

The idea of the affiliation was that the two independently governed institutions would at first exist side by side, each with its own Board and its own finances and administration. The ultimate long-term aim was to have one institution, perhaps called "The King's University." This institution would incorporate the essentials of the missions of the Institute and of The King's as developed in practice by each since their founding. The new university would have a subunit designated as an "Institute" of The King's University, to serve as a centre for foundational studies in the reformational tradition and provide graduate programs, including worldview studies. There would eventually be one Board of Governors and one Senate. All continuing members of the faculty of both schools would become members of the new unified faculty.

A joint two-day meeting of the faculties of the Institute and The King's was held in Edmonton in August to get the two groups to know each other. This meeting was highly appreciated by all. It was widely agreed that the task forces did excellent work in preparing a plan for the move and the amalgamation of the two institutions. They had proposed a plan as good as could be worked out.

Many questions, however, arise when such a major change is considered. Some Institute people wondered whether the historic task and mission of the Institute would, in the long term, receive sufficient emphasis. They were concerned that perhaps too much energy of the Institute faculty would be drawn into the undergraduate program, allowing less emphasis on research and scholarly writing, though these were highly valued by The King's as well as by the Institute.

There was also concern that the graduate degrees of the Institute might not be accredited in Alberta. That accreditation would require a change in Alberta's Universities Act, which, at the time, allowed private undergraduate colleges but not private universities.

Further, there was the question about financing the graduate program, since about sixty percent of the Institute's donations come from the eastern half of North America. If the Institute became part of a small university located in the northwest, would the move jeopardize its support base?

A good number of Institute faculty members said they would be willing to move to Alberta, but the personal costs would be high. All of them had deep academic, family, and kinship connections in the Toronto area, and in some cases these extended over thirty years. But the professional cost would be high also because of the loss of their direct access to resources and contacts available to many through the University of Toronto. While Institute faculty members were willing to consider moving away from this, they did not welcome it.

At the Institute each component group—students, administrative staff, faculty, Senate, and Board—voted separately on the affiliation proposal. Faculty members voted on the proposal and were also asked to indicate a willingness to move with the Institute to Edmonton if the recommendation passed. An affirmative response of at least sixty percent from the faculty, both in favour of affiliation and a willingness to move to Edmonton, was needed to proceed with affiliation. An affirmative vote of seventy-three percent by Board members (by eleven of the fifteen members) was required.

There were not enough affirmative votes at the Institute to carry the affiliation. Many people at The King's were disappointed that the Institute, which had initiated the proposal, in the end had voted against it. A key issue was the Institute's moving to Edmonton, causing it to leave its advantageous location literally right across the street from the University of Toronto campus and causing the disruption of families deeply involved in activities in Toronto. But the decisive issue for the Institute was probably the fear that eventually the graduate school component would be swallowed up by the undergraduate. That cost was seen as being too high.

Membership in the Toronto School of Theology of the University of Toronto

When the discussions about affiliation with The King's University College ended, a formal relationship with the Toronto School of Theology (TST), centred at the University of Toronto, began to look attractive. Harry Fernhout already had relationships with some of its leaders, and the question of some kind of Institute membership was reopened. In 2005, TST consisted of seven member institutions, all theological colleges, plus three affiliate members.

Fernhout told Jean-Marc Laporte, Director of TST, that one of the hurdles that ICS would need to overcome if it affiliated with TST was that for twenty years the Institute had been at pains to demonstrate to the world, particularly to the Ontario government and the University of Toronto, that it was not a theological college. Fernhout said to TST, "We don't think of ourselves as a theological college, and you are the sponsors of theological education, so we need to see what kind of place we would have in TST, and whether we would have a place at all." Laporte replied, "If you don't think that what ICS is doing is theological education, that is fine with me, but as long as you are willing to accept that from our perspective we understand what you are doing to be theological education, we'll get along fine." TST wanted the unique strength in philosophy that ICS could bring to the table, plus its Calvinist intellectual tradition.

In May 1999, the Institute Board approved a Memorandum of Agreement with the Toronto School of Theology of the University of Toronto, opening the door to extensive academic cooperation between the two institutions. Fernhout's view of this action was that "As a freestanding graduate school the Institute runs the risk of isolation. This agreement will greatly enhance our recognition on the academic map." With affiliate membership in TST, Institute courses became available to the hundreds of students taking Toronto School of Theology programs, and Institute students could take TST courses.

The Institute's developing relationship with the TST brought about major changes at ICS, and gave ICS a much larger profile in the broader academic community. With the affiliation, ICS faculty members were considered for cross-appointment to the faculty of TST. Most were cross-appointed to the Advanced Degree Faculty, others to the Basic Degree faculty. Coupled with the affiliation was a whole new set of requirements. The writing of course proposals, for example, was about a year earlier than the ICS faculty was used to doing it. And course descriptions could only be so many characters long.

The TST affiliation brought with it the requirement that the Institute abide with rules and regulations that were not of its own making but nevertheless had a certain justification. Related to that were transitions in leadership positions in the Institute faculty, with Lambert Zuidervaart becoming Academic Dean. Zuidervaart had come to the Institute a year earlier, after twenty years of experience in a highly developed institution, Calvin College. He brought with him a certain ethos as to how the system of higher education works, which ICS benefited from. Gone were the days when the Institute made up its own ways of doing things without regard to what other schools did.

The TST affiliation played significantly into major changes in ICS, as well as to the effort in 2003 to prepare material that enabled the Ontario government's Postsecondary Education Quality Assessment Board (PEQAB) to conduct a rigorous examination of the Institute's organizational structure and academic quality. Its positive recommendation of ICS led to changes in the Institute's degree capability, with a more acceptable title for the academic master's degree and the right to award the Ph.D. on the authority of the Institute. Preparation for this extensive outside examination meant that in various policy areas, the Institute had to get its house in order. At issue was how the Institute handled matters not only like course descriptions but also faculty promotion, student record keeping, program development, grievance procedures, and ethical research policies. The Institute now needed to handle all those according to generally accepted standards in the academic world.

A development with the TST connection that the Institute did not foresee was that TST quickly latched onto ICS faculty members as supervisors for TST graduate students. ICS gets a small amount of financial credit for that, but that was a workload factor that ICS did not fully anticipate. Overall, there has been a small net financial benefit to ICS for services offered to TST that are larger than services ICS receives from TST. A great benefit the ICS has received from membership of the Institute with TST is the increase in its public profile. For example, the ICS affiliation with TST was very positively noted in the evaluation by the PEQAB examiners, by which they understood that Institute work and policies were at a high level.

Looking Ahead

If ICS wishes to benefit from public funding through the University of Toronto, it will need to become a full member of TST. To become a full member, the Institute would need to sign on to the TST relationship to the University of Toronto. One of the Institute's concerns with such a relationship is in the area of faculty tenure and dismissal. Disagreement with the founding religious statements of the Institute, including its Educational Creed, does not constitute formal grounds for dismissal under university policy. This is an issue the ICS needs to come to terms with as it considers whether to continue its affiliate membership in TST or to become a full member. Since the Institute does not want to be or be seen as a theological college, affiliation with the University of Toronto Philosophy Department might be another option to consider. However, the Institute handles philosophy much differently than does the university, and unlike the university's Philosophy Department, ICS offers courses in Biblical studies and in education.

Looking to the future in 2005, a major issue concerning institutional context is whether the Institute remains as an independent, freestanding graduate school. TST has given clear signals that it would welcome full membership of the Institute in TST. Alternatively, the Institute could revisit the issue of a significant link with an undergraduate Christian college in the Reformed family. ICS could also consider a strategic alliance in which ICS would provide a context for undergraduate college faculty members to do some graduate teaching and student supervision, as well as for some ICS professors to do undergraduate teaching. This might also bring financial benefits for the Institute if the partner institution could help ICS access new sources of funding.

16

Institute Appraisal and Influence

The Institute has required enormous amounts of time, energy, and money from those who support it. From the first stirrings in 1955 to the official opening of the Institute in 1967 to the present, the question is whether the significant effort is worth it. Has the Institute developed the academic strength to match its high-sounding goals? Do people outside of the Institute give it a good evaluation? Does it have a strong effect on people's lives as well as an important role in the lives of institutions? In short, what can be said about what the Institute has achieved?

In our scientific age, we would like quantitative answers to this question. The value of a school, however, goes much beyond what numbers can show. There are instances of great effectiveness resulting from the Institute's work. But the effectiveness of this kind of ministry lies in intimate personal changes and in subtle and rather invisible changes in communal insights and attitudes, that is, in individual lives and the contributions to communities. The anecdotes in this chapter represent a sampling of the ways that the Institute has effected change in the lives of those associated with it.

External Evaluations

The response in 1983 by about fifty prominent university professors to whom Thomas McIntire wrote to ask their support for the Institute's application for a charter from the Ontario legislature offered a glowing statement about the Institute's quality. The letters were written by professors at the University of Toronto, from many other universities in Ontario, throughout Canada and various parts of the world.

Institute academic programs received many positive and interesting comments from professors at secular universities written in response to the Institute's application for a $59,000 grant it received from the Social Science and Humanities Research Council of Canada in 1992 for interdisciplinary research on pluralism. On the basis of the application, the judges expressed confidence that Institute scholarship is "rigorous and of high quality." The evaluators said they could clearly sense the "creative tension" in which the Institute works. One reviewer noted that many contemporary scholars may dismiss the proposal to explore the theme of pluralism from a Christian point of view as "preposterous." "How could a group of scholars committed to a particular moral outlook shed light on the questions of pluralism and its significance in modern secular society?" The reviewer concluded, however, that in our society today this Christian voice must be heard, for if pluralism cannot be justified from within the religious tradition that shaped modern culture, then "genuinely pluralistic modern societies must rest on incoherent moral foundations."

Another evaluator recognized that the grant application came from a particular community which he labelled "Dutch Calvinist." He emphasized, however, that a grant application from a particular community should not be denied simply because it is "contrary to the liberal-individual ideology which is dominant within academia. Indeed the issue of 'bias' would probably not even be raised if all the members of a team shared the dominant ideology."

Report from Ontario's Quality Assessment Board

In 2004, the Institute felt that the time was right for it to be granted enlarged educational powers from the Ontario government. By that time, the provincial services in higher education had developed to the point where it had a strong and broadly based program for evaluating programs in higher education. A service had been set up called the Postsecondary Education Quality Assessment Board (PEQAB). That Board agreed to a full assessment of the Institute, to result in a report to the province on its findings. A team was appointed consisting of three university professors: Robert Gibbs, philosophy professor from the University of Toronto; Wesley Cragg, professor of business ethics from York University; and Timothy Noone, philosophy professor from the Catholic University of America.

The examiners had received a very large volume of written materials, and the three of them spent a full day at the Institute in February 2004. They met with Lambert Zuidervaart, the Academic Dean who oversaw preparation of the written materials; had half-hour meetings with six other full-time faculty members; by pairs and singly, met with four students for fifteen minutes each; and had a final, extensive meeting with the President, the Academic Dean, and the Associate Academic Dean.

The examiners wrote in their report, "We discussed a wide range of issues with the faculty and administration, and with the students and alumni we focused quite naturally on the student experience and the issues of expectations for courses." Their written section on the program's strengths and weaknesses reads:

> The carefully structured and diverse program in philosophy offers an excellent graduate education. There is thorough academic planning and oversight. The classes are small and engaged, and in addition there is good access to guided reading courses. Mentoring of students, both during course work and in supervision of theses, is intensive and constructive. The interdisciplinary nature of the program, and particularly the "Interdisciplinary Seminar" are valuable.
>
> The faculty are not only devoted teachers, but have a strong record of research and provide learning opportunities for the students on the basis of their research. Moreover, there is a strong commitment to the creation and maintenance of a positive, open, critical, interactive, learning environment. The result is a successful formal and informal integration of traditional scholarly research and teaching values into a supportive, open, inclusive, tolerant, interactive learning environment capable of adapting to a variety of academic and cultural backgrounds of students, academic visitors and faculty.
>
> The weaknesses are slight in comparison. The panel was concerned that the standards for the students were too high, requiring more course work than in many comparable programs in philosophy, and thus delaying the completion of the program. The process of review for non-continuing faculty (in their first six years) may benefit from some adjustments.

Public comments from other university professors included the concern of a York University professor that unlike other Ontario universities ". . . the Institute might not explicitly encourage a critical, questioning perspective on the material studied and the consideration of a range of alternative points of view." In response, the panel reported that it had found ". . . that ICS does engage in a rigorous and profound critical questioning. . . ." They accepted the response of Dean Zuidervaaart to the professor's concern when he said that ". . . ICS is a philosophy program, and that the Dutch Reformed Protestant tradition is committed to just this kind of critical questioning, as well as the consideration of a wide-range of alternative perspectives. He further suggested that the rootedness in a Protestant tradition offered resources for philosophical reflection that allowed members at ICS to draw critical relations to their own tradition. The Dean compared the situation to Catholic universities where the Catholic tradition was a resource and a context for scholarly inquiry."

The Students

No doubt the greatest benefit from the Institute has been received by its students. They have gone into a great variety of positions of service, in part because the Institute has not focused its study on preparation for a specific kind of work. Perhaps the only focus on preparing students for a profession is on academic work. In 2004, some ninety-three former Institute students were serving in institutions of higher education, either Christian or secular.

A small taste of what the Institute has offered to students is shown by the way the Institute appealed to two early students from Japan. One was Rev. Koichiro (Ko) Takariki from Japan, a graduate of Japan Christian College and Kobe Reformed Seminary. Part of his reason for coming to the Institute, he said, was that "I found deeply disturbing the very fact that only Marxism exists today as a total life principle, and that the original Christian faith and its early potential have largely disappeared. Christianity, I found, had been reduced to the inner life, to the sectarian—and at best, propositional things. It didn't exist as a guiding principal for all of life." While studying at seminary in Japan, he came across some Association publications and found them liberating. After his studies at the Institute were completed, Takariki became Professor of Cultural History at Rio Grande University in Japan.

A few years later, the Japanese student Kiyotaka Doi came to the Institute. He was raised in a deeply Buddhist and Shintoist tradition. He studied economics, but always felt something lacking. He turned to philosophy, hoping that it could give him the insight and spiritual base he was seeking. After he converted to Christianity, he found that base. One of his professors, Sumito Haruna, who had translated into Japanese Dooyeweerd's book *In the Twilight of Western Thought,* told him about the Institute. After his graduation, Doi also returned to Japan as a professor. Similar stories can be told about students from cultures different from that of the Institute. For that matter, coming to the Institute even presented a significant religious cultural change for committed Christian students living in North America, since the Institute's idea of what Christian faith meant for academic study was much different from what these students had experienced earlier.

Relations with Churches and Other Organizations

The Institute's influence on churches and other agencies, through the leadership of its professors and their ideas, has always been significant. The Institute's Dutch Reformed founders wanted it to be the heart of the subculture they aimed to develop in Canada following their immigration from the Netherlands. There is no question that the Institute has given direction to that group and has built the Christian strength of its people. The Institute has been a blessing to many pastors, Christian school teachers, and university professors, in addition to its students. Institutions like churches and Christian schools have been vitalized with fresh vision from the Institute.

That vision, even fifty years later, lives and leads in pervasive and surprising ways. The Institute affirmed its commitment to the Christian vision of its founders through the quotation of its Mission Statement in 2003 by President Henry Fernhout: "To provide Christian graduate education that addresses the spiritual foundations of learning and equips Christians around the world to be effective leaders in the academic arena and other areas of society."

In 1979, some twenty-five years after planning for the Institute started, Rev. Arie Van Eek noted publicly that the Christian Reformed Church in Canada grew up with the Institute. He said that the church would have developed very differently without the Institute. The great effect that the Institute had on the church was at times resented and resisted. The Institute forced the church to face a number of hard questions that many people would have preferred not to face. People liked their church the way it was, and they were often not happy with the Institute taking the role of prophet and goading church people out of their complacency.

The fervour and faith of Institute people came with a vision deep and broad, continued Van Eek. The forces of conservatism and reaction were very strong in the church. The Institute helped the church move away from a mentality that saw the church as almost the only agency that could work at building the Kingdom of God to a broader vision of the involvement of the church in the world. At the same time, the Institute focused on the Word of God in the context of the world. The Institute helped many people, immigrants particularly, clarify or redirect their goals in a foreign society. Yet at the same time there was a concerted effort by many church people to put the Institute on the defensive. After a few decades, however, it is clear that these immigrant church members have been led by the Institute to an insight deeper than they would have had from the limited education that most of them had received.

Another major influence of the Institute has been to lead Christian day school teachers to come together and work at developing scripturally directed curricula. Private Christian schools offering education from kindergarten through high school were an extremely high priority for Dutch Reformed immigrants. The Institute led to the formation of the Curriculum Development Centre, funded in significant part for some years by the Institute. In this Centre, teachers and school principals developed integrated curricula for elementary and secondary schools that expressed their Christian view of life. Many teachers and schools throughout the world started using the fruits of this work and have been enriched by them. In addition, people very close to the Institute have spoken at annual Christian school teacher's conventions in various parts of the world and have led workshops in summer programs to prepare teachers to carry on the work in their own schools.

The Institute has made a special mark in serving social action organizations through its faculty and through its graduates. Faculty members have served on boards and as resource people in many social service organizations, where they have been extremely valuable. Leadership in their research and writing have been tremendously helpful. In the early years, Institute faculty members were frequent keynote speakers at major meetings of organizations like the Christian Labour Association of Canada and Citizens for Public Justice and at Christian school events.

Very quickly, the work of the Institute reached beyond the Dutch immigrants of the Christian Reformed Church in Canada. Professors and pastors from many churches were attracted to its vision of study and life filled with the presence of God. From the start, the Institute had a great and surprising international influence. Its vision of academic research and higher education struck a responsive chord all over the world. The early books that published the lectures at the summer academic conferences traveled worldwide and brought responses from places not dreamed of. When the Institute invited students to come and study, some of the first students were from Lebanon, Cyprus, Japan, South Africa, England, Sweden, Jamaica, Australia, Indonesia, New Zealand, and even the Netherlands.

By 1987, the Institute had active personal contacts in the following countries: Sweden, Switzerland, South Africa, Singapore, Sierra Leone, Scotland, Peru, Nigeria, New Zealand, the Netherlands, Mozambique, Mexico, Malawi, Korea, Japan, Jamaica, Italy, Ireland, Indonesia, India, Greece, Ghana, England, Cyprus, Australia, and Argentina (and the USA). At that time, the Institute's quarterly newsletter, *Perspective*, was regularly mailed to people in fifty-seven countries.

There is no doubt that the Institute has a constructive effect on the few independent postsecondary Christian schools that exist in Canada.

From its early years, the Institute has had mutually supportive relations with Regent College and Trinity Western University, as well as with The King's and Redeemer, both of which are Reformed university colleges. The Institute faculty and also its graduate students have had a significant presence in the professional academic societies of Canada, presenting papers at each annual Spring meeting which is now called the Congress of Social Sciences and Humanities. The Institute is taking a leading role in the developing the Association of Institutions of Christian Higher Education in Canada.

Satellite Centres Throughout the World

The vision of Christian higher education and cultural leadership of the Institute was received with considerable excitement in various places around the world and resulted in the establishment of a number of study and research centres. Often stimulated by people who had studied at the Institute, various study, teaching, and literature centres were established to enrich and develop Christians and local institutions. Among those were the center started and staffed by Tom Forman at the University of Kansas; the Irish Christian Study Centre; Zadok Centre in Australia; Christian Faith and Action Trust started by ICS alumnus Chris Gousmett in New Zealand; Christian Educational Services Northwest organized by Trace James in Minneapolis; The Center for Christian Studies directed by Jon R. Kennedy in California; the Center for Christian Studies founded by Kenneth Hermann in Champaign-Urbana, Illinois; and the Institute for Christian Leadership and Renewal in Oregon. In addition, two other places deserve special note.

One of these was College House, located in eastern England, started by ICS alumnus Steve Shaw and some of his friends. They persuaded Bible teacher John Peck to join them in a teaching ministry. They were major supporters of the Greenbelt Arts Festival held each summer, which in 1981, for instance, drew over 22,000 people. A number of Institute people were lecturers and visitors at College House. College House also set up an ambitious correspondence course program, highlighted by an excellent Christian Worldview course.

Peter Steen set up an extraordinary student ministry in western Pennsylvania in the late 1970s after being on the staff of the Coalition for Christian Outreach, headquartered in Pittsburgh. A very effective speaker, Steen regularly visited thirty-nine college and university campuses in western Pennsylvania at which he promoted the Institute's Christian view of academic study. He worked on campuses that were full of individualism and narcissism, which the traditional style of campus Christian ministries did not touch. He had an enormous influence on large numbers of students, more than thirty of whom at one time or another came to Toronto to study at the Institute.

Affirmation from Nicholas Wolterstorff

In 1992, at the close of the Institute's international conference celebrating its twenty-fifth year of existence, Nicholas Wolterstorff presented this toast to the Institute:

> I speak with affection, in gratitude to God
> –for the vision of wholeness of faith and scholarship out of which the Institute for Christian Studies was born and by which it has lived all these years
> –for the courage it has shown in realizing and sustaining that vision, often when success seemed implausible
> –for the creativity it has displayed in how and what it taught
> –for its intense devotion to God's people in their need for learning that sheds light on their path
> –for the endurance of the agony of hostile criticism and the boredom of innumerable meetings
> –for the willingness to live at risk, on the margins of acceptability in quasi-poverty
> –for the enthusiasm, the seemingly unquenchable enthusiasm
> –for the mellowing of spirit, the increase of charity, and the growth in ability to discern faith and wisdom in more places than at first recognized
> –for intense devotion to the God who calls and promises
> –in gratitude to God for all this we say to you, on this 25th anniversary of the founding of the Institute for Christian Studies, that we are deeply thankful you are here.
>
> We pray for your continued flourishing. And we say to you with all our heart: Do not leave the fire of the Spirit!

17

Today and Tomorrow

In the past five to ten years, a significant development at the Institute has been the generational change in the faculty. Calvin Seerveld was the first to retire, in 1995. Hendrik Hart followed in 2000, and James Olthuis and George Vandervelde retired in 2004. Along with Bernard Zylstra, Albert Wolters, Arnold De Graaff, and Thomas McIntire, they were the first generation on the faculty of the graduate school, starting in 1968. They were emblematic of the growing phase of the Institute.

An important moment in that phase came with the presentation to the Institute of the Greystone Report in 1985 (see Chapter 11), which said that the Institute really needed to make up its mind about the kind of institution it ought to be. Would it continue to be a movement, or would it focus on being a graduate school?

An effort to focus the mission of the Institute away from being an ill-defined movement toward being a graduate school came in 1977, when the Board of Trustees gave priority to being a graduate school centred on teaching and research that had a theoretical, that is, a philosophical base. At the same time, the Board gave secondary priority to the service of teaching Christian perspective courses on university campuses and of communicating the results of Institute research to the widest possible range of people through conferences, short courses, public lectures, and written materials. These educational services were largely dropped in 1987 because of a chronic shortage of money (see Chapter 9). This meant that the Institute's resources would be largely limited to teaching and research. It would no longer be a "University for the People" in the sense that many of its founders envisioned.

The recent faculty changeover is symbolic of that decision for change. The ICS is now clearly committed to being a graduate school, but one that maintains a close spiritual bond with its constituency, preparing leaders for society in special ways through scholarly research and teaching with concern for the community's thinking and life attitudes. This transition is a dimension of institutional maturity.

Full Degree-Granting Status

In June 2005, the Ontario government passed a bill allowing the Institute "to advertise and offer in Ontario a Master of Arts (Philosophy) program and a Ph.D. in Philosophy program."

The Institute had worked hard to get this authority for thirty-five years, which could only be given by the provincial government. For a number of years, the Institute had authorization from the government to offer two master's degrees and a program of studies toward the Ph.D., provided the doctoral degree itself would be awarded by another institution. For over twenty years, that institution was the Free University in Amsterdam. The Institute's application to the government for this award needed to be extremely detailed, but when completed it drew high praise from the people who evaluated it for the government.

Worldview Studies. In 1992, the Institute received a modification in its charter permitting it to offer the degree of Master of Worldview Studies. It was publicly stated that the program ". . . is designed to help professionals develop a Christian approach to their vocations so that their relationship with God is not only personally engaging but culturally relevant as well. The program is directed to people in various professions who already have an undergraduate degree but want to develop their Christian perspective in their work."

Although there was not much change in the courses offered and degrees granted in the Institute's master's and doctoral programs in the years that followed the enlargement of its powers, there is still an unresolved discussion of the Master of Worldview Studies degree program. The place of that program in relation to the Institute's more focused academic studies is an issue that has been with the Institute for a long time. President Clifford Pitt pushed to create that program and then to get degree credit for it. The first faculty member directing Worldview Studies, Brian Walsh, bought considerable acclaim and success to the program. Walsh left the Institute in 1994 and was succeeded for four years by Caroll Guen Hart. Since that time, the Worldview Studies program has not had someone specifically identified as its director.

The Worldview Studies program continues to attract students, even though it has not had a full-time director. Faculty members share in teaching the distinctive courses in the program. As all Institute students do, Worldview students take the basic course that used to be called Philosophical Foundations, but is now Religion, Life, and Society, and the basic Biblical Foundations course. The other Worldview courses are distinct from those of other degree programs. Each faculty member is expected to teach one course each year in the Worldview program. There is an Education component in the program that is attractive to in-service teachers in Christian schools, who take the courses part-time. Some of those Education courses can be taken through the Internet.

Dooyeweerd's Philosophical Heritage

Institute professors have made some changes over the years as to how they handle their work in relation to the philosophy of Herman Dooyeweerd. Currently, the creative engagement with the Dooyeweerd tradition is as lively as its ever been. Robert Sweetman very consciously has moulded himself as a historian of philosophy, particularly working creatively with issues in the tradition of Dirk Vollenhoven, Dooyeweerd's colleague and close associate. In 2006, Jonathan Chaplin wrote the essay "Towards an Ecumenical Social Theory: Revisiting Herman Dooyeweerd's Critique of Theories," a chapter in the book *That the World May Believe*. In Zuidervaart's course on the introduction to philosophy required of all first-year students, he actively works with Dooyeweerd's thinking, as do Adrienne Chaplin and Doug Blomberg.

The Institute is very active in the Dooyeweerd Centre, started at Redeemer University College. Harry Fernhout and Jonathan Chaplin are members of the Board of the Dooyeweerd Centre, which has been changed to be a voting and governing board rather than being an advisory board governed by the Dooyeweerd family. The main project of the Centre is translating into English and publishing Dooyeweerd's works, along with organizing conferences and contributing to the programs of various other conferences.

The Institute recently created two named chairs as a way of positioning itself in relation to the thinking of Dooyeweerd and of the reformational movement. Jonathan Chaplin was appointed to the Herman Dooyeweerd Chair in Social and Political Philosophy, funded by members of the Dooyeweerd family. The other is the H. Evan Runner Chair in the History of Philosophy, held by Robert Sweetman, which recognizes the vision of the philosopher who tirelessly promoted the Institute in its planning stages and who championed the Christian philosophical insights of Dooyeweerd.

Distance Learning

Distance learning and the Faith and Learning Network are both still being developed, and the Institute is involved in several creative ventures that involve institutions of Christian higher education throughout the world. Formative in these developments was a conference of the International Association for the Promotion of Christian Higher Education (IAPCHE) held in 2000, attended by more than one hundred people from twenty-six countries. What struck home was having people from distant places telling how Christian higher education in their areas is bursting forth. Few of them have a Reformed basis, but all are asking what Christian higher education can mean for them. They are desperate to have professors who have a sense of what Christianity means in their academic fields and to have Christian resources for the development of their vision. The Institute for decades has been developing many of the resources these people are calling for. Since it is not possible to send Christian professors to all parts of the globe to enable students to complete graduate degrees and to develop a Christian academic perspective, the idea arose of sending courses and written materials over the Internet.

In response to this need, IAPCHE has set up a program of five categories of courses that will lead to a new Christian Academic Studies Certificate. To receive the Certificate, students will need to complete five courses, one course in each category. As part of this program, the Institute has arranged for Kenn Hermann to set up the Institute's Worldview Foundations course for use on the Internet. This program started with eleven courses in the fall of 2005.

Courses for the program can be set up by professors at Christian colleges or universities anywhere in the world. A member institution needs to evaluate each course and recommend its inclusion in the Certificate program. Then a Steering Committee, which includes one person from each of the five international regions that IAPCHE has identified, needs to approve the course, based on recommendations from qualified professors in the field of the course. The institution from which the course arises receives tuition payment for each course taken, and it pays the writer of the course to evaluate the student work. There is one lead Christian institution in each of the five world regions; the Institute is the lead institution for North America. The Institute's goal is for each Institute professor to have an introductory course in their field online to be used in this program.

The worth of the Certificate, which is equivalent to half of a Master of Worldview Studies degree at the Institute, resides in the worth the institution employing the Certificate holder gives it. The Certificate basically says that the person receiving it has some grounding in Christian worldview studies, the history of Christian thought, and Christian philosophy. The Certificate is designed for people who have not had their advanced education in a Christian institution.

This activity shows that there is a beautiful growth and coming together of Christian higher education throughout the world. The Institute has a special role in contributing to worldwide higher Christian education because it already has courses with Christian philosophical insight in a variety of subject areas.

The Ontario Christian School Teachers Association (OCSTA) also has a Certificate program for Ontario Christian school teachers who have not received their bachelor's degree from a Christian college. Doug Blomberg has set up a series of courses on Christian day school education on the Internet that are a significant part of that program. Library materials, bibliographies, and printed texts can also be transmitted over the Internet.

The Free University in Amsterdam

The relation between the Institute and the Free University in Amsterdam is of vital importance to the Institute. In late 2004, when the Ontario government gave the Institute the right to award the Ph.D. on its own authority, it became necessary to reconsider the nature of that relationship. The Institute recognized the importance of maintaining a formal and working partnership with the Free University. At the time this privilege was granted in 2004, the Institute had about twenty students in the doctoral program who came in with the expectation of getting a degree from the Free University. These students will have the option of receiving the degree from the Free University, as all previous Institute's doctoral students have done, or of simply receiving the degree from the Institute.

When the Institute was in the process of going through Ontario government's Postsecondary Education Quality Assessment Board (PEQAB) evaluation in preparation for a major change in granting its own degrees, President Fernhout was in communication with the Free University saying that whatever the results of the ICS evaluation would be, some changes in the agreement with the Free University would need to be made. They responded that their doctoral regulations include provision for a double degree conferral with foreign institutions with which they have a cooperative relationship. Thus, a new agreement with the Free University will provide for a conjoint Ph.D., granted simultaneously by both institutions. ICS will then no longer need to model its doctoral curriculum on that of the Philosophy Department of the Free University, but it would simply give assurance to the Free University that ICS doctoral candidates had met requirements equivalent to those at the Free University at the predoctoral stage.

Another change in the Institute's relation with the Free University could be that the ICS partnership with the Free University would become university-wide, no longer just with the Philosophy Department. That would mean that any Free University professor with appropriate expertise, whether a member of the Free University Philosophy Department or not, could be asked to supervise, alongside an ICS professor, the work of an ICS doctoral student. This is attractive to the Institute because there are Free University professors not in the Philosophy Department who are close in heart and mind to the ICS.

Institute Enrolment

Until recent years, most students were drawn to the Institute through reading faculty publications. That has changed with the Institute's receiving significant numbers of students from colleges where ICS alumni are teaching. A good network is growing up between the Institute and many undergraduate Christian colleges. Students continue to come to the Institute with excellent academic backgrounds.

In the year 2004–2005, the Institute enrolled 136 students for one or more courses. Of these, twenty-nine students were enrolled in the Master of Philosophy program and twenty-seven in the Ph.D. program. Thirteen people were students in the Philosophy Department at the University of Toronto and twenty-eight were students at the Toronto School of Theology. About half of that number of Institute students took courses at TST or the University of Toronto, since ICS students are now able to access graduate courses in various university departments through TST. An increasing number of the Institute's graduating master's degree students are now applying to stay at the Institute for the Ph.D. Although that is a welcome development, this also means that higher donation income for the Institute is needed because educating students at the doctoral level is expensive for the school.

Financial Issues

Graduate schools typically offer doctoral students more financial assistance in the form of tuition relief, scholarships, and work/study opportunities than they offer master's degree students. Doctoral students also need this extra financial help for a longer time. The Institute welcomes larger numbers of doctoral students, but the cost of their education is significantly higher than for master's degree students.

The Institute not only needs to expand its base of donors who contribute each year, but also to develop long-term sources of funding to reduce its reliance on the ups and downs of annual donations.

The Institute definitely needs to build a solid endowment fund of, say, $10 million dollars. That would give Institute supporters the confidence that the school is stable and likely to exist for many years ahead. Limited-term endowments are possible where, for example, over ten years, ICS could use up both the principal and interest. That option could be attractive to donors who would not wish their money to be used in perpetuity at a school that might not in the distant future hold the donor's religious convictions.

In certain ways, the question comes up each year whether the Institute can continue to survive. The Institute wants to think that the money will always be there. But ICS receives no government funding, and a graduate school cannot pay its bills with tuition income. ICS is unique in its almost complete reliance on donations to pay its expenses. Donations are always hard to come by in the amounts needed for the education of people for master's and doctor's degrees. The Institute seems to be more a ministry of faith than any other school. Thus far, the years of development at the Institute show that the impossible dream of its founders included a rich vision, even though the Institute has not been rich in financial resources.

Current Status

Times certainly change. In its early years, the Institute (or the ARSS, as people in those days called it) was combative. Its countercultural attitude attacked not only secular Canadian society but also the churches and Christian schools that led its Christian community. Its weekend conferences drew many hundreds of people, and its traveling lecturers brought an exciting vision of Christian living and thinking that was almost a competitor of churches. The Institute has mellowed as it has grown stronger and developed greater confidence in its ability to make a change in its Christian community. The Institute has become a beacon among its people with a vision that gives them a spirit of wisdom and hope.

Among both Christians and non-Christians, there seems to be a wider acceptance today that academic study is not irreligious but that all of learning inevitably contains within it attitudes and thinking that lie outside of the usual definition of the academic field. It is not as common today for secular scholars to say, as Institute people often heard in the past, "If it is Christian, it is not academic, and if it's academic, it's not Christian." In the past, secular people could only think of the Institute as being a Bible college or a seminary, not as a school teaching the same subjects as the university but with a Christian philosophy underlying them.

Today, there seems to be a quickening among Christians in higher education, leading them to ask passionately how one's thinking can change to accept a Christian understanding of science and all academic study. These scholars have left positivism and are asking for help as they seek to know just how God works throughout all of academic study, the things and the ideas that he has created. Indeed, there is a growing realization that Calvinistic education has moved further than others with that kind of thinking and may have some directions for further reflection.

The Institute has made a breakthrough in thinking deeply about how religious faith affects academic work. It is now poised to give worldwide leadership to people of all kinds of theologies who are seeking answers to this basic question. The heart of the Institute's direction is the insight that the roots of all reflection lie in philosophy that is entirely submissive to God's creative and sustaining power. The Bible says that "the fear of the Lord is the beginning of wisdom," and the vision of the Institute is that this "fear of the Lord" needs to be articulated today in Christian philosophy undergirding all scholarly work.

To start studying philosophy, a person needs to stand on a worldview. It is now common for Christian scholars to speak of worldview as an essential part of Christian thinking in their work. The Institute has given international leadership in worldview studies, and its leadership continues today.

A special characteristic of the Institute is its worldwide influence. From the start, it has drawn students from many parts of the world, and the international origins of its students continues to be very strong. It is not surprising, then, that the ministry of the Institute has reached all parts of the globe, both through its publications but also through people who have brought its insights in person, and a new means of reaching the world comes through the Internet. As President Harry Fernhout wrote in 2005,

> Wherever the seed of the gospel has been planted and borne fruit in areas such as Africa and Asia, people are now busy with the second wave: building institutions and developing a new generation of leaders to carry the faith forward. Few places in the world offer these emerg-

ing leaders what the ICS does: non-seminary graduate education with a profound grasp of the role of Christian faith in shaping an integral understanding of various fields of learning. By the grace of God, new communication technologies make it possible for us to share our experiences and resources so that we can contribute to the movement of the Spirit around the world.

The Institute started as a "university for the people," a place where people without advanced education as well as scholars could develop a Christian culture, a Christian mind-set. The Dutch immigrants who started the Institute are now Canadian and have become comfortable in their new home, and their children and grandchildren are receiving education beyond high school. Immigrants are now comfortable with the English language, and there is much Christian literature that will build their insight.

The Institute has also found it appropriate to sharpen its focus to be a graduate school for people who wish to engage in advanced study. This has meant that it is no longer "a university for the people" in the sense of its original vision.

The Institute has had a significant effect in shaping attitudes and on building Christian culture, starting with its Dutch immigrant culture and spreading to other cultures in many distant places. In the end, its effect on human lives cannot be measured or even estimated, but must be left in the hands of God.

Appendix 1
Institute Basis and Educational Creed

Preamble

In humble awareness of our dependence upon the Triune God, who called all things into being to his own glory and proclaimed to men, after they had transgressed his Law, his forgiving love, which was revealed to us fully in the sending of his Son, Jesus Christ, we do, out of gratitude for his undeserved favour and in conforming with his requirement that we consecrate ourselves and all things to him, establish in accordance with the principles and provisions herein set forth, an association for the promotion of scripturally-directed higher learning. To this end we beseech of him that he graciously grant us both now and in the future men and women equipped for our task with special gifts of heart and mind together with the means to enable them to do this work, and that he always bless our association to his honour and to the salvation of his people, particularly in Canada and the United States of America, in order that they may be a blessing to both lands and all their inhabitants.

Purpose

The purpose of the association shall be to undertake or promote whatever activities it shall deem conducive to the development of scripturally-directed higher learning and scholarly enterprise, and particularly to establish, control and develop a Christian university, and in these ways to equip men and women to bring the Word of God in all its power to bear upon the whole of life.

Basis

The supreme standard of the association shall be the Scriptures of the Old and New Testaments, here confessed to be the Word of God in the sense of the historic creeds of the Protestant Reformation.

Educational Creed

Believing that Scripture reveals certain basic principles intensely relevant to education, we confess:

Life. That human life in its entirety is religion. Consequently, scholarly study unfolds itself as service either of the one true God or of an idol.

Scripture. That Scripture, the Word of God written, in instructing us of God, ourselves and the structure of creation, is that integral and active divine Word or Power by which God, through his Spirit, attaches us to and enlightens us in the Truth, which is Christ.

Christ. That the Christ of the Scriptures, the Word of God Incarnate, is the Redeemer and Renewer of our life in its entirety and therefore also of our theoretical thought.

Reality. That the essence or heart of all created reality is the covenantal communion of human beings with God in Christ.

Knowledge. That true knowledge is made possible by true religion and arises from the knowing activity of the human heart enlightened through the Word of God by the Holy Spirit. Thus religion plays its decisive ordering role in the understanding our everyday experience and our theoretical pursuits.

Scholarship. (a) That the diligent pursuit of theoretical thought in a community of scholars is essential to the obedient and thankful response of God's people to the cultural mandate. The task of the scholar is to give a scientific account of the structure of creation and thereby promote a more effective ordering of the everyday experience of the entire community. (b) That because of God's gracious preservation of creation after the fall, those who reject the Word of God as the ordering principle of life provide many valuable insights into the common structure of reality; nevertheless the central religious antithesis of direction in life remains. We therefore reject the possibility of the synthesis of scripturally-directed thought with any other system of thought.

Academic Freedom. That scholarly pursuits are to be undertaken in the God-given freedom of a complete and voluntary submission to the Word of God and the divine laws that govern human life. The responsible freedom of the scholar must be protected against any constraint or domination of church, state, industry or other societal structure.

Summary. That all scholarship pursued in faithful obedience to the divine mandate will heed the normative direction of God's Word, will acknowledge his Law to which creation in all its spheres is subject, and will bow before Christ's Kingship over all scientific work.

Appendix 2

Speakers for Annual Summer Student Conferences 1959-69

1959
The Relation of the Bible to Science, by Hendrik Van Riessen
The Relation of the Bible to History, by Allan Leonard Farris
The Relation of the Bible to Learning, by H. Evan Runner

1960
Scientific and Pre-Scientific, by H. Evan Runner
Sphere Sovereignty, by H. Evan Runner
Absolute Truth and the Relativism of History, by W. Stanford Reid
Pragmatism, by S.U. Zuidema
Existentialistic Communication, by S. U. Zuidema

1961
Organic Life and the Evolutionistic World and Life View, by J. J. Duyvene de Wit
Philosophy, by Hendrik Van Riessen
Scriptural Religion and Political Task, by H. Evan Runner

1962
The University and its Basis, by Hendrik Van Riessen
Facts and Values, by Remkes Kooistra
A Christian Critique of Art, by Calvin Seerveld

1963
A Christian Critique of Literature, by Calvin Seerveld
The Meaning of Ethos, by F. H. Von Meyenfeldt
The Nature of Religion. by Paul G. Schrotenboer

These lectures by the speakers indicated, as well as some lectures by other speakers given in following years, have been published in a series of books called Christian Perspectives. In later years these summer lectures became widely attended by many people who were not students and who may not have had university-level education. Speakers at summer

Appendix 2

conferences sponsored by the Institute in the years and provinces or states indicated through 1969 follow.

1963 (September) F. H. Von Meyenfeldt, Calvin Seerveld and H. Evan Runner
1964 (Ontario, August) Johan Vander Hoeven, H. Evan Runner and Remkes Kooistra
  (Ontario, September) Johan Vander Hoeven, H. Evan Runner, Calvin Seerveld and Herman Dooyeweerd
  (British Columbia) Johan Vander Hoeven and H. Evan Runner
1965 (Ontario, August) Harry Vander Laan, Maarten Vrieze, H. Evan Runner and Calvin Seerveld
  (Ontario, September) Harry Vander Laan and Maarten Vrieze
  (British Columbia) Harry Vander Laan and H. Evan Runner
1966 (Ontario) Maarten Vrieze, Harry Vander Laan and Calvin Seerveld
  (Alberta) Hendrik Hart and Maarten Vrieze
  (British Columbia) Hendrik Hart and Maarten Vrieze
1967 (Ontario)
  (Barrie, Ontario) John Vander Stelt, Bert Witvoet and Adrian Peetoom
  (British Columbia) Hendrik Hart and Peter Schouls
  (Pennsylvania) Hendrik Hart, Robert Knudsen, William White and John Olthuis
1968 (Ontario) Arnold De Graaff and Hendrik Hart
  (Alberta) Hendrik Hart and Calvin Seerveld
  (British Columbia (Hendrik Hart and Calvin Seerveld)
  (Pennsylvania) Paul Schrotenboer, James Skillen and James Olthuis
1969 (Ontario) Arnold De Graaff and Bernard Zylstra
  (Alberta) H. Evan Runner and James Olthuis
  (Pennsylvania) H. Evan Runner and James Olthuis
  (Holland, Michigan) Arnold De Graaff and Bernard Zylstra

Appendix 3
Summer Academic Conferences, Workshops and Seminars

Starting in 1970 the Institute undertook to set up a very considerable number of one or two week academic conferences, seminars and courses. The aim was to bring scholars together to contribute to building insight into a Christian academic understanding of reality. Some of these programs were:

1970	"Foundations of the Natural Sciences," a three-week seminar by Hendrik Hart, M. Dirk Stafleu and E.D. Fackerell
1972	"Economics and Politics," a seminar led by Bob Goudzwaard, Bernard Zylstra and Sander Griffioen
1974	"Economic Theory and Policy" by Bob Goudzwaard and A.B. Cramp
1975	"Affirming Creation and History," a conference with Regent College (Vancouver)
1975	"The Philosophy of the Physical Sciences" by M. Dirk Stafleu and Arie Leegwater
1975	"History of Economic Theory," by Bob Goudzwaard
1977	"Studies in Aesthetics," two week seminar by Calvin Seerveld and others
1978	"The Relevance of Christian Studies for the Social Sciences," coordinated by Bernard Zylstra and Elaine Botha
1979	"The Methodology and Roots of Modern Science," coordinated by Albert Wolters
1979	"Descartes, Locke and Modern Science," by Peter Schouls
1980	"Seminar on Economics" by Bob Goudzwaard
1980	"Christianity and Capitalism," six sessions by Bernard Zylstra
1981	"Interpreting an Authoritative Scripture," with Fuller Theological Seminary
1981	"Rationality in a Calvinian Context," a conference with Calvin College
1982	"Conference on Liturgy and Music" (COLAM), co-sponsored with Redeemer University College and Calvin College
1982	"Art History and the Problems of Method," 3 week course by

Appendix 3

	Calvin Seerveld and Graham Birtwhistle of the Free University
1983	"Economics in Christian Perspective," a one week course by A.B. Cramp
1983	"Justice and Peace for Christians One Century after Kuyper," six lectures by Nicholas Wolterstorff
1983	"Riding the Third Wave: The Impact of Technology on our Lives," eight sessions
1983	Faculty Lecture Series of six lectures in Toronto and London, Ontario
1984	"The Spirit—Empowering Presence," four day conference led by George Vandervelde
1984	"Christianity and the Classics," three day conference led by Wendy Helleman
1984	"Responsible Citizenship," eight presentations co-sponsored by Citizens for Public Justice
1985	"The Legacy of Herman Dooyeweerd," three day conference
1985	"Theories in Science," a two-week course led by M. Dirk Stafleu
1987	A two-day consultation on biology attended by about twenty persons from eastern North America interested in Christian perspective in the biological sciences, which included many biology teachers in Christian schools looking for assistance in teaching about evolution in their schools
1988	"The Church and Canadian Culture," three day conference
1988	"Canadian Culture and the Christian Reformed church, three day conference
1989	"Land in Biblical Perspective," two day conference with John Stek
1991	"Rumours of Glory: Bruce Cockburn and the Christian Faith in a Postmodern World," two day conference led by J. Richard Middleton and Brian Walsh
1991	"Christianity and the Classics II—Beginnings: In the Context of Hellenistic Judaism and Gnosticism," led by Wendy Helleman
1991	"The People of the Book," two day conference with N. Thomas Wright as speaker
1991	"Connecting Economics and Ethics: Afterthought or Starting Point?", two week conference led by Bob Goudzwaard
1992	"An Ethos of Compassion and the Integrity of Creation," international conference celebrating the 25th Anniversary of

	the Institute for Christian Studies
1992	"Teaching the Elementary Language Arts: Theory and Practice in Christian Perspective," a two-week course by Robert Bruinsma
1993	"Integral Learning and Faith/Learning Integration," a two week course by Ken Badley
1993	"Youth and Spirituality," a two day conference with Donald Posterski
1995	"Christianity and the Classics III," led by Wendy Helleman
1996	Dooyeweerd Symposium, one day with Elaine Botha, Danie Strauss, Hendrik Hart and James Olthuis
1996	Dooyeweerd Conference of four days organized by Danie Strauss
1997	"Trust and Suspicion: Hermeneutics in a Broken World," led by James Olthuis.

Workshops for pastors included these:

1972	Seminar on biblical hermeneutics, led by James Olthuis and Henk Geertsema of the Free University at Amsterdam
1979	"The Challenge of Liberation Theology," coordinated by George Vandervelde
1980	"Modern Theological Trends," a two-day discussion with lectures by Jaap Klapwijk and George Vandervelde
1984	"Preaching from the Gospels" by Bastiaan Van Elderen of Calvin Theological Seminary
1989	"Land in Biblical Perspective" by John Stek of Calvin Theological Seminary

Appendix 4
Books Co-Published for the Institute by University Press of America between 1983 and 1997

1983   *Rationality in the Calvinian Tradition*, edited by Hendrik Hart, Johan van der Hoeven and Nicholas Wolterstorff

1984   *Understanding our World*, by Hendrik Hart

1985   *The Legacy of Herman Dooyeweerd*, edited by C.T. McIntire

1986   *Telling the Next Generation: Educational Development in North American Calvinist Christian Schools*, by Harro van Brummelen

1987   *A Hermeneutics of Ultimacy: Peril or Promise*, by James H. Olthuis with Donald G. Bloesch, Clark H. Pinnock and Gerald T. Sheppard

1987   *Theories at Work: On the Structure and Functioning of Theories in Science, in Particular during the Copernican Revolution*, by Marinus Dirk Stafleu.

1988   *Social Science in Christian Perspective*, edited by Paul A. Marshall and Robert E. VanderVennen

1989   *Stained Glass: Worldviews and Social Science*, edited by Paul A. Marshall, Sander Griffioen and Richard J. Mouw

1990   *Norm and Context in the Social Sciences*, edited by Sander Griffioen and Jan Verhoogt

1990   *Search for Community in a Withering Tradition: Conversations between a Marxian Atheist and a Calvinian Christian*, by Kai Nielsen and Hendrik Hart

1990 *Christianity and the Classics: The Acceptance of a Heritage*, edited by Wendy E. Helleman

1991 *Church and Canadian Culture*, edited by Robert E. VanderVennen

1991 *Langdon Gilkey: Theologian for a Culture in Decline*, by Brian J. Walsh

1991 *Bringing into Captivity Every Thought*, edited by Jacob Klapwijk, Sander Griffioen and Gerben Groenewoud

1993 *Educating Christians for Responsible Discipleship*, edited by Peter P. De Boer

1994 *"The Woman Will Overcome the Warrior": A Dialogue with the Christian/Feminist Theology of Rosemary Radford Ruether*, by Nicholas John Ansell

1994 *Political Theory and Christian Vision: Essays in Memory of Bernard Zylstra*, edited by Jonathan Chaplin and Paul A. Marshall

1994 *Hellenization Revisited: Shaping a Christian Response within the Greco-Roman World*, edited by Wendy E. Helleman

1995 *An Ethos of Compassion and the Integrity of Creation*, edited by Brian J. Walsh and Robert E. VanderVennen

1997 *Decomposing Modernity: Ernest Becker's Images of Humanity at the End of an Age*, by Stephen W. Martin

Printed in the United States
111758LV00003B/37-69/P